interactive
SCIENCE

A hummingbird's wings in flight produce the humming sound that gives the birds their name.

SAVVAS
LEARNING COMPANY

Authors

You are an author!

You are one of the authors of this book. You can write in this book! You can take notes in this book! You can draw in it too! This book will be yours to keep.

Fill in the information below to tell about yourself. Then write your autobiography. An autobiography tells about you and the kinds of things you like to do.

My Photo

Name

School

Town, State

Autobiography

ISBN-13: 978-0-328-87140-7
ISBN-10: 0-328-87140-0
16 2020

ON THE COVER:
A hummingbird's wings in flight produce the humming sound that gives the birds their name.

Program Authors

DON BUCKLEY, M.Sc.
Director of Technology & Innovation,
The School at Columbia University, New York, New York
Don Buckley has transformed learning spaces, textbooks, and media resources so that they work for students and teachers. He has advanced degrees from leading European universities, is a former industrial chemist, published photographer, and former consultant to MOMA's Education Department. He also teaches a graduate course at Columbia Teacher's College in Educational Technology and directs the Technology and Innovation program at the school. He is passionate about travel, architecture, design, change, the future, and innovation.

ZIPPORAH MILLER, M.A.Ed.
Coordinator for K-12 Science Programs, Anne Arundel County Public Schools.
Mrs. Zipporah Miller served as a reviewer during the development of Next Generation Science Standards and provides national training to teachers, administrators, higher education staff and informal science stakeholders on the Next Generation Science Standards. Prior to her appointment in Anne Arundel, Mrs. Miller served as the Associate Executive Director for Professional Development Programs and Conferences at the National Science Teachers Association (NSTA).

MICHAEL J. PADILLA, Ph.D.
Eugene P. Moore School of Education, Clemson University, Clemson, South Carolina
A former middle school teacher and a leader in middle school science education, Dr. Michael Padilla has served as president of the National Science Teachers Association and reviewed the Next Generation Science Standards. He is a former professor of science education at Clemson University. As lead author of the *Science Explorer* series, Dr. Padilla has inspired the team in developing a program that promotes student inquiry and meets the needs of today's students.

KATHRYN THORNTON, Ph.D.
Professor, Mechanical & Aerospace Engineering, University of Virginia, Charlottesville, Virginia
Selected by NASA in May 1984, Dr. Kathryn Thornton is a veteran of four space flights. She has logged more than 975 hours in space, including more than 21 hours of extravehicular activity. As an author on the *Scott Foresman Science* series, Dr. Thornton's enthusiasm for science has inspired teachers around the globe.

MICHAEL E. WYSESSION, Ph.D.
Associate Professor of Earth and Planetary Science, Washington University, St. Louis, Missouri
An author on more than 50 scientific publications, Dr. Wysession was awarded the prestigious Packard Foundation Fellowship and Presidential Faculty Fellowship for his research in geophysics. Dr. Wysession is an expert on Earth's inner structure and has mapped various regions of Earth using seismic tomography. He is known internationally for his work in geoscience education and research, and was an author of the Next Generation Science Standards.

Instructional Design Author

GRANT WIGGINS, Ed.D.
President, Authentic Education, Hopewell, New Jersey
Dr. Wiggins is a co-author with Jay McTighe of *Understanding by Design, 2nd Edition* (ASCD 2005). His approach to instructional design provides teachers with a disciplined way of thinking about curriculum design, assessment, and instruction that moves teaching from covering content to ensuring understanding.
UNDERSTANDING BY DESIGN® and UbD™ are trademarks of ASCD, and are used under license.

Activities Author

KAREN L. OSTLUND, Ph.D.
Past President, National Science Teachers Association, Arlington, Virginia
Dr. Ostlund has over 40 years of experience teaching at the elementary, middle school, and university levels. She was Director of WINGS Online (Welcoming Interns and Novices with Guidance and Support) and the Director of the UTeach/Dell Center for New Teacher Success with the UTeach program in the College of Natural Sciences at the University of Texas at Austin. She also served as Director of the Center for Science Education at the University of Texas at Arlington, as President of the Council of Elementary Science International, and as a member of the Board of Directors of the National Science Teachers Association. As an author of Scott Foresman Science, Dr. Ostlund was instrumental in developing inquiry activities.

ELL Consultant

JIM CUMMINS, Ph.D.
Professor and Canada Research Chair, Curriculum, Teaching and Learning Department at the University of Toronto
Dr. Cummins's research focuses on literacy development in multilingual schools and the role technology plays in learning across the curriculum. *Interactive Science* incorporates research-based principles for integrating language with the teaching of academic content based on Dr. Cummins's work.

Reviewers

Program Consultants

William Brozo, Ph.D.
Professor of Literacy, Graduate School of Education, George Mason University, Fairfax, Virginia.
Dr. Brozo is the author of numerous articles and books on literacy development. He co-authors a column in The Reading Teacher and serves on the editorial review board of the Journal of Adolescent & Adult Literacy.

Kristi Zenchak, M.S.
Biology Instructor, Oakton Community College, Des Plaines, Illinois
Kristi Zenchak helps elementary teachers incorporate science, technology, engineering, and math activities into the classroom. STEM activities that produce viable solutions to real-world problems not only motivate students but also prepare students for future STEM careers. Ms. Zenchak helps elementary teachers understand the basic science concepts, and provides STEM activities that are easy to implement in the classroom.

Content Reviewers

Brad Armosky, M.S.
Texas Advanced Computing Center
University of Texas at Austin
Austin, Texas

Alexander Brands, Ph.D.
Department of Biological Sciences
Lehigh University
Bethlehem, Pennsylvania

Paul Beale, Ph.D.
Department of Physics
University of Colorado
Boulder, Colorado

Joy Branlund, Ph.D.
Department of Earth Science
Southwestern Illinois College
Granite City, Illinois

Constance Brown, Ph.D
Atmospheric Science Program
Geography Department
Indiana University
Bloomington, Indiana

Dana Dudle, Ph.D.
Biology Department
DePauw University
Greencastle, Indiana

Rick Duhrkopf, Ph. D.
Department of Biology
Baylor University
Waco, Texas

Mark Henriksen, Ph.D.
Physics Department
University of Maryland
Baltimore, Maryland

Andrew Hirsch, Ph.D.
Department of Physics
Purdue University
W. Lafayette, Indiana

Linda L. Cronin Jones, Ph.D.
School of Teaching & Learning
University of Florida
Gainesville, Florida

T. Griffith Jones, Ph.D.
College of Education
University of Florida
Gainesville, Florida

Candace Lutzow-Felling, Ph.D.
Director of Education
State Arboretum of Virginia & Blandy Experimental Farm
Boyce, Virginia

Cortney V. Martin, Ph.D.
Virginia Polytechnic Institute
Blacksburg, Virginia

Sadredin Moosavi, Ph.D.
University of Massachusetts Dartmouth
Fairhaven, Massachusetts

Klaus Newmann, Ph.D.
Department of Geological Sciences
Ball State University
Muncie, Indiana

Scott M. Rochette, Ph.D.
Department of the Earth Sciences
SUNY College at Brockport
Brockport, New York

Ursula Rosauer Smedly, M.S.
Alcade Science Center
New Mexico State University
Alcade, New Mexico

Frederick W. Taylor, Ph.D.
Jackson School of Geosciences
University of Texas at Austin
Austin, Texas

Chapter 1

Energy and Heat

You use many different forms of energy, such as light and electrical energy, every day.

SavvasRealize.com

Go online for engaging videos, interactivities, and virtual labs.

Chapter 2

Motion

The force of the cyclists pushing on the pedals helps their bikes move.

SavvasRealize.com

Go online for engaging videos, interactivities, and virtual labs.

Chapter 3

Electricity

*Storms often have lightning,
a form of electricity.*

SavvasRealize.com

**Go online for engaging
videos, interactivities,
and virtual labs.**

Chapter 4

Plants and Animals

To survive and grow, these plants need sunlight, water, carbon dioxide, and nutrients from the soil.

SavvasRealize.com

Go online for engaging videos, interactivities, and virtual labs.

Chapter 5

Ecosystems

Animals get energy by eating plants or other animals.

SavvasRealize.com

Go online for engaging videos, interactivities, and virtual labs.

Earth's Resources

Salt water can cause
weathering that changes
Earth's surface.

SavvasRealize.com

**Go online for engaging
videos, interactivities,
and virtual labs.**

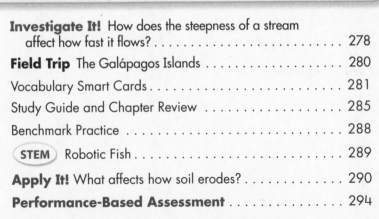

Skills Handbook

Part 1

The Nature Science

This scientist is recording observations.

SavvasRealize.com

Go online for engaging videos, interactivities, and virtual labs.

Technology and Design

This satellite is technology that helps people communicate.

SavvasRealize.com

Go online for engaging videos, interactivities, and virtual labs.

"This is your book. You can <u>write</u> in it!"

interactive SCIENCE

Big Question

At the start of each chapter you will see two questions—
an **Engaging Question** and a **Big Question.**
Just like a scientist, you will predict an answer to the
Engaging Question. Each Big Question will help you
start thinking about the Big Ideas of science. Look for the
symbol throughout the chapter!

Why do kangaroos carry their young?

Living Things

Try It! How can shells be classified?

STEM Activity Bird Feather Cleaning

Lesson 1 How can you classify animals?

Lesson 2 How are offspring like their parents?

Lesson 3 What are the life cycles of some animals?

Investigate It! What do leaves have in common?

Chapter 4

When a kangaroo is born, it is blind and has no
fur. It is about the size of a peanut. It climbs into
its mother's pouch to finish developing. The young
kangaroo stays there for months to eat, sleep,
and grow.

Predict What might happen if a baby kangaroo
left its mother's pouch too soon?

How do living things grow
and change?

PearsonRealize.com

Let's Read Science!

You will see a page like this toward the beginning of each chapter. It will show you how to use a reading skill that will help you understand what you read.

Sequence
- **Sequence** is the order in which events take place.
- Clue words such as *first, next, then,* and *finally* can help you figure out the sequence of events.

Let's Read Science!

Classify Animals
Scientists can classify animals according to their behaviors, such as how they act, and their physical characteristics, such as hair. Scientists may classify a slug such as the one below. Scientists may first identify whether or not the slug has a backbone. Next, they can find out what the slug eats. Finally, scientists can compare and contrast the slug to other animals.

Practice It!
Complete the graphic organizer to show the sequence of classifying animals.

First

Next

Finally

sea slug

PearsonRealize.com   155

Vocabulary Smart Cards

water cycle
precipitation
weather
climate
atmosphere
severe weather

Play a Game!
Cut out the Vocabulary Smart Cards.

Work with a partner. Choose a Vocabulary Smart Card.

Say as many words as you can think of to describe the vocabulary word.

Have your partner guess the word.

Have your partner repeat with another Vocabulary Smart Card.

279

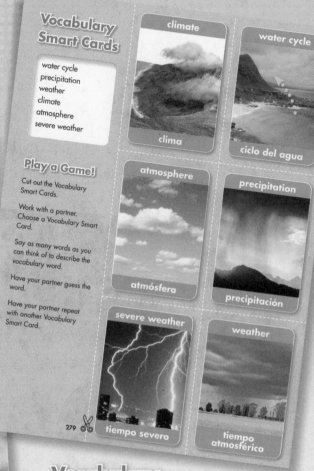

climate — clima
water cycle — ciclo del agua
atmosphere — atmósfera
precipitation — precipitación
severe weather — tiempo severo
weather — tiempo atmosférico

Vocabulary Smart Cards

Go to the end of the chapter and cut out your own set of **Vocabulary Smart Cards.** Draw a picture to learn the word. Play a game with a classmate to practice using the word!

SavvasRealize.com

Go to **SavvasRealize.com** for a variety of digital activities.

"Engage with the page!"

interactive SCIENCE

Envision It!

At the beginning of each lesson, at the top of the page, you will see an **Envision It!** interactivity that gives you the opportunity to circle, draw, write, or respond to the Envision It! question.

Lesson 2

How are offspring like their parents?

Envision It!

Circle the two pictures that show behaviors an animal must learn.

Draw an ✗ on the pictures that show behaviors an animal is born knowing how to do.

I will know that some characteristics and behaviors are inherited and some are learned or acquired.

Words to Know

inherit
instinct

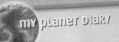

MY PLANET DIARY DISCOVERY

Karl von Frisch

A honey bee scout flies out of the hive to look for food. It finds flowers full of sweet nectar. How can the scout communicate to the other bees where the food is? Beginning in the 1920s, Karl von Frisch studied bee behavior. He discovered that the scout bee performs a dance. The dance tells other bees where to find the food. The bees in the hive are born knowing what the dance means.

What do you think the bees will do after they see the scout's dance?

Both Alike and Different

Why do kittens look like cats and not like dogs? Why does a corn seed grow into a corn plant and not a tomato plant? Most young plants and animals grow to look like their parents. Some plants and animals look like their parents even when they are very young.

The young antelope in the picture shares many characteristics with its parent. For example, the young antelope has the same body shape as its parent. Its fur is about the same length too.

The young antelope is also different in some ways. For example, its horns are much smaller than its parent's horns. The young antelope's horns will grow larger as it gets older. But even then, its horns may not have the exact shape or size of its parent's horns.

1. ◎ **Compare and Contrast** Describe other ways in which the young antelope and its parent are alike and different.

PearsonRealize.com

169

168

MY PLANET DIARY

My Planet Diary will introduce you to amazing scientists, fun facts, and important discoveries in science. They will also help you to overcome common misconceptions about science concepts.

Read See DO!

After reading small chunks of information, stop to check your understanding. The visuals help teach about what you read. Answer questions, underline text, draw pictures, or label models.

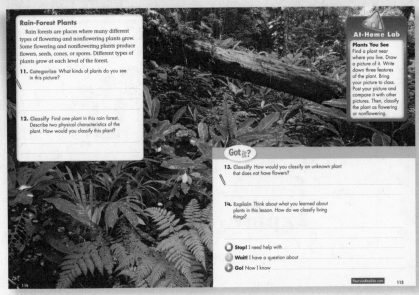

Do the math!

Scientists commonly use math as a tool to help them answer science questions. You can practice skills that you are learning in math class right in your *Interactive Science Student Edition!*

Got it?

At the end of each lesson you will have a chance to evaluate your own progress! At this point you can stop or go on to the next lesson.

"Have fun! Be a scientist!"

interactive SCIENCE

▷ Try It!

At the start of every chapter, you will have the chance to do a hands-on inquiry activity. The activity will provide you with experiences that will prepare you for the chapter lessons or may raise a new question in your mind.

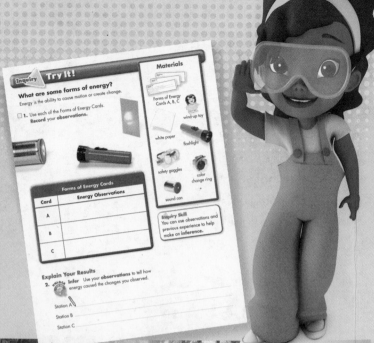

Inquiry **Try It!**

What are some forms of energy?
Energy is the ability to cause motion or create change.

☐ **1.** Use each of the Forms of Energy Cards.
Record your observations.

Materials

Forms of Energy Cards A, B, C

wind-up toy

white paper

flashlight

safety goggles

color change ring

sound can

Forms of Energy Cards	
Card	**Energy Observations**
A	
B	
C	

Inquiry Skill
You can use observations and previous experience to help make an **inference**.

Explain Your Results
2. **Infer** Use your observations to tell how energy caused the changes you observed.

Station A

Station B

Station C

2

Lesson 2
How do plants use leaves to make food?

Envision It!

Tell how you think leaves help plants.

UNLOCK
I will know that leaves help plants live, grow, and make food.

Words to Know
photosynthesis
carbon dioxide
oxygen

Inquiry **Explore It!**

How does sunlight affect plant survival?

☐ **1.** **Observe** a green leaf on a plant. Gently fold a piece of foil completely around the whole leaf. Be sure the foil cannot fall off.

☐ **2.** Place the plant near a sunny window. Wait one week.

☐ **3.** Take off the foil. Observe. Compare what you observed before and after the leaf was covered.

Materials

plant

foil

Be careful! Wash your hands when finished.

Explain Your Results
4. **Infer** What do you think happened to the leaf? Explain.

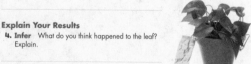

What Plants Need

Plants need food, air, water, and space to live and grow. Many plants live and grow in soil. The four main parts of a flowering plant are leaves, roots, stems, and flowers. In different kinds of plants, these parts may look alike. They may also look different.

Unlike animals, plants make their own food. Plants need energy from the sun to make food. Food is made in a plant's leaves, using the sun's energy. This food helps plants grow.

1. ⊙ **Text Features** Look at the text features on this page. Identify one text feature and the clue it gives you.

Text feature	Clue
Heading	It tells me that I'll read about what plants need.

Bromeliad plants are like other plants. They use energy from the sun to make food.

116

PearsonRealize.com

▷ Explore It!

Before you start reading the lesson, **Explore It!** activities provide you with an opportunity to first explore the content!

Design It!

The **Design It!** activity has you use the engineering design process to find solutions to problems. By finding a problem and then planning, drawing, and choosing materials, you will make, test, and evaluate a solution for a real world problem. Communicate your evidence through drawings and prototypes and identify ways to make your solution better.

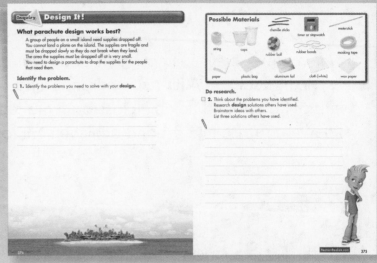

Investigate It!

At the end of every chapter, a Directed Inquiry activity gives you a chance to put together everything you've learned in the chapter. Using the activity card, apply design principles in the Guided version to Modify Your Investigation or the Open version to Develop Your Own Investigation. Whether you need a lot of support from your teacher or you're ready to explore on your own, there are fun hands-on activities that match your interests.

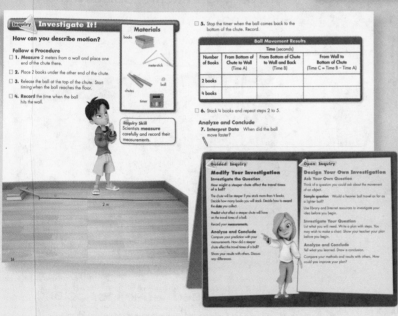

Apply It!

These Open Inquiry activities give you a chance to plan and carry out investigations.

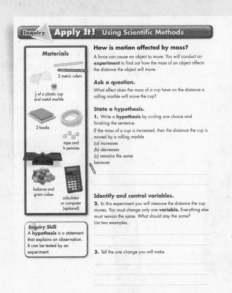

What is Savvas Realize?

Interactive Science is now part of Savvas' brand-new learning management system, Realize! With rich and engaging content, embedded assessment with instant data, and flexible classroom management tools, Realize gives you the power to raise interest and achievement for every student in your classroom.

Engaging Videos

Engage with science topics through videos! Start each chapter with an Untamed Science video.

Savvas Flipped Videos for Science give you another way to learn.

Interactivities and Virtual Labs

Practice science content with engaging online activities.

At **SavvasRealize.com** go online and conduct labs virtually! No goggles and no mess.

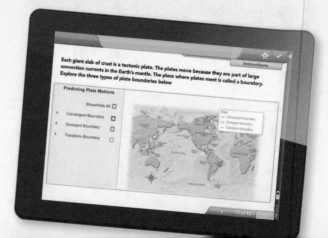

Connect to What You Know

Check what you know at the end of each lesson and chapter.

Get More Practice on skills and content, based on your performance.

Predict your exam readiness with benchmark assessments.

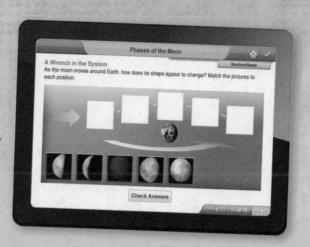

Savvas Realize offers powerful classroom management functionality, including:

Standards-aligned content — search by standard

Powerful Search tools — search by keyword, topic or standards

Customizable curriculum — reorder the table of contents, uploadfiles and media, add links and create custom lessons and assessments

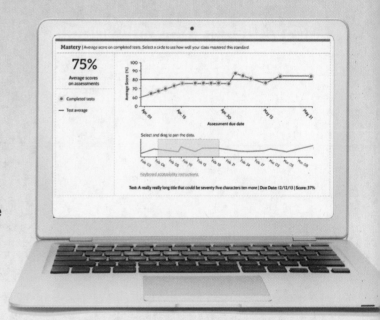

Flexible class management tools — create classes, organize students, and create assignments targeted to students, groups of students, or the entire class.

Tracks student progress — instantly access student and class data that shows standards mastery on assessments, online activity and overall progress.

Track Your Learning Online.

SavvasRealize.com

Quest

Make a Human Body Road Map

Your Quest is to make a model or road map using a human body. Identify how the various human body systems are involved in the consumption of food.

Quest Kick-Off
Make a Human Body Road Map
Watch a video about human body systems.

Quest Check-In 1
Follow the Flow
Watch a movie on the blood's journey through the circulatory system. Make a model of how blood moves in your body.

Quest Check-In 2
Digested: Tale of the Eaten Apple
Write a comic strip. Show how the parts of the digestive and circulatory systems work together to transport nutrients, water, and waste throughout the body.

Quest Check-In 3
Systems That Help You Move
Learn about how your muscles and bones work. Think about activities you do such as sports. How do the bones and muscles move?

Quest Check-In 4
How do parts of the body work together like a system?
Work through daily activities and see how your body systems work together.

Quest Check-In 5
A System for All Systems
Learn about the endocrine system. Complete an interactivity to show how the body processes sugar from food.

Quest Findings
Show Where Nutrients Go
Make a map or model of how nutrients, water, and waste move throughout human body systems.

SavvasRealize.com Go online for all Quest digital interactivities and hands-on labs

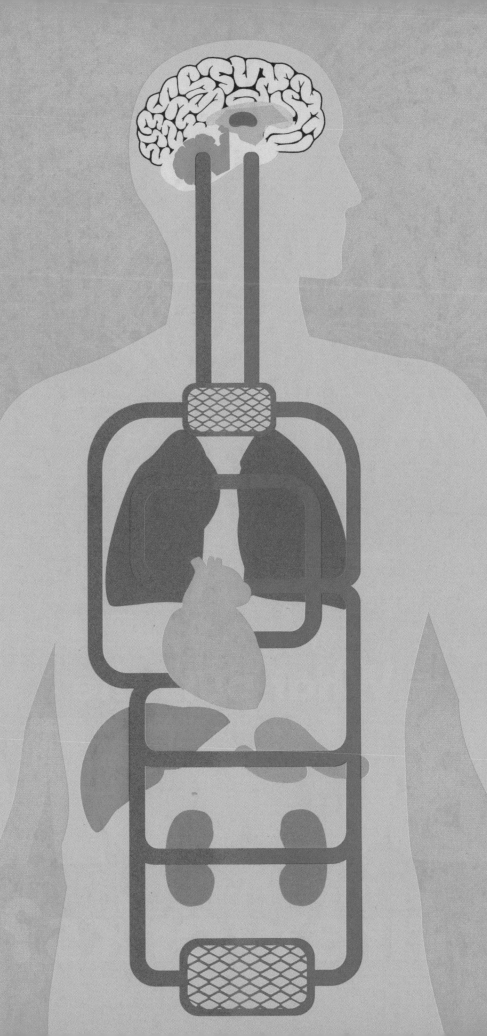

What puts the

BOOM
in fireworks?

Energy and Heat

Chapter 1

Try It!   What are some forms of energy?

STEM Activity   Is It Cold in Here?

Lesson 1   What are forms of energy?

Lesson 2   What is sound energy?

Lesson 3   What is light energy?

Lesson 4   What is heat?

Investigate It!   Which material is the better heat conductor?

When fireworks go off they can be louder than a jet engine. Even if you watch from a safe distance, a fireworks display can be loud enough to make you shake!

Predict   What forms of energy are at work in a fireworks display?

....

....

....

THE BIG ?   How does energy cause change?

What are some forms of energy?

Energy is the ability to cause motion or create change.

☐ **1.** Use each of the Forms of Energy Cards.
Record your **observations.**

Materials

Forms of Energy
Cards A, B, C

wind-up toy

white paper

flashlight

safety goggles

color
change ring

sound can

Forms of Energy Cards

Card	Energy Observations
A	
B	
C	

Inquiry Skill
You can use observations and previous experience to help make an **inference.**

Explain Your Results

2. **Infer** Use your **observations** to tell how energy caused the changes you observed.

Station A

Station B

Station C

⊙ Main Idea and Details

- The **main idea** is the most important idea in a reading selection.
- **Details** help to explain or support the main idea.

A Hot Job!

Steelworkers work in one of the world's hottest jobs. At the mill where they work, iron ore is heated with other substances in giant furnaces to become liquid steel. Workers must wear suits that protect them from heat, but they can still sense the warm air around them.

Practice It!

Complete the graphic organizer below to show the main idea and two details in the example paragraph.

Main Idea

Steelworkers have the worlds Hotest Jobss

Detail

they were Suits to protce t them

Detail

they work at the mill

Is It Cold in Here?

Did you feel that breeze? How did I feel a breeze if I'm inside a building? Buildings can leak cold or warm air. By finding and fixing these leaks, people can cut back on how much energy they use. The less energy people use to heat or cool their homes, the more money they save. Burning fewer fossil fuels, such as oil and coal, also reduces air pollution. You have been invited to participate in an international contest to design a device to detect drafts in buildings.

Identify the Problem

☐ 1. What is your task? _fixing leaks_

☐ 2. What problem will your device help to solve? _fixing leaks and have warm air._

Do Research

Walk around the room and put your hand near walls, windows, and outside doors to feel for drafts.

☐ 3. Why might drafts be a problem? _because they could blow cold air or warm air._

☐ 4. Why might some drafts be harder to detect than others? _be cause some could be tiny._

Go to the materials station(s). Pick up each material one at a time. Think about how it may or may not be useful in your design. Leave the materials where they are.

☐ 5. What are your design constraints? _fixing leaks_

Develop Possible Solutions

☐ **6. Describe** two ways you could combine some of the materials to build a draft detector.

You can build a fan

_____

_____

_____

_____

Choose One Solution

☐ **7. Draw** your device. **Label** all the parts. **Describe** how you will build it.

_____

_____

_____

☑ **8. List** the materials that you will need. _____

_____

_____

_____

Design and Construct a Prototype

Gather your materials and a metric ruler. **Build** your device. Use the metric ruler to measure the length and width of the paper and the length of the stick, if you are using one. Round your measurements to the nearest millimeter.

☑ **9. Record** the measurements of your prototype. _____

_____

_____

Test the Prototype

Test your device by holding it up to a window, window frame, windowsill, or outside doorframe. **Observe** it carefully for movement.

Communicate Results

☑ **10.** Rate your draft detector on a scale of 0 to 2 with 0 being no movement, 1 being slight movement, and 2 being a lot of movement. **Tell** why you rated your detector as you did.

My rating: _____

_____

_____

Evaluate and Redesign

☑ **11.** What changes could you make to your design to make it work better?

_____

_____

_____

☑ **12.** Make your changes and **record** the new measurements. _____

_____

_____

☑ **13.** Did your revised prototype work? Explain. _____

_____

_____

What are forms of energy?

Tell what sounds and movements you think this plane might make.

MY PLANET DIARY
FunFact

Fireflies know the secret, but eventually people discovered it. The secret is how to make light with a chemical reaction that does not produce much heat.

Glow sticks are made in two sections. One chemical, along with a dye, fills the outer section. Another chemical fills the inner section. When the glow stick is bent, the inner section breaks open. This lets the chemicals mix. The reaction that follows gives off energy in the form of light. The light can last for hours.

What do you think are two or three uses for glow sticks?

light 1.
fun 5
colorsy

I will know what energy is and some forms it can take. I will know what energy can do.

Words to Know

energy
kinetic energy
potential energy

Energy

Turn on a light switch. Rub your hands together to warm them. Roll a pencil across your desk. You are using energy! **Energy** is the ability to cause motion or create change. Whenever the position, chemical structure, or look of something changes, energy is required.

There are many forms of energy. Some energy takes the form of light or sound. Electrical energy is another type of energy you use every day.

1. ◎ **Main Idea and Details** Complete the graphic organizer below. Write details about energy.

2. **Analyze** What is changing about the dog and the toy?

Main Idea

> Energy is the ability to cause motion or create change.

Kicking

Clapping

Detail

Detail

Forms of Energy

Energy cannot be made or destroyed. It is transferred from form to form. Energy also moves from one object to another. Energy can exist in many forms. Here are some common forms of energy.

Electrical energy is energy caused by the movement of electrically charged particles. This movement is also called an electric current. When you flip on a light switch, turn on the radio, or use the toaster, you are using electrical energy. The energy is transferred from place to place. Electricity flows through the devices to produce motion, sound, heat, or light.

Thermal energy is energy due to randomly moving particles that make up matter. You can feel the flow of thermal energy as heat. The faster particles move, the more thermal energy is produced. People use thermal energy to heat or cook food. The thermal energy causes changes in the food as the food cooks.

Sound energy is the energy of vibrations carried by air, water, or other matter. You use sound energy when your alarm clock wakes you up, or when you listen to your favorite music.

3. **Describe** Write an example of sound energy in your home.

the HW

Kinetic energy is the energy of motion. Anything moving has this kind of energy. A moving swing at the playground or a hurricane both have kinetic energy.

4. **Describe** Write an example of kinetic energy in school.

   trowing the ball

Light energy travels as waves and can move through empty space. Some light energy comes from the sun and travels to Earth. These sunflowers use this light energy to help make their own food.

Potential energy is energy that is stored in an object. When an object is in motion, its potential energy is released as other forms of energy. For example, when a truck burns fuel, the potential energy in gasoline is released as sound, heat, and motion.

5. **Conclude** Circle the names of the forms of energy in use when you turn on a fan in your home.

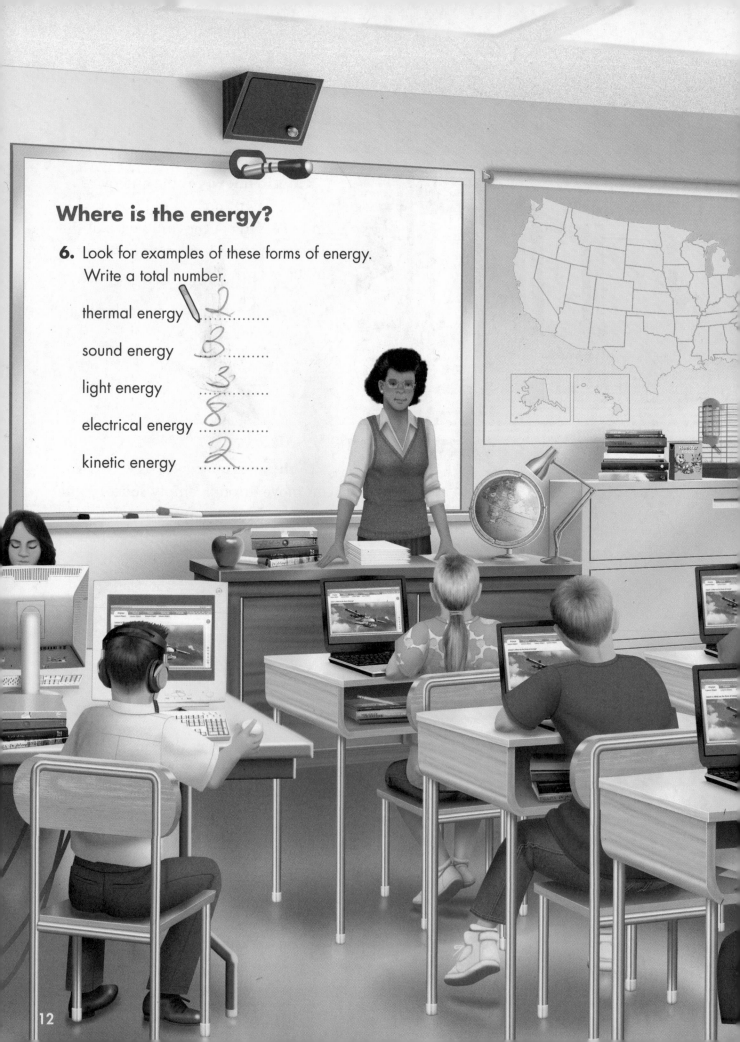

Where is the energy?

6. Look for examples of these forms of energy.
Write a total number.

thermal energy ....2....

sound energy ....3....

light energy ....3....

electrical energy ....8....

kinetic energy ....2....

Go Green

Energy Savers
Look around your
classroom. Describe some
forms of energy. How
could you save energy?
Write a list. Share your
list with the school.

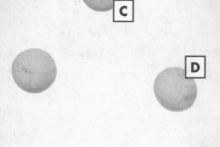

Energy and Motion

All moving things have kinetic energy. The amount of kinetic energy depends on the speed and mass of the object. Look at the time-lapse photo of the boy tossing an orange. The harder he throws the orange, the more kinetic energy it has. An object with greater mass would also have more kinetic energy.

When the boy throws the orange, he gives it kinetic energy. As the ball rises, it slows down. Its kinetic energy is gradually converted to potential energy. As the orange falls, the potential energy is converted back to kinetic energy.

7. Explain Use the photo at left to complete the captions.

Forms of Potential Energy

There are different forms of potential energy. Some forms have to do with an object's position. Other forms have to do with an object's makeup. When people say something "produces energy," they mean that the energy is converted from potential energy to a useful form.

Gravitational

A raised object has what is called gravitational potential energy. The orange the boy is throwing has this kind of potential energy. The higher or heavier an object is, the more gravitational potential energy it has.

8. Hypothesize Does the orange have more gravitational potential energy in the boy's hand or high in the air? Explain.

potenfail energy the higher it goes the more potentail it gets.

Chemical

Chemical potential energy is stored in the connections that hold particles together. A car uses chemical energy when it burns gasoline. The food you eat has chemical energy. When your body digests food, chemical energy turns into other forms of energy that you use to move, talk, and live.

A The orange is at rest in the boy's hand. He gives the orange kinetic energy when he throws it.

B As the orange rises, its kinetic energy changes to

....

C At the top of the throw, the orange has its maximum potential energy.

D As the orange falls, its potential energy changes back into

....

Elastic

A stretched rubber band or a compressed spring have potential energy. This is called elastic potential energy. The more a rubber band is stretched, the more potential energy it has. If you bounce, kick, or hit a ball, the ball also has this kind of potential energy. The ball's material and the air inside it compress like a spring. Elastic potential energy can change into sound energy and kinetic energy.

The golf club's kinetic energy is transferred to the ball as elastic potential energy. The club compresses the ball.

9. Hypothesize Look at the picture of the golf club striking the golf ball. Will the ball's elastic potential energy change into kinetic energy? Explain.

Yes it will.

Got it?

10. Categorize What forms of energy taught in this lesson are produced by a television set?

11. Analyze Suppose you throw a basketball in the air. Instead of catching it, you let it bounce on the court. What kinds of energy are in use as the ball travels?

◻ **Stop!** I need help with ....

❙❙ **Wait!** I have a question about ....

▶ **Go!** Now I know ....

Lesson 2

What is sound energy?

Circle the instruments that you think make a high sound.
Draw boxes around those that make low sounds.

MY PLANET DIARY

How does an acoustic guitar make sound? It starts with plucking the guitar's strings. Plucking causes the strings to vibrate. The vibrations first move through the saddle. Then they move through the bridge to the soundboard. The soundboard is the wooden piece that makes up the front of the guitar's body. The entire soundboard then vibrates. The body of the guitar is shaped in a way that makes the sound louder. These sounds come out through the sound hole, producing the sound you hear when someone plays a guitar.

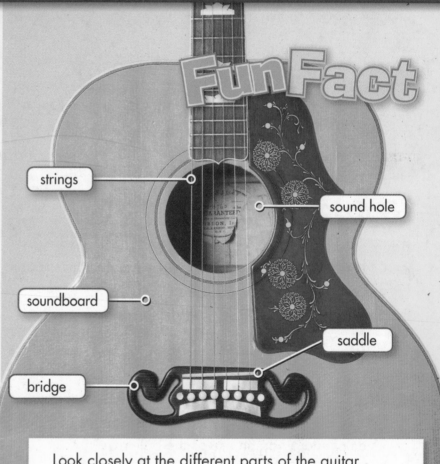

Fun Fact

strings

sound hole

soundboard

saddle

bridge

Look closely at the different parts of the guitar.
Suppose the sound hole were covered up.
How do you think the sound would change?

It would sound diferene

16

I will know what sound
energy is and how it is
produced.

Words to Know

sound	pitch
frequency	volume
wavelength	amplitude

Sound Energy

The blare of an alarm clock, the beep of a car horn, the quack of a duck, and the rumble of thunder during a storm are all sounds. **Sound** is energy in the form of vibrations *Pretty important* passing through matter. A vibration is a quick back-and-forth movement. Sounds occur when objects vibrate. Sound travels through solids, liquids, and gases. Sound cannot travel through empty space, where there is no matter. Matter is needed for sound, because collisions between particles in matter can cause some energy to be transferred into the air. The air gets heated, and sound is produced.

Pluck a guitar string, and the string starts to vibrate. The vibrating string collides with the particles in the air around it and passes energy to the air. The sound energy travels outward as sound waves. A sound wave is a disturbance that moves sound energy through matter. When the waves reach your ears, the waves make your eardrum vibrate, and you hear the sound made by the guitar string.

1. **Underline** words that tell what sound is.

2. **Explain** A plucked guitar string will make a sound until the string stops vibrating. How might you play a short note?

   Pull the string a little bit.

How Sound Travels

As sound waves move through matter, they set particles into motion. The moving particles form a pattern. Areas with groups of particles that are bunched together alternate with areas of particles that are farther apart. The areas where particles bunch together are called compressions.

Sound waves travel at different speeds through matter. Sound waves travel quickly through most solids and liquids. Sound waves tend to travel more slowly in gases.

3. Identify Circle the compression images in this picture.

4. ⊙ Main Idea and Details Circle the main idea in the first paragraph above. **Underline** three details.

Do the math!

Read a Graph

This graph shows the speed of sound through some common materials. Use the graph to answer the following questions.

Approximate Speed of Sound

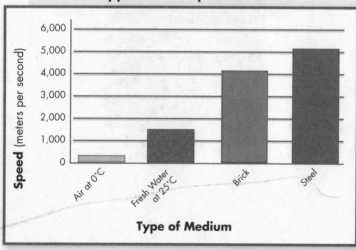

① Compare Does sound travel faster in air or in fresh water?

....

② Compute About how many meters per second faster is the speed of sound in steel than in brick?

....

....

Frequency and Wavelength

Waves can travel in different ways. They can carry different types and amounts of energy. But all waves have certain properties. Frequency and wavelength are two of these properties. The **frequency** of a wave is the number of waves that pass a point in a certain amount of time. Frequency is often described as the number of complete cycles a wave makes in one second. A cycle is one vibration. **Wavelength** is the distance between a point on one wave and a similar point on the next wave.

Studying Sound

One way scientists study sound is by using oscilloscopes. An oscilloscope is a device that takes sound waves and displays the shape of the waves on a screen. Look at the oscilloscope screen below. The signals are displayed onscreen in the form of a wave. Compressions in a sound wave show up on screen as crests, or high points on the wave. The spaces between compressions show up as troughs, or low points on the wave.

Notice how the pattern resembles ripples in water. Waves like this one can be made in water by tapping the surface of the water. The ripples are the crests and troughs of the waves.

5. **Analyze** Which has a higher frequency, a wave that makes 6 cycles per second or one that makes 10 cycles per second? Explain your answer.

6 cycles. When I looked back I look back at the word frequency and it said

Wavelength can be measured between two crests or between two troughs. The slower an object vibrates, the longer its wavelength and the lower its frequency will be.

If this screen represented one second, this wave's frequency would be 2 cycles per second.

6. **Label** Where are the compressions in both images to the left?

Pitch

People experience the frequency of sound as its pitch. **Pitch** is how high or low a sound is. Pitch depends on the frequency of the sound wave. Objects that vibrate more quickly have higher frequencies. Those objects have a higher pitch. Objects that vibrate more slowly have a lower frequency and a lower pitch.

The material of the object making the sound and its size and shape affect the pitch you hear. A tuba, for example, is a musical instrument made of many feet of brass tubing. Tubas make low-pitched sounds. Some sounds are too low-pitched or too high-pitched for humans to hear.

7. **Apply** Put your hand on your throat and make a low-pitched sound. Then make a high-pitched sound. Explain how your throat adjusts while making these sounds.

low pitch sounds like your
voice hurts
hi

A dolphin communicates by making high-pitched sounds.

8. **Explain** Are dolphin sounds high or low frequencies?

Volume

When you describe a sound, probably one of the first things you think about is loudness, or volume. You know that some sounds are louder than others. A jet engine, for example, makes much more noise than a car. What, exactly, is volume? **Volume** is a measure of how strong a sound seems to us. The more energy there is in the sound wave, the louder the sound and the higher the volume.

The volume of a sound is related to its amplitude. **Amplitude** is the height of a wave measured from its midline. The higher the amplitude of a wave, the more energy it has, and the louder it sounds. Suppose you turn down the volume on the TV as soft as it will go. You can barely hear it. Then you turn it up as high as it will go. Now you have to hold your ears so they don't hurt! You have not changed the pitch of the sound. You have changed its amplitude and its volume.

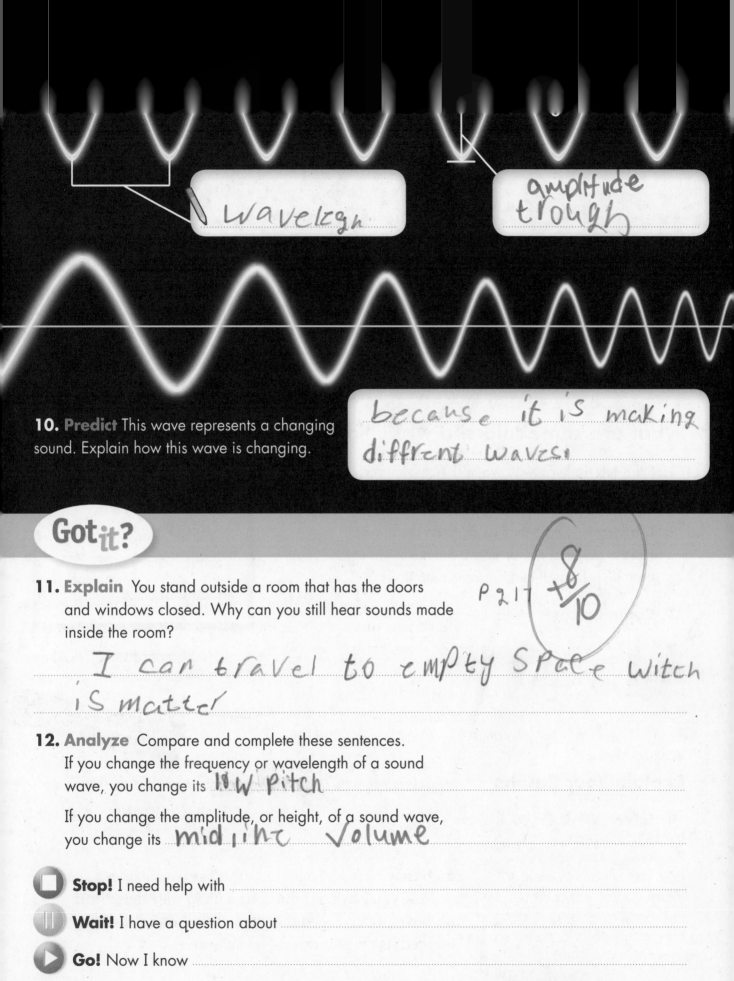

wavelegn (handwritten)

amplitude (handwritten)
trough (handwritten)

10. Predict This wave represents a changing sound. Explain how this wave is changing.

because it is making diffrent waves. (handwritten)

Got it?

11. Explain You stand outside a room that has the doors and windows closed. Why can you still hear sounds made inside the room?

_P 217_ (handwritten)   _8/10_ (handwritten, circled)

I can travel to empty space witch is matter (handwritten)

12. Analyze Compare and complete these sentences.

If you change the frequency or wavelength of a sound wave, you change its _low pitch_ (handwritten)

If you change the amplitude, or height, of a sound wave, you change its _midiine volume_ (handwritten)

⏹ **Stop!** I need help with ....

⏸ **Wait!** I have a question about ....

▶ **Go!** Now I know ....

What is light energy?

Envision It!

Describe how the frog looks. Tell why you think it looks this way.

Inquiry Explore It!

What are some colors in white light?

☐ **1.** Fill a tub halfway with water. Place a mirror in the water at an angle.

☐ **2. Observe** Shine the flashlight on the mirror. Hold a piece of paper above the flashlight so that the reflected light bounces onto it.

☐ **3. Communicate** What colors do you see?

....

....

Materials

mirror

plastic tub
$\frac{1}{2}$ full of water

flashlight

white paper

metric ruler

Hold paper about 30 to 60 cm above the flashlight.

Set mirror at about this angle.

Shine flashlight here.

Explain Your Results

4. Infer What do you think causes the white light to spread into colors?

....

....

....

Put flashlight here.

Chemical energy in the battery changes to electric energy, which changes to light energy.

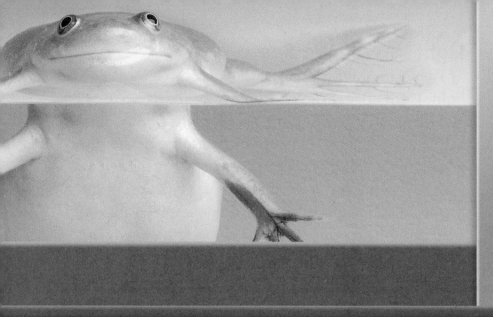

UNLOCK THE BIG ?

I will know how light bends when it passes through different materials.

Words to Know

refraction   reflection
absorption

Sources of Light

The sun is an important source of light energy on Earth. Without constant light energy from the sun, Earth would be a dead planet. It would be too cold and dark for any kind of life. For example, plants convert sunlight into chemical energy, which they use to make food. Without plants, animals could not survive.

Besides the sun, there are sources of light on Earth. For example, some animals give off light called bioluminescence. This light is a result of chemical reactions inside the animal's body. In addition, humans discovered long ago that they could make their own light. The discovery of fire changed how people lived. They could light a campfire and work even after dark.

firefly

2. **Explain** Describe how this firefly can be a source of light energy.

The animal

1. ◉ **Draw Conclusions** Write in the graphic organizer facts that support the conclusion about the sun.

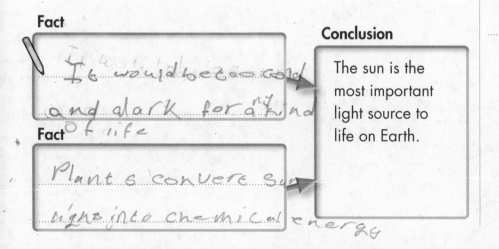

Fact

It would be too cold and dark for any kind of life

Fact

Plants convert sunlight into chemical energy

Conclusion

The sun is the most important light source to life on Earth.

At-Home Lab

Rainbows in Light
Look at the back of a compact disc in a well-lit room. Describe what you see. How does a compact disc act like a prism?

Light Waves We See

The form of light energy that we can see is called visible light. Light energy travels from its source as waves. Like all waves, light waves have wavelengths and frequencies. White light, such as the light from a lamp or the sun, is actually a blend of colors. The colors are red, orange, yellow, green, blue, and violet. These colors make up the visible light spectrum. The colors of the visible light spectrum always appear in the same order in which they appear in a rainbow and are arranged by their wavelengths and frequencies.

3. **Explain** Why does the visible light spectrum have different colors?

The colors make up visible light spectrum

red   orange   yellow   green   blue   violet

Prisms

A piece of glass called a prism separates white light into its different wavelengths. A prism lets you see the colors. As you move from red to blue on the visible light spectrum, wavelength decreases and frequency increases.

4. Describe Explain how raindrops and prisms are similar.

light waves bend when they enter the prism

5. Apply Raindrops can cause light waves to bend. What other substances can cause a rainbow to form?

Soap and bubbles

Light waves bend when they enter the prism at an angle.

Different wavelengths bend at different angles. The different colors separate from each other when light leaves the prism.

6. Describe Light rays refract as they travel from the pencil to the water to the glass to the air. Explain how the pencil looks.

It is cut in half.
or Seperaced

Light and Matter

Light rays travel in straight lines—as long as nothing is in their way! But when light rays strike an object, they may pass through it, reflect off it, or be absorbed by it.

Refraction

Light changes speed when it passes into a new medium. When this happens, the light bends. This bending is called **refraction.** The change in speed causes the light to refract, or bend. Refraction causes the white light striking a prism to bend. The white light separates into individual colors you can see because each color bends differently.

Reflection

Light waves reflect at least a little off most objects. **Reflection** occurs when light rays bounce off, or reflect from, a surface. Objects with smooth, shiny surfaces, such as still water, reflect more light rays than other objects. When you brush your teeth in front of a mirror, the smooth, shiny surface of the mirror reflects almost all the light rays that hit it. All light rays reaching the mirror from the same direction are reflected in the same new direction, so you see a clear image, or reflection, of your toothpaste-filled mouth.

halo

Halos around the sun are formed where ice crystals in Earth's atmosphere refract light.

Absorption

Objects may absorb some light waves. **Absorption** occurs when an object takes in a light wave. After a light wave is absorbed, it becomes a form of heat. Look at the photo of the pencil in the glass on the previous page. The pencil is an object that absorbs most light waves.

7. ⊙ **Draw Conclusions** What happens to an object that absorbs a lot of light?

It becomes hot

8. **Explain** Tell what you see in the photo at right. Explain what you see.

I refects of the surface

Got it?

9. **Describe** What happens during refraction of light as light passes through a prism?

The diffrent colors seperate from each other when the light leaves the prism.

10. **Summarize** Describe how light bends, or refracts, when traveling through different objects.

Light waves bend when they enter the prism.

⬛ **Stop!** I need help with ....

❚❚ **Wait!** I have a question about ....

▶ **Go!** Now I know ....

Lesson 4

What is heat?

In this kind of photograph, different temperatures show up as different colors.

Inquiry Explore It!

How does heat move?

1. Fill a paper cup with warm water. Cover it. Push a thermometer through the lid and hold it in place with clay. **Record** the temperature. _____ °C.

2. Fill a foam cup $\frac{1}{4}$ full with very cold water. Record the temperature. _____ °C.

3. Place the paper cup inside the foam cup. Record the temperature in each cup every minute for 10 minutes.

Materials

paper cup with lid   foam cup

clay   2 thermometers

clock with a second hand   warm water   very cold water

	Heat Movement Observations										
	Water Temperature (°C)										
	Start	1 min	2 min	3 min	4 min	5 min	6 min	7 min	8 min	9 min	10 min
Paper cup											
Foam cup											

Explain Your Results

4. **Observe** What happened to the temperatures? _____

5. **Infer** Tell which way heat moves between objects with different temperatures.

28

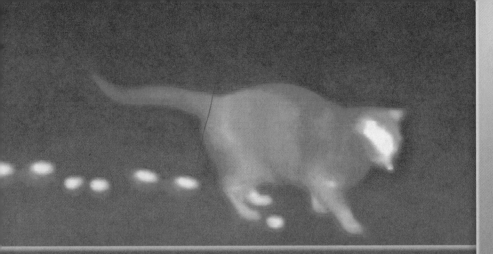

Tell which colors you think represent warmer areas.

I will know that heat flows from hot objects to cold ones. I will know that some materials are good conductors of heat and others are not.

Words to Know

conduction   radiation
convection

Conduction

Thermal energy flows from something warm to something cool. The transfer of thermal energy between matter of different temperatures is heat. Energy is present whenever there is heat. A heat source is anything that gives off energy that particles of matter can take in.

When you go to bed at night, does your pillow feel cool on your face? Is the pillow warm when you wake up? That is thermal energy moving! Your body is the heat source. Thermal energy transfers from your body to your pillow. When solids touch, thermal energy moves by conduction. **Conduction** is the transfer of heat that occurs when one thing touches another.

A bird warming its eggs in a nest is another example of conduction. The bird's body is the heat source. Conduction transfers thermal energy from the bird to the eggs, which are cooler.

1. Visualize Draw an ice cube sitting on a counter top on a hot day. Draw an arrow showing which direction thermal energy flows. Describe how the heat is transferred.

At-Home Lab

Heat on the Move
Put a thermometer in various places around your home. Record your findings. Think about why some places are cooler or warmer than others. Where might heat be moving in or out of a home?

A Conduction Example

Have you ever eaten hot oatmeal for breakfast? Suppose that you eat a bowl of hot oatmeal with a metal spoon. Why does the metal spoon begin to feel warmer? The particles of the spoon that touch the oatmeal start to move. As they move more quickly, they crash into other particles in the spoon. Soon, thermal energy from the oatmeal moves throughout the spoon. Heat transfer continues until the oatmeal and the spoon are at the same temperature.

2. Exemplify How do you know that heat from the oatmeal has moved?

the thermal energy from the oatmeal moves throught the spoon

3. Describe Suppose cold milk is poured into a warm glass. What will happen to the milk's temperature? Why?

The milk gets warmer.

Convection

Have you felt how warm a kitchen gets when the oven is on? You feel the heat indirectly as the heat moves through the room from convection. **Convection** is the transfer of thermal energy as matter moves. In convection, a gas or a liquid moves from place to place. The oven heats air inside it. Particles in the warm air move faster and travel upward into the rest of the kitchen. Then cooler air enters the oven to be warmed up.

Radiation

When the sun warms your skin or you sit near a fire, you feel another kind of energy. This energy is radiant energy, or radiation. **Radiation** is energy that is sent out in waves. When radiant energy hits you, the particles in your skin move more quickly. The radiation is converted to thermal energy and you feel warm. Radiation can travel through matter and through empty space.

4. **Summarize** Complete the captions on the greenhouse below.

Radiation from the sun warms the ground in _____ the greenhouse below.

Convection moves warmer air upward.

convection moves cooler air downward.

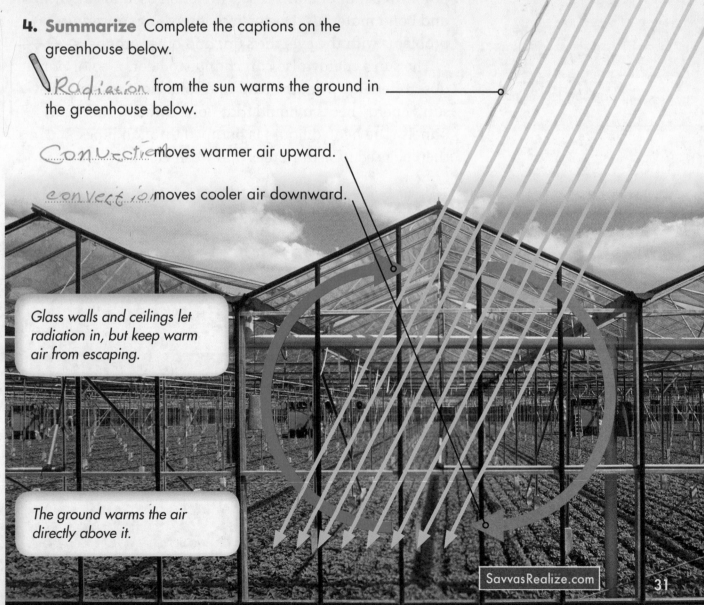

Glass walls and ceilings let radiation in, but keep warm air from escaping.

The ground warms the air directly above it.

Changes of Other Energy to Heat

Where does heat come from? Sometimes, other forms of energy change and give off heat. This heat can be used in many different ways.

Fossil Fuel to Heat

Fossil fuels are a source of heat. Coal, natural gas, and oil are all fossil fuels. When these fuels are burned, they produce useful heat. People often use this heat in their homes, schools, and other buildings.

Light to Heat

Have you ever noticed that a black T-shirt gets warm on a hot, sunny day? Objects that are black absorb all the colors of visible light. When the light is absorbed, it becomes a form of heat. So, the black T-shirt warms up.

Laser light produces a great deal of heat. A laser is a powerful beam of light. Lasers are often used to cut, drill, and bond materials. Doctors use lasers to treat certain problems with the eye, the skin, and other organs.

The sun's energy also can change to heat. A solar panel absorbs energy from the sun. In a solar heat system, the sun's energy heats a liquid that flows through the solar panels. The heated liquid is pumped through pipes. It can then be used to heat homes and wash clothes.

5. **Predict** What do you think could be one important use of solar panels, such as the ones on this home?

The sun's energy heats a liquid is pumped through pipes.

Friction to Heat

Try rubbing your hands together quickly. The heat you feel is an effect of friction. Friction occurs when two surfaces rub together. As a result of friction, heat is produced. For example, when a person skates on ice, the ice and skate rub together. This friction gives off heat.

6. **Infer** The skates of this ice skater cause friction. What might you see that would show that the friction of an ice skate sliding on ice causes heat?

When a person skates on ice, the ice and skate rub together.

Got it?

7. **Classify** How is thermal energy transferred in these examples?

A cold drink left in the sun gets warm. *It will absorb all the colors of visable lighto*

You eat a warm bite of food. *The heat is traveling to your mouth.*

After you get out of a long shower, the bathroom is warm. *The mirror blurs.*

8. **UNLOCK THE BIG ?** How does heat travel during conduction?

Soon thermal energy moves throughout the spoon.

⬛ **Stop!** I need help with ....

⏸ **Wait!** I have a question about ....

▶ **Go!** Now I know ....

Which material is the better heat conductor?

Follow a Procedure

☐ **1.** Place $\frac{1}{4}$ of a spoonful of margarine on the handles of each spoon. Stick a bead into the margarine on each spoon. Place both spoons in an empty cup.

☐ **2.** Pick up the cup filled halfway with very warm water. Gently pour it into the cup with the spoons.

Be careful! Use water that is a safe temperature.

Materials

2 small beads   margarine

metal spoon

plastic spoon

plastic cup $\frac{1}{2}$ full of very warm water

timer, stopwatch, or clock with second hand

empty plastic cup

Inquiry Skill
Carrying out an investigation carefully and observing closely help you make accurate **inferences.**

3. Observe Watch the beads closely.
Time how long it takes for each bead to fall.

4. Record your **data** below.

Heat Conductor Observations	
Material	Observations and Melting Time
Plastic spoon	
Metal spoon	

Analyze and Conclude

5. Write an explanation for your **observations.**

....

....

....

6. Infer Which of the materials would be better for a cooking pot? Explain how you made your inference.

....

....

7. **UNLOCK THE BIG ?** What do your observations teach you about how energy moves?

....

....

....

Sound and Temperature

Did you know that you can usually hear sounds better at night than during the day? You can investigate the properties of sound at home. During the day, have a friend stand 50 meters away and make a sound using a whistle. Describe the volume of the sound. During the evening after the temperature has decreased, repeat this activity and describe what you hear. The speed and direction of the sound waves are affected by the temperature of the air. In many places, the temperature of the air is warmer during the day than it is in the evening.

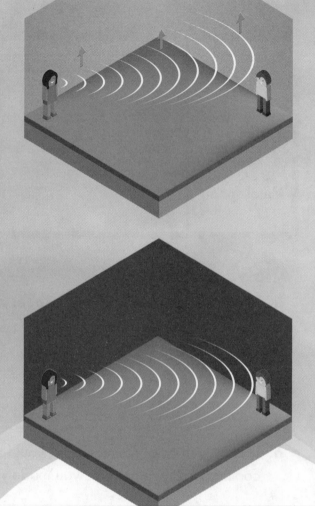

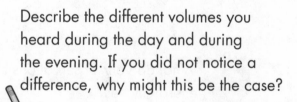

Describe the different volumes you heard during the day and during the evening. If you did not notice a difference, why might this be the case?

....

....

....

....

Lesson 1

What are forms of energy?

- There are basic forms of energy, including light, sound, electrical, and the energy of motion.
- Energy has the ability to cause motion or create change.

Lesson 2

What is sound energy?

Sound is produced by vibrating objects. The way an object is made and the way it vibrates affect the type of sound we hear.

A sound wave's frequency and energy also affect the sound we hear.

Lesson 3

What is light energy?

- Visible light is made up of waves with different wavelengths and frequencies.
- Light can be refracted, reflected, or absorbed.

Lesson 4

What is heat?

- Heat is the transfer of thermal energy.
- Heat can move by conduction, convection, or radiation.
- Other forms of energy can change to heat.

Chapter Review

 How does energy cause change?

Lesson 1

What are forms of energy?

1. **Vocabulary** The energy of motion is called
   A. potential energy.
   B. kinetic energy.
   C. chemical energy.
   D. thermal energy.

2. **Analyze** What two kinds of energy are you using when you play on a slide?

   Potential energy.
   thermal energy.

Lesson 2

What is sound energy?

3. Sound travels through cold air at about 1,190 kilometers per hour. That means that a sound can travel the length of three football fields in about a second. Some machines, such as jet planes, can travel faster than sound. The world's fastest train can travel 574.8 kilometers per hour. How much faster would it have to go to match the speed of sound in air?

   615.2 km per hour

4. **Summarize** Sound cannot travel through
   A. water.
   B. metal.
   C. air.
   D. empty space.

Solar Cooking

In some parts of Africa, people use wood to cook food. But wood is sometimes hard to find, and other fuels can be very expensive. Solar Cookers International (SCI) is a group that helps people learn to cook with the sun's energy. SCI needs to know where solar cooking can best be used.

One of NASA's energy management programs uses satellites to study Earth from space. NASA's Surface Solar Energy (SSE) information lets people use their latitude and longitude to learn the amount of solar energy available for cooking and many other purposes.

NASA's SSE information helps people use the sun, a natural resource and great source of energy, to cook. Then the people do not need to hunt for wood or spend what little money they have on fuel.

With the sun's energy, people use solar cookers to prepare meals. The sun is a safe and clean heat source. Solar cooking does not cost much. It does not cause a lot of smoke or air pollution in the environment. Solar cooking helps people harness some of the sun's power!

What properties should solar cookers have to make them work well and be useful?

....

....

....

What affects motion?

◉ Sequence

- **Sequence** refers to the order in which events happen *more time*
- Words such as *first, next, then, after,* and *finally* signal sequence.

Gracie

Ramp and Marble

(First) my friend gave me a ruler with a groove in the center. Next, I put one end of the ruler on the floor. Then, I propped the other end on a book to form a ramp. Finally, I put a marble in the groove at the high end of the ruler and let it go.

Practice It!

(Circle) clue words in the above reading. Then complete the graphic organizer to show the sequence in which things happened.

First

First, my friend gave me a ruler with a groove in the center.

Next

Next, I put one end of the ruler on the floor. then I prop the other

Then

Then, I propped the other end on a book to form a ramp

Finally

Finally, I put a marble in the groove at the high end of the ruler and let it go.

Let's Glide Away!

A glider is an aircraft that flies without an engine. Most gliders are towed into the air by a powered airplane. When the glider is released, the forces of thrust, drag, lift, and gravity act on the craft. Lift opposes gravity because air under the wings pushes the glider up. Like other aircraft, glider wings have a curved upper surface. Air moves faster over the wing than under it, causing the glider to rise. Air moving parallel to the airplane's wing has lower pressure than non-moving air. The faster air moves, the lower the pressure. Higher pressure under the wing lifts the glider.

Drag, which is caused by friction between the glider and the air, slows the glider down. Glider pilots can keep these craft in the air for hours by riding thermals—rising columns of warm air—to provide additional height throughout the flight.

You probably have made simple gliders before. Paper airplanes are gliders. Like gliders that carry people, a paper airplane's design determines how long, how far, and the speed it can fly. To make a model of a fuel-efficient way to fly, an airline company has asked you to work in a group to build a paper glider, test it, and then modify its design for maximum flying time and distance.

Identify the Problem

☐ **1.** What is your task? _are task is to make it fly._
_One ____ with it_

Do Research

Examine pictures of different aircraft.

☐ **2.** How are the designs of the aircraft the same? _big and fast_
_____

☐ **3.** How are the designs of the aircraft different? _One start's_
with it's size and the other
it with it's sped

Hold the short end of a strip of paper up to your mouth. Blow over the top of it.

☐ **4.** What happened to the paper? _____
_____

5. How is this similar to what makes a powered airplane fly? _It's creating_ _force_

Work with a group. Use a sheet of letter-sized copy paper and the directions below to **build** a glider.

1. Fold the paper in half lengthwise. Unfold the paper and smooth it out.

2. Fold one corner over so that it lines up with the center fold. Do the same with the other corner across the short side of the paper.

3. Fold the corners over again.

4. Fold the paper along the center fold again. Then, to make wings, fold the top half of each side down.

5. Use a small piece of tape to hold the wings together. Tape the keel (the paper under the wings) together at the plane's tail. Clip about 1 cm off the nose of your glider.

Use the spring scale to weigh your glider. **Record** the glider's weight: _____

Now, stick a piece of masking tape to the floor. Stand at the tape line, hold your glider from the back of the keel and throw it three times. For each throw, **record** how many seconds it is in the air and how many meters it flies. Use the chart below.

Trial	Time (seconds)	Distance (meters)
1	3.000 sec	28
2	5.000 sec	9
3	8.000 sec	12

Add up and ÷ by 3

6. What is the average time your glider stayed in the air? _8.000 sec_

7. What is the average distance your glider flew? _28_

Go to the materials station(s). Think about how each material may or may not be useful to modify the design of your glider so that it stays in the air longer and flies farther. Leave the materials where they are.

problem or restiction.

☐ **8.** What are your design constraints? Like to be able to fly very high

Develop Possible Solutions

☐ **9. Describe** two ways that you could modify the glider's design to make it fly longer and farther. _____

_____

_____

Choose One Solution

☐ **10. Draw** a diagram of your modified glider. **Label** its parts. **Describe** how you will build it.

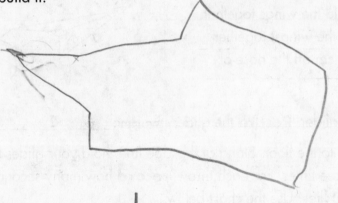

I would _____

_____

_____

_____

_____

☐ **11. List** the materials that you will need. Tape _____

_____

Design and Construct a Prototype

Gather your materials and a ruler. **Measure** the size of the paper you chose. Then, **build** your glider and weigh it using a spring scale.

☑ **12. Record** the design details of your prototype. I want my glider to fly 27 seconds and meters 55.

Test the Prototype

Test your glider. Again run three trials and **record** your results below.

Trial	Time (seconds)	Distance (meters)
1	3,000 sec	20 M
2	5,000 sec	9 M
3	9.00 6	10 M

☑ **13.** What is the average time your modified glider stayed in the air? 9000 t

☑ **14.** What is the average distance your modified glider flew? 20 meters

Communicate Results

☑ **15.** Did your modified design have the desired effect? Explain. No

Evaluate and Redesign

☑ **16. Explain** how you would further modify your design to make your glider fly better.
It flew very high and it made it better

What is motion?

Draw the path that the bouncing ball takes.

MY PLANET DIARY

//// MISCONCEPTION ////

Have you ever felt sick in a car, boat, train, or airplane? You may have had motion sickness. Some people think that motion sickness is a problem related to the stomach. However, motion sickness happens when a person's sense of balance is thrown off. Balance is controlled by the inner ear. Sometimes the inner ear and the eyes process riding in something, such as a car or airplane, in different ways. This can cause a person to get pale, to get sweaty, or to vomit.

What do you think people with motion sickness could do to feel better?

....

....

....

I will know what motion is. I will know that motion is relative and is affected by forces.

Words to Know

motion	force
reference point	gravity

Motion

All kinds of things around you move in different ways. Objects can move in a straight line, in a curved path, back and forth as a vibration, or as a rotation. You can describe and measure their motion in different ways. **Motion** is a change in the position of an object.

Look at the toy car and track in the picture to the right. First, the car moves in a straight path. Next, the car moves in curves around the track. Finally, the car moves back to the starting line.

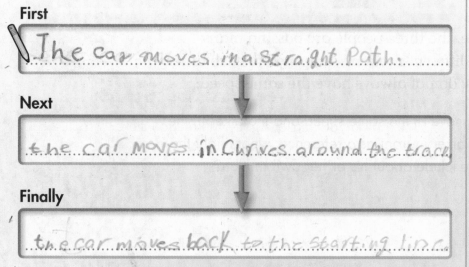

Sometimes toy cars move in a curved path.

Sometimes the cars move in a straight path on the track.

1. ◉ **Sequence** Describe the sequence of events of the yellow race car as it travels around the track.

2. **Identify** Of the types of motion discussed in this section, which types are not shown in the picture above?

car and race track

First

The car moves in a straight Path.

Next

the car moves in Curves around the track

Finally

the car moves back to the starting line

Relative Motion

As you ride your bicycle or walk down a street, you pass trees, buildings, and other things that do not move. They are fixed in place. When you pass a fixed object, you know you are moving. When you stand still, you can tell that a car you see moves if it changes position. Every day, you compare objects that change position with objects that do not. The change in one object's position compared with another object's position is called relative motion.

In the picture above, the three people are passing many trees. They also have different motions compared to each other, because they probably do not always have the same speed.

3. **Infer** If the bikers move at the same speed and the biker in the back uses only the biker in front as a reference, what might the biker in the back conclude about his or her own motion?

The biker in the book may
not be able to tell wheather
he or she is moving

Frame of Reference

How do you know if a person on a water slide moves? How do you know if the water moves? You look at the changing positions of the person and the water. You compare the person's changing positions with the fixed position of the slide. You use the relative motion of the objects around you to decide what is moving and what is not moving.

Objects that do not seem to move define your frame of reference. Your frame of reference is like your point of view. How an object seems to move depends on your frame of reference.

One way to help you describe your motion is to find a reference point. A **reference point** is a place or object used to determine if an object is in motion. For example, when you ride in a car, you can tell your car is moving by observing a sign, a tree, or a building. Many objects can be reference points.

4. ◉ Sequence **Underline** the steps you take to tell if a person on a water slide moves. Then number each step.

5. **Locate Draw** an ✗ on a reference point for the girl. **Circle** a moving object.

A moving marble hits a blue marble that is standing still.

6. Explain What do you think the contact force will do to the yellow marble above?

It will knock the 2 marbles and fall then it will slow down

Forces Affect Objects

Forces make objects move or stop. A **force** is any push or pull. Force can make an object that is standing still start to move in the direction of the force. It can also make a moving object move faster, slow down, stop, or change direction.

Some forces act only on contact. A contact force must touch an object to affect it. A marble on a level surface will not move until you hit it with your finger or another object. When your finger collides with the marble, you transfer energy from your finger to the marble to make it move. The collision of your finger and the marble also transfers some energy to the surrounding air, making a sound that you hear.

Pushing or pulling can change both the position and motion of an object. The size of the change depends on the strength of the push or pull. For example, the harder you push a swing, the higher and faster it will move.

All forces have size and direction. Notice the dogs pulling on the rubber toy. They are pulling in opposite directions, but with the same amount of force. As long as they pull with forces that are the same size, the forces are balanced, and the toy will not move. If one dog pulls with more force, the forces will be unbalanced. The toy will move toward the dog pulling with greater force.

7. Locate Underline in the first paragraph the five ways a force can affect motion.

A person applies a force to bike pedals. The pedals transfer this force to the chain and then to the tires. This causes the bike to move.

Force and Motion

Force causes a change in motion in an object. The amount of force acting on an object affects how that object changes speed, direction, or both. When you ride a bike, you push the pedals. If you push harder, the bike goes faster. You turn the handlebars. The bike changes direction. Pedaling and turning change the bike's motion.

A moving object changes its motion only when a force acts on it. If balanced forces are applied to a moving object, it will keep moving at the same speed and in the same direction. The moving object will not slow, speed up, or turn until the forces acting on it become unbalanced. An example is when you continue to pedal your bike with the same force. The bike will continue to move at the same speed because the same force is acting on it. If the moving bike collides with another object, the bike will slow down or stop. The contact forces from the collision transfer energy and change the bike's motion.

Balanced forces that act in opposite directions cancel each other. For example, if you apply the same force to the brake and pedal at the same time, the motion of the bike will not change.

8. Demonstrate Describe an example of balanced forces that cancel each other.

....

....

....

The brakes produce a force that slows or stops the bike when necessary.

Lightning Lab

The Wrecking Ball
Work with a partner. Roll a ball across the floor. Note what is changing—the ball's position, its direction, or both. Roll the ball again. Have your partner roll another ball at it so that they collide. Note what is changing—the first ball's position, its direction, or both.

Force and Mass

How an object moves also depends on how much mass it has. More force is needed to change the motion of an object with more mass. You can easily move an empty shopping cart. As you fill the cart with groceries, the cart gains mass. So, you have to use more force to move the cart.

9. Evaluate Suppose one pumpkin is taken out of the wagon. How will the force needed to pull the wagon change?

Less force will be needed

Force of Gravity

The force that pulls all objects toward each other is **gravity.** The strength of the force of gravity depends on the masses of the objects and how much distance is between them. You do not notice or feel the force of gravity between everyday objects. The force of gravity increases as objects increase in mass. It also increases as objects get closer.

Gravity and Mass

Gravity is the force that makes an object such as a ball fall to the ground. When you drop a ball, it falls to the ground because Earth's large mass pulls on it. The ball pulls on Earth, too, but the ball's mass is too small to affect Earth in any noticeable way.

10. Apply Gravity keeps Earth orbiting the sun. Earth is about 150,000,000 km (93,205,679 miles) from the sun. What does this distance tell you about the masses of Earth and the sun?

The masses are very great

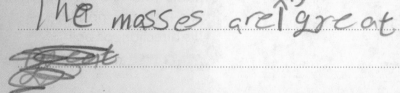

Gravity pulls this apple to the ground.

Rank the animals from fastest to slowest. Put a *1, 2,* or *3* next to each animal.

UNLOCK THE BIG ?

I will know how to find, describe, and graph the speed of an object.

Words to Know

speed
velocity

Speed

The rate at which an object changes position is called **speed.** Speed measures how fast an object moves. Moving objects have energy. The faster an object moves, the more energy it has. For example, a car moving at a high speed has more energy and changes position faster than a car moving at a slow speed. The unit for speed is a unit of distance divided by a unit of time, such as kilometers per hour.

Many animals run faster than humans. The fastest land mammal is the cheetah. It can run at speeds around 70 miles per hour or 112 kilometers per hour. A peregrine falcon is also very fast. When it swoops to capture prey, the falcon moves at almost 275 miles per hour! In the pictures above, which animals do you think are faster than you?

1. **Locate** (Circle) the main idea in the second paragraph above. **Underline** the details.

2. **Compute** How much faster is the top speed of a peregrine falcon than that of the cheetah?

205 mph

$$\begin{array}{r} 275 \\ - 70 \\ \hline 205 \end{array}$$

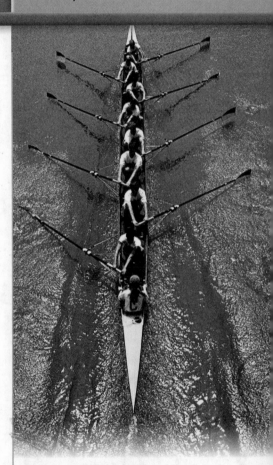

3. **Tell** Describe the speed of this rowboat.

The boat is probily moving fast b/c many people rowing.

Calculate Average Speed

The speed of most objects changes. For example, when you ride your bike, you do not always travel at the same speed. At different points on your trip, you will have different speeds. However, you can calculate the average speed of your trip. To find an object's average speed, divide the distance the object moves by the total time spent moving.

To calculate average speed, you use this equation:

$$\text{Average Speed} = \frac{\text{total distance}}{\text{total time}}$$

Look at the map on these pages. The map shows the route a car traveled from point A to point D.

Point A

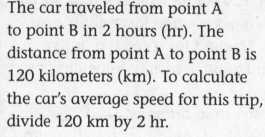

Point B

The car traveled from point A to point B in 2 hours (hr). The distance from point A to point B is 120 kilometers (km). To calculate the car's average speed for this trip, divide 120 km by 2 hr.

$$\text{Average Speed} = \frac{120 \text{ km}}{2 \text{ hr}}$$

$$\text{Average Speed} = \frac{60 \text{ km}}{1 \text{ hr}}$$

$$\text{Average Speed} = 60 \frac{\text{km}}{\text{hr}}$$

So the car traveled at an average speed of 60 kilometers per hour from point A to point B.

At-Home Lab

On a Roll

Work in an open area. Mark a starting point. Roll a ball from the starting point. Mark where the ball stopped. Roll the ball from the starting point again. Use more force. Make a statement about the speed of the ball. Base your statements on your observations.

| 20 mi |
| 20 km |

The car traveled 231 kilometers from point B to point C in 3 hours.

$$\text{Speed} = \frac{231 \text{ km}}{3 \text{ hr}}$$

 3⟌231

4. Calculate What was the average speed for this leg of the trip? Show your work.

77 $\frac{Km}{hr}$

The car traveled 90 kilometers from point C to point D in 2 hours.

5. Calculate What was the average speed for this leg of the trip? Show your work.

2⟌90

Point D

Point C

6. CHALLENGE What was the average speed for the entire trip from point A to point D? Show your work.

12 Km + 231 Km + 90 Km = 441 Km

2hr + 3 hr + 2hr = 7hr

441 Km = 63 Km
7hr

63 $\frac{Km}{hr}$

Velocity and Acceleration

Some objects change speed and direction. **Velocity** combines both the speed and the direction an object is moving. Some words that describe direction are *north, south, east,* and *west.* Others are *left, right, up,* and *down.*

Any change in the speed or direction of an object's motion is acceleration. Starting, speeding up, and slowing down are accelerations. The roller coaster accelerates as it speeds up or slows down. It is changing speed. A roller coaster on a curved path accelerates even if its speed does not change. That is because it changes direction as it moves around the curve.

7. **Summarize** What are two things that must be measured in order to find an object's velocity?

....

....

....

8. **Illustrate** Look at the roller coaster on the opposite page. **Draw** a solid arrow where the roller coaster slows down, and a dotted arrow where the coaster speeds up.

Do the math!

Make a Graph

The chart shows the distance a cyclist has traveled in 4 hours. Use the data in the chart to graph the distance traveled by the cyclist.

Distance Traveled by a Cyclist				
Time (hours)	1	2	3	4
Distance (kilometers)	15	32	40	60

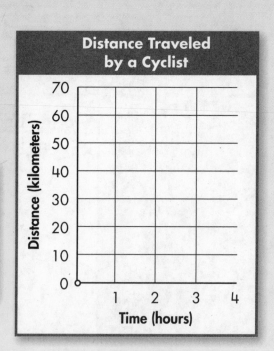

Distance Traveled by a Cyclist

Got it?

10. **Produce** How do you calculate average speed?

11. **UNLOCK THE BIG ?** How do speed and velocity help to describe and measure motion?

⬛ **Stop!** I need help with

⏸ **Wait!** I have a question about

▶ **Go!** Now I know

How does friction affect motion?

Follow a Procedure

☐ **1.** Tape sandpaper to a piece of cardboard.

☐ **2.** Put a toy car and eraser at the top of the ramp. Have another student hold the Ramp Angle Protractor.

☐ **3.** Slowly raise the ramp by hand. When each object reaches the bottom of the ramp, **record** the angle. Repeat 2 more times.

Materials

sandpaper

tape

scissors

cardboard

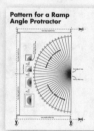

waxed paper

Pattern for a Ramp Angle Protractor

calculator or computer (optional)

eraser

toy car

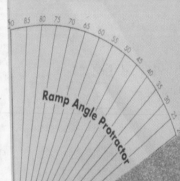

Ramp Angle Protractor

Inquiry Skill
You can use a bar graph to help you **interpret data.**

4. Tell what would happen if you used waxed paper instead of sandpaper. Test your **prediction** 3 times. Record your results.

Trial	Angle When Object Reached Bottom of Ramp (degrees)			
	Sandpaper Surface		**Waxed-Paper Surface**	
	Car	**Eraser**	**Car**	**Eraser**
1				
2				
3				
Average				

Effect of Friction on Motion

5. Find the average angles. Make a bar graph of your results.

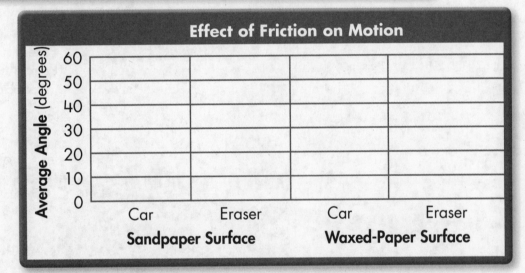

Analyze and Conclude

6. Interpret Data How did changing surfaces affect the angle you recorded?

....

7. Describe how friction affected the motion of the objects on each surface.

....

....

....

STEM

SmartPlane™

What if an airplane became damaged in mid-flight? What if software could help control the damaged airplane? Engineers are working on just such software! It is called the Intelligent Flight Control System. This technology helps damaged airplanes fly. For example, if a bird flew into an engine and damaged the engine, the software could help the pilot safely land the plane. The software technology would know how an airplane should fly. If the airplane started having problems, the system would adjust controls, such as engine thrust.

Determine How do you think engineers might use science and math to develop the software?

....

....

....

Future commercial airplanes could use this technology to avoid crashes and to save lives.

Vocabulary Smart Cards

motion
reference point
force
gravity
speed
velocity

Play a Game!

Cut out the Vocabulary Smart Cards.

Work with a partner. Choose a Vocabulary Smart Card. Write several sentences using the vocabulary word. Have your partner repeat using a different Vocabulary Smart Card.

gravity

gravedad

motion
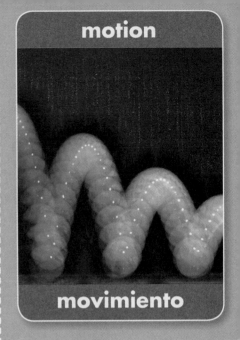
movimiento

speed

rapidez

reference point
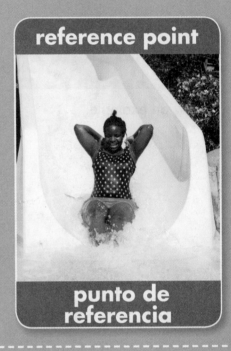
punto de referencia

velocity

velocidad

force

fuerza

a change in the position of an object

Write an example.

The motion Of the basket ball curved as its entcved the.

cambio en la posición de un objeto

---

the force that pulls all objects toward each other

Write a sentence using this word.

The force of gravity with effect an objects weight

fuerza que atrae a todos los objetos entre sí

---

a place or object used to determine if an object is in motion

Draw an example.

bike

lugar u objeto usado para determinar si algo está en movimiento

---

the rate at which an object changes position

Write a sentence using this word.

The car Speed was 35m per hour

ritmo al cual cambia la posición de un objeto

---

any push or pull

Draw an example.

she is pushing the table

empujón o jalón

---

the speed and the direction an object is moving

Write a sentence using this word.

The truck volosity was 50 miles per hour heading north.

rapidez y dirección en que se mueve un objeto

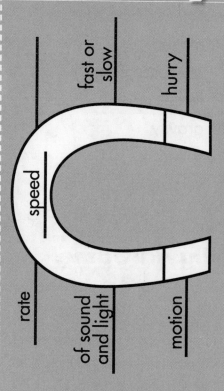

fast or slow

hurry

speed

rate

of sound and light

motion

Make a Word Magnet

Choose a vocabulary word and write it in the Word Magnet. Write words that are related to it on the lines.

Study Guide

REVIEW THE BIG ? How can motion be described and measured?

Physical Science

Lesson 1

What is motion?

- Objects move in straight lines, in curved paths, or back and forth.
- The mass of an object affects the force needed to change its motion.
- The force of gravity pulls objects to Earth.

Lesson 2

What is speed?

- Speed is the rate at which an object changes position.
- Velocity describes the speed and direction of a moving object.
- Acceleration is the change in speed or direction of an object.

SavvasRealize.com

Lesson 1

What is motion?

1. **Vocabulary** Motion occurs when one object changes _____ in relation to another object.
   A. reference
   B. position
   C. force
   D. time

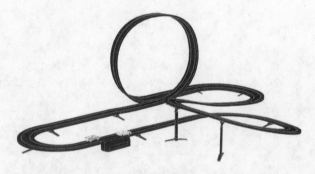

2. **Predict** If you are in a car that is going to the supermarket, how do you know when the car is moving?

   I look for a reference point. Such as a building When the car moves away, from it's potion

3. **Analyze** What makes objects move? How would you make a lawnmower move?

4. **Sequence** Read the paragraph. Then, fill in the graphic organizer to show the sequence of events.

   The car that I saw was really cool. First, it drove in my direction while I was on the sidewalk. Next, it drove past me and messed up my hair. Before going out of sight, it moved away from me.

   First I saw a cool car.

   ↓

   Next it drove past me and messed up my hair.

   ↓

   Then it moved away from me.

   ↓

   Finally, the cars was out of sight.

5. **Write About It** Why do you need to use force to move a ball up a ramp when it moves downward by itself?

   Gravity is the force that causes the ball to roll down the ramp. You need a force to overcome the force of gravity to push the ball up the ramp.

Lesson 2

What is speed?

6.  The chart shows how far a runner races in 4 minutes. Use the data in the chart to graph the distance traveled by the runner.

Distance Traveled by a Runner

Time (minutes)	Distance (meters)
1	200
2	400
3	600
4	800

Distance Traveled by a Runner

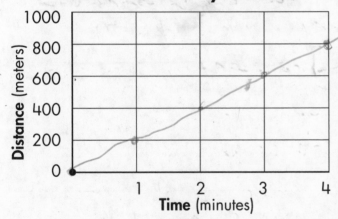

7. **Explain** What is velocity?

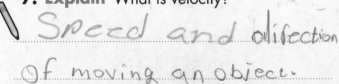

Speed and direction of moving an object.

8. **Explain** How does the speed of an object relate to the energy of the object?

The faster an object moves, the greater the energy.

9. **Apply** Circle the place on the ruler where the marble has the greatest speed.

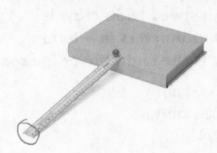

10. **APPLY THE BIG ?** **How can motion be described and measured?**

Think about the motion of an airplane. Describe its speed and acceleration before and during takeoff.

Before takeoff, an airplane is not moving or moves slowly. During takeoff, an airplane accelerates when its speeds up and changes direction of the runway and of the ground.

Benchmark Practice

Read each question and choose the best answer.

1 Gravity is a force that makes objects

    A push apart.
    B pull toward each other.
    C stop moving.
    D move uphill.

2 A high-speed train travels 1,000 kilometers in 4 hours. What is the train's average speed?

    A 4,000 km/hr
    B 1,000 km/hr
    C 250 km/hr
    D 150 km/hr

3 What happens to the energy of an object when the speed of the object decreases?

    A It increases.
    B It decreases.
    C It stays the same.
    D It first decreases and then increases again.

4 Which of the following is an example of velocity?

    A walking 28 km
    B walking 28 km/hr quickly
    C walking 28 km/hr north
    D walking 28 km/hr

5 This picture shows the brakes on a bicycle. Explain how the use of the brakes changes the motion of the bicycle. How does the mass of the bicycle affect the force that needs to be applied to the brakes?

The breakes slows or Stops the bike. The greater the mass of the bike, the greater the force that it needs to be applied to the brakes to make the bike slows or stop

A Trip Along the San Juan Skyway

The San Juan Skyway is a scenic road in Colorado. The road winds through national forests and through the San Juan Mountains. Drivers must travel slowly and carefully in places where the road gets steep. Drivers may also go slowly to enjoy the views of the mountains.

There is, however, another reason to travel at or below the speed limit. Did you know that most cars use less gas when they are traveling more slowly? Cars are most efficient when they are moving at a certain speed. A car's gas mileage decreases rapidly when it travels faster than 60 mph. For most cars, the most efficient speed is between 35 and 45 mph.

Place a check mark next to the items that your family does to save fuel.

Save Fuel in an Automobile

- [ ] Do not accelerate too quickly from stoplights or stop signs.
- [ ] Keep tires filled with the right amount of air.
- [ ] Have the vehicle serviced on a regular basis.
- [ ] Use bicycles or walk when the distance is not far.

What LIGHTS the night?

Electricity

Try It! What can electricity flow through?

STEM Activity How Can You Keep Liquids Warm or Cold?

Lesson 1 How do electrical charges flow in a circuit?

Lesson 2 How can energy change?

Investigate It! How does a circuit board work?

Physical Science

Apply It! Which is the best way to slow the rate at which ice melts?

This is what the United States looks like at night. Can you find a city near where you live?

Predict How does electrical energy help to light the cities of the United States?

....

....

....

THE BIG ? How is electrical energy transferred and transformed?

What can electricity flow through?

☐ **1.** Make the circuit as shown.

☐ **2. Predict** Choose one of the objects to complete
the circuit. Will it allow the bulb to light up or not?
Record your predictions for each object.

....

....

....

☐ **3.** Test each object. **Observe.**

*Touch the free ends of the wires
to the material being tested.*

Be careful! **Wear safety goggles.**

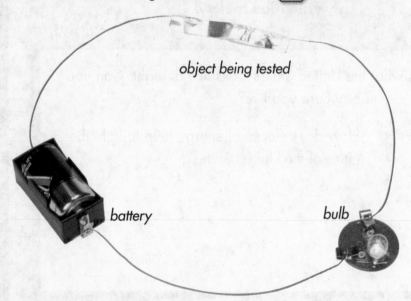

object being tested

battery   bulb

Materials

flashlight bulb and holder

3 pieces of wire

plastic spoon

battery and battery holder

paper clip

foil

penny

index card

safety goggles

Inquiry Skill You **classify** objects when you sort them according to properties you observe.

Explain Your Results

4. Classify Electricity flows through ....

....

Electricity does not flow through ....

....

Cause and Effect

- A **cause** is why something happens. An **effect** is what happens.
- When you read, sometimes clue words such as *because* and *since* signal a cause-and-effect relationship.

Heat Lamps and Chicks

A farmer flips the switch on a heat lamp. Electricity begins to flow, the lamp lights up, and the lamp heats up. The farmer puts newly hatched chicks under its warm glow. Because the lamp gives off heat, the chicks will stay warm and be able to grow.

Practice It!

Use the graphic organizer below to list one cause and one effect found in the example paragraph.

Cause

Effect

How Can You Keep Liquids Warm or Cold?

Suppose you and your classmates are packed together in a tight space. You start to wiggle. What happens? The people around you would move when you bumped into them. The people next to them would also move, and so on.

Conduction works in the same way. Conduction is the movement of thermal energy from one molecule to another. When a particle of an object warms, it moves faster. As moving particles bump into neighboring particles, these particles move faster. The particles of good conductors are close together. They can bump into each other easily. The particles of good insulators are farther apart. Insulators slow conduction. For example, if the same friends spread out in a large room, one could wiggle without affecting the others.

After complaints from customers, a local coffee shop asked you to design and test a cup insulator that keeps cool things cool and hot things hot.

Identify the Problem

☐ **1.** What problem will your cup insulator help to solve? _____

_____

Do Research

Examine a foam cup, a vacuum flask, and a soft drink's can cover. These are all good insulators. They keep cold things cold and hot things hot. **Write** your observations about each one.

☐ **2.** Foam cup: _____

_____

☐ **3.** Vacuum flask: _____

_____

☐ **4.** Can cover: _____

_____

☐ **5.** Do you think air or metal is a better insulator? Explain. _____

_____

6. Why can the same material keep cool things cool and hot things hot?

_____

_____

Go to the materials station(s). Pick up each material one at a time. Think about how it may or may not be useful in your design. Leave the materials where they are.

7. What are your design constraints? _____

_____

Develop Possible Solutions

8. List two different ways you could combine some of the materials to solve the problem.

_____

_____

Choose One Solution

9. Describe your cup insulator and how you will build it. _____

_____

_____

10. List the materials that you will need. _____

_____

Design and Construct a Prototype

Gather enough materials to build two insulators, plus four paper cups, a ruler, four thermometers, and a spring scale. **Measure** each material using the appropriate units of measurement. **Build** your insulators and place each one on a cup.

11. Record the design details of your prototype. _____

_____

_____

Test the Prototype

Test your insulator.

☐ **12.** First, fill two of your paper cups—one with an insulator and one without—with hot water. Snap on the lids. The cup without the insulator is your control. Push a thermometer through the hole in each lid, and measure the temperature of the water. Wait at least 30 seconds in order to get an accurate reading. **Record** your initial reading in the table below. Leave the thermometers in the cups.

Time	Control (°C)	Insulated Cup (°C)
Initial reading		
10 minutes		
20 minutes		
30 minutes		
40 minutes		

☐ **13.** Fill the other two cups with ice water. Use the strainer to strain the ice out of the water as you fill the cups. Snap on the lids. The cup without the insulator is your control. Push a thermometer through the hole in each lid, and measure the temperature of the water in the cups. Wait at least 30 seconds in order to get an accurate reading. **Record** your initial reading in the table below. Leave the thermometers in the cups.

Time	Control (°C)	Insulated Cup (°C)
Initial reading		
10 minutes		
20 minutes		
30 minutes		
40 minutes		

In 10-minute intervals, **measure** the temperatures of the water in each cup four more times. **Record** your data in the tables above.

Communicate Results

Graph the data in your tables. Label the x-axis "time" and the y-axis "temperature." Each graph will have two lines, one for the control and one for the cup with the insulator. Make the line that represents the control cups a different color than the line that represents the cups with the insulators.

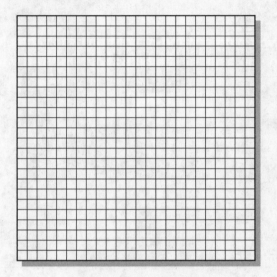 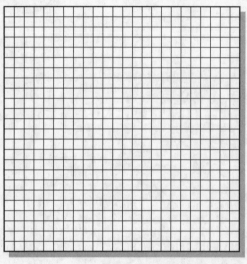

☐ **14. Summarize** each graph, including how temperature changed over time in each of the cups.

_____

_____

_____

Evaluate and Redesign

☐ **15.** What do your graphs help you see about your insulator? _____

_____

☐ **16. Explain** how you would change your design to make your insulator work better. ____

_____

_____

How do electric charges flow in a circuit?

Envision It!

When you plug a string of light bulbs into an electric outlet, why do you think all the bulbs light up? **Tell** your answer.

MY PLANET DIARY

Science Stats

If you have seen lightning, then you know it can be an incredible sight. Lightning strikes the ground in the United States more than 20 million times in a year. A flash of lightning can heat the air around it to about 30,000 degrees Celsius (about 54,000 degrees Fahrenheit). That is five times hotter than the sun's surface! One flash of lightning also has enough electricity to light an incandescent light bulb for more than three months.

About how many times did lightning strike the ground between when you were born and your most recent birthday?

2 X 9 = 180000000

Lightning can strike as far as 16 kilometers away from a rainstorm.

Words to Know

electric current	series circuit
conductor	parallel circuit
insulator	

Electric Charges

You dash across a carpet and touch a metal doorknob. *Ouch!* A jolt of static electricity startles you. To understand what happened, start with atoms, the tiny building blocks of everything. Most atoms have three different particles. Some particles have a positive charge (+). Some have a negative charge (–). Some have no charge. Atoms usually have the same number of positive and negative particles.

Charged particles can move between objects that are close to each other. Static electricity happens when positive and negative charges no longer balance. *Static* means "not moving," but eventually the static electricity does move. It may move gradually or it may move very quickly. Moving charges generate electrical energy, which can change into sound energy, light energy, or heat.

2. **Infer** Name an object that may have caused the static electricity in this child's hair.

Silde
Trampoline

1. ◉ **Cause and Effect** Complete the graphic organizer below. Write the cause of static electricity.

hi Gracie it is 12/13/21

Cause

and
+ − charges are no longer in balnce

Effect

Static electricity happens.

Classify Conductors and Insulators

Look at objects at your desk and around your classroom. Think about what material each object is made of. Make a list of objects that are conductors and a list of objects that are insulators.

How Electric Charges Flow

Most electricity is on the go. Energy can be moved from place to place by moving objects or through sound, light, or electric currents. An electric charge in motion is called an **electric current.** An electric current flows quickly and invisibly from one place to another.

Conductors

The flow of electric charge is not the same in all materials. An electric current flows through some kinds of atoms more easily than others. These materials are called conductors. A **conductor** is a material through which an electric charge can move easily. Most metals, such as copper, gold, and silver, are good conductors. Other conductors include metal scissors and the lead, or graphite, in your pencil.

3. ◉ **Cause and Effect** In the text, **underline** what causes some materials to be good conductors of electricity.

4. **Explain** The computer part below is made of gold conductors. Will gold allow electric charges to flow easily in this computer part? Why or Why not?

Yes, electric charges and moves easily

Insulators

Other materials do not allow an electric current to move easily through them. An **insulator** is a material through which an electric charge moves with difficulty. Plastic, rubber, glass, and dry wood are good insulators. Other insulators are the eraser on your pencil and the chalk you may use to draw.

5. Analyze Why are glass insulators used on power lines?

Plastic, rubber, glass, and Dry wood are good insulators.

glass insulators

6. Infer Electricians often wear special shoes with thick, rubber soles. Why?

Why because if you were in regular shoes those they will burn that is why they wear boots.

plastic insulator

conductor

The plug and the wires inside this electrical cord are conductors. The plastic insulator makes the cord safe to handle.

Circuits

For a current to flow, electric charges must complete a loop, or circuit. A current cannot flow if the circuit has any gaps, or breaks. A cut wire and an off switch are examples of breaks. A circuit is open if it has at least one break. It is closed if it has no breaks. For example, if a switch in a flashlight is turned off, the circuit is open.

A circuit has many parts. Its energy source provides the energy to move electric charges. Batteries and electrical outlets are energy sources. A circuit has wires through which the charges flow. It also has resistors such as light bulbs or machines. Resistors transform energy to other forms of energy. They use the energy that flows through the circuit. A circuit may also have a switch. The symbols below are used to represent the parts of a circuit.

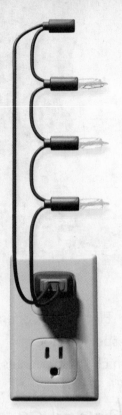

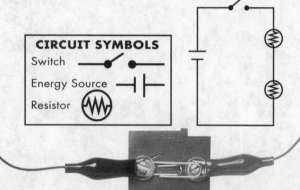

CIRCUIT SYMBOLS
Switch
Energy Source
Resistor

7. Conclude Think about what you read about series circuits. Why are the bulbs in the series circuit above not lit?

The missing bulb opens in circuit.

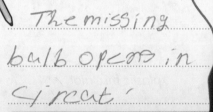

energy

circuit

Series Circuits

One type of circuit is called a series circuit. In a **series circuit,** electric charge can flow in only one circular path. When the power source is turned on, the charged particles in the wire flow in one direction around a single loop. Any break in the loop, such as a burnt-out or missing bulb, stops the current from flowing.

8. Recognize Label the parts of this series circuit.

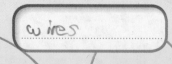

wires

90

Parallel Circuits

Another type of circuit is a parallel circuit. A **parallel circuit** has two or more paths through which electric charges may flow. Each path leaves from the power source and returns to it. The current that flows through one path does not have to flow through the other paths. Therefore, if one loop in the circuit is broken, the current will still flow through the other loops.

9. Locate (Circle) the loop that is broken.

In a parallel circuit, one missing or burnt-out bulb does not open the circuit.

Got it?

10. Classify How can you classify materials as conductors or insulators?

Well electric charges moved difficulty for an insulator and a conductor can move easaly. so I think a conductor.

11. Cause and Effect Explain how a switch can affect the flow of an electric current in a circuit.

When it's open it flows when site is closed burnt Stop Passing bulb, stops the current from flowing

Stop! I need help with ....

Wait! I have a question about ....

Go! Now I know ....

Lesson 2

How can energy change?

Tell how electricity is important to the plants in this tank.

Inquiry Explore It!

How can a switch make a complete circuit?

☐ **1.** Make a circuit as shown.

☐ **2.** Make a switch as shown.

top side

Punch two fasteners into an index card. Attach a paper clip to one of the fasteners.

bottom side

Wrap a wire around the arms of two metal fasteners.

Materials

safety goggles

3 pieces of wire

bulb and holder

battery and holder

paper clip

pencil with eraser

2 fasteners

index card

☐ **3. Predict** what will happen when the paper clip touches the other fastener.

☐ **4.** Use the pencil eraser to touch the paper clip to the other fastener. **Observe.**

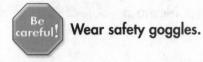

Be careful! Wear safety goggles.

Explain Your Results

5. Draw a Conclusion How did the paper clip act as a switch?

92

I will know how energy changes form. I will know how electricity changes to light and gives off heat.

Word to Know

filament

Energy Changing Form

There are many different forms of energy. Electricity, light, sound, and energy of motion are some forms of energy. Energy is never lost. It cannot be made or destroyed. However, energy can transform, or change form. Wind can change to electricity. After electrical energy is transferred from one place to another by an electric current, it can be transformed to another type of energy, such as motion, sound, heat, or light. These examples are only some ways that energy can change.

Many objects transform energy as they work. A lamp transforms electrical energy to light. If you pluck a guitar string, the energy of motion transforms to sound energy.

You experience energy changing form when you rub your hands together quickly. The energy of motion causes friction. Friction is a force that acts when two surfaces rub together. As a result of friction, heat is given off. So, your hands warm up.

1. **Exemplify** Name an object that transforms electrical energy to sound energy.

....

A wind turbine transforms energy of motion into electrical energy, which can form electric currents.

2. **Recognize** Write how energy is transformed by a wind turbine. Fill in the blanks.

....

energy changes to

....

Light from Electricity

Televisions, computers, and light bulbs all use electricity. These objects are resistors that use the energy in a circuit. Most resistors transform electrical energy to heat and light. The filament in an incandescent light bulb is its resistor. A **filament** is a thin, coiled wire that can get very hot without melting. Most of the electricity passing through the filament is changed into heat. But the filament is a strong resistor. The filament becomes so hot that it glows, also giving off light.

3.  **Cause and Effect**
Underline the cause of electricity being changed into light in a filament.

Fluorescent light bulbs do not use a filament. They produce less heat than incandescent light bulbs and use less electricity.

incandescent light bulb

Do the math!

Using Percents

Electrical energy is measured in units called kilowatt-hours. About 10 percent of the energy in an incandescent light bulb is used for light. The rest is heat. About 75 percent of the energy of a fluorescent light bulb is given off as light.

1 If an incandescent light bulb burns for 1,000 kilowatt-hours, how much energy is used for light?

....
....

2 If a fluorescent light bulb burns for 1,000 kilowatt-hours, how much energy is used for light?

....
....

3 **Conclude** Which bulb is more energy efficient at producing light?

....
....

Heat from Electricity

When electrical current passes through a resistor, it often gives off heat. This change is why electrical wires sometimes become hot. Some types of wires are good resistors. Many appliances have coils of these wires. More coils allow an appliance to become hotter. The resistors of some appliances get so hot that they produce a red glow. This glow happens in toasters.

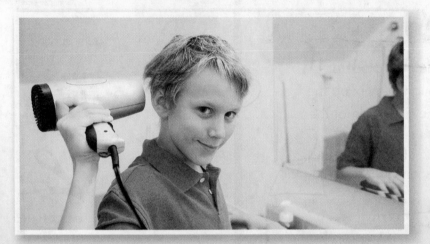

At-Home Lab

Motion and Heat
Rub an eraser quickly across a table several times. Touch the eraser. Then describe how it feels.

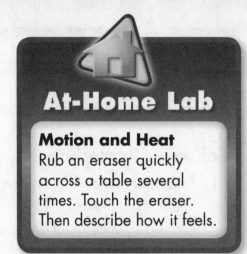

4. **Infer** Many hair dryers use heating coils as resistors. Explain why.

So the coils can become hotter.

Got it?

5. **Summarize** Describe how a filament in an incandescent light bulb transforms electrical energy.

6. **UNLOCK THE BIG ?** How can objects transform electrical energy?

_I___ by sound and light._

◻ **Stop!** I need help with ....

❚❚ **Wait!** I have a question about ....

▶ **Go!** Now I know ....

How does a circuit board work?

Follow a Procedure

☐ **1.** Fold an index card. Cut along the fold lines to make 12 squares. Write 6 science questions and 6 answers on the squares.

☐ **2.** Glue the questions on the left side of a piece of cardboard. Number them 1 through 6. Mix up the answers. Glue the answers on the right side of the cardboard. Label them A to F.

☐ **3.** **Record** the correct answer for each question.

Answers to Science Questions	
Question	Correct Answer
1	
2	
3	
4	
5	
6	

☐ **4.** Punch a hole to the left of each question and to the right of each answer. Put a fastener through each hole.

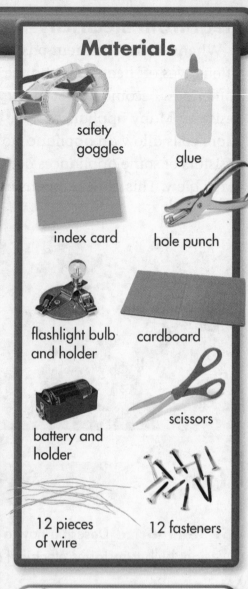

Materials

safety goggles

glue

index card

hole punch

flashlight bulb and holder

cardboard

scissors

battery and holder

12 pieces of wire

12 fasteners

Inquiry Skill Using the right tool can make it easy to **observe** energy flow.

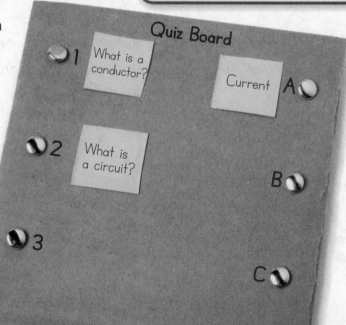

Quiz Board

1 What is a conductor?

Current A

2 What is a circuit?

B

3

C

5. Turn the cardboard over. Label the fasteners with the correct numbers and letters. Use a wire to connect the fastener for each question to the fastener for the correct answer.

Be careful! **Wear safety goggles.**

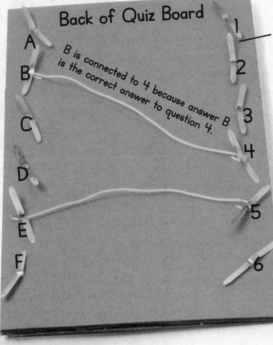

Back of Quiz Board

A
B *B is connected to 4 because answer B is the correct answer to question 4.*
C
D
E
F

1
2
3
4
5
6

Make sure fasteners do not touch!

Turn the board over. Touch one wire to a question and the other wire to the correct answer. Does the bulb light?

6. Make the simple circuit as shown.

7. Observe Touch a testing wire to a question fastener. Touch the other wire to the correct answer.

Analyze and Conclude

8. Infer What can you infer from your observations in Step 7?

....

....

9. **UNLOCK THE BIG ?** What kind of energy transformation took place when a question was answered correctly?

....

....

Electrician

You flip a switch and a light goes on. Every time this happens, you have an electrician to thank.

Electricians run the wires that carry current throughout your home, your school, and any building that has electricity. Some electricians work mainly in houses and other small buildings. Others work in office buildings, where they might install telephones and cables for computers as well as electrical wiring. Still others work in large factories, where they might repair robots or fix machine tools.

Electricians check to make sure that electrical systems are safe. They usually spend much of the workday on their feet. Sometimes they need to climb ladders or crawl into small spaces to put up or repair wires. They must work carefully because poor wiring can cause electrical shocks and fires.

If you like to work with your hands and are good at problem solving, you might like to become an electrician.

Apply Why do you think it is important for electricians to be good at problem solving?

....

....

Vocabulary Smart Cards

electric current
conductor
insulator
series circuit
parallel circuit
filament

Play a Game!

Cut out the Vocabulary Smart Cards.

Work with a partner. Choose a Vocabulary Smart Card. Do not let your partner see your card.

Draw a picture to show what the word means. Have your partner guess the word. Take turns drawing and guessing.

series circuit

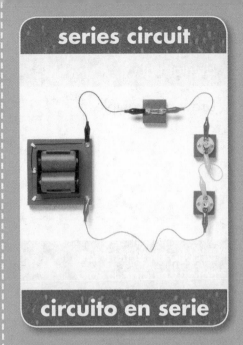

circuito en serie

electric current

corriente eléctrica

parallel circuit

circuito en paralelo

conductor

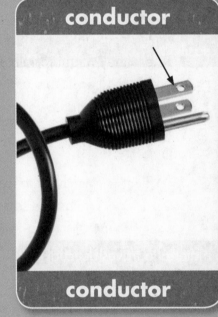

conductor

filament

filamento

insulator

aislante

an electric charge in motion

Write a sentence using this term.

....

....

....

....

carga eléctrica en movimiento

---

a circuit in which electrical charge can only flow in one circular path

Draw an example.

circuito en el cual las cargas eléctricas sólo pueden fluir en una trayectoria circular

---

Interactive Vocabulary

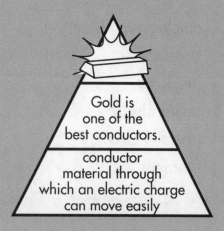

Gold is one of the best conductors.

conductor material through which an electric charge can move easily

Make a Word Pyramid!

Choose a vocabulary word and write the word and definition in the base of the pyramid. Write a sentence in the middle of the pyramid. Draw a picture of an example, or of something related, at the top.

---

a material through which an electric charge can move easily

Draw an example.

material a través del cual las cargas eléctricas pueden moverse con facilidad

---

a circuit that has two or more paths through which electrical charges may flow

Write an example.

....

....

....

circuito que tiene dos o más vías por las que pueden fluir las cargas eléctricas

---

a material through which an electric charge moves slowly

Draw an example.

material a través del cual las cargas eléctricas se mueven muy lentamente

---

a thin, coiled wire that can get very hot without melting

Write a sentence using this word.

....

....

....

alambre fino y enrollado que puede calentarse mucho sin derretirse

Study Guide

REVIEW THE BIG ? How is electrical energy transferred and transformed?

Physical Science

Lesson 1

How do electric charges flow in a circuit?

- An electric charge flows through conductors easily.
- An electric charge flows through insulators with difficulty.
- For a current to flow, electric charges must complete a circuit.

Lesson 2

How can energy change?

- Electrical, light, and energy of motion are some forms of energy.
- The energy of motion can cause friction and give off heat.
- Electrical energy can change to light energy and give off heat.

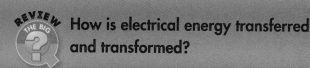
Lesson 1

How do electric charges flow in a circuit?

1. **Vocabulary** An electric charge in motion is called
   - A. an electric current.
   - B. an insulator.
   - C. a parallel circuit.
   - D. an energy source.

2. **Interpret** Look at the circuit diagram. Is it a series circuit or a parallel circuit? Explain your answer.

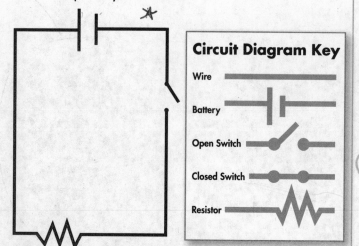

Circuit Diagram Key

Wire	
Battery	
Open Switch	
Closed Switch	
Resistor	

How I knew is was a series circut becauss It is Shaped in a Square and a parnici is shaped in a diffrant Shape.

3. **Cause and Effect** Circle a cause and **underline** its effect in the paragraph below.

Electric charges move more easily through some materials than others. Conductors are materials with atoms that easily become charged. As a result, an electric charge can move easily through a conductor. Most metals are good conductors.

4. **Predict** Suppose you have a set of lights that are wired in a parallel circuit. What will happen to the circuit if one bulb burns out?

The bulbs will stay unto circut.

5. **Write About It** A flashlight is a series circuit that has a battery as its energy source. Describe what happens in a flashlight when the switch is turned from *off* to *on*.

When it is open The light bulb will light when Ia When it is off

Lesson 2

How can energy change form?

6. Vocabulary The resistor in a light bulb is called

  A. an insulator.

  B. an electric charge.

  C. a filament.

  D. a power source.

7. Apply List three appliances that transform electrical energy into another form of energy. Identify the form or forms of energy each produces.

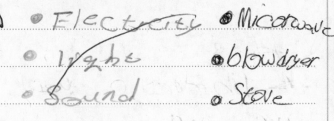

- Electricity
- light
- Sound
- Microwave
- blowdryer
- Stove

Do the math!

8. Calculate About 75 percent of the energy that passes through a fluorescent bulb is used as light. If a fluorescent bulb uses 2,000 kilowatt-hours, how much energy is used as light?

9. APPLY THE BIG ? **How is electrical energy transferred and transformed?**

Look at the picture. Describe how electrical energy moves in this circuit. Include how the energy changes form.

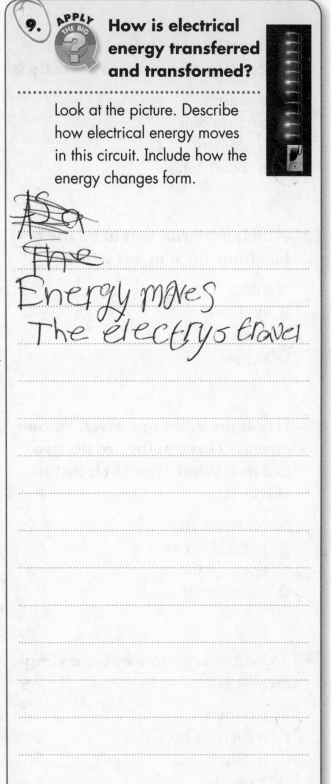

Energy moves
The electrys travel

Benchmark Practice

Read each question and choose the best answer.

1 A material through which an
electric charge can move easily is

   A a resistor.
   B an insulator.
   C a filament.
   D a conductor.

2 Which material would be the **best**
insulator for a metal wire?

   A silver
   B graphite
   C glass
   D copper

3 Five light bulbs are wired on one
circuit. Three bulbs are lit, two
are not. What type of circuit is
this?

   A series circuit
   B parallel circuit
   C open circuit
   D short circuit

4 A good energy source for a simple
circuit is

   A a battery.
   B a copper wire.
   C a light bulb.
   D a switch.

5 How does energy change as it
moves through this circuit?

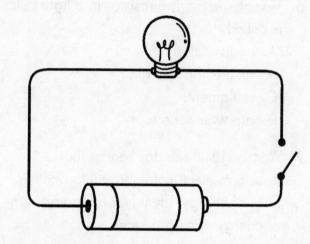

In the filimene
it Theres a open
circut and it not
going to go.

SavvasRealize.com

UNPLUG IT!

Did you know that a television continues to use energy, even when it is turned off? Computers, cell phone chargers, and electric toothbrushes do too. These devices continue to use energy because they are still plugged into a power source. The energy that flows through them, even when they are off, is called phantom energy. Phantom energy makes up part of a household's energy use. A household may spend about $100 each year on phantom energy.

You can make a difference. To conserve energy, plug your computer and other electronics into a power strip. When you are not using the electronics, switch off the power strip. Or unplug the electronics altogether. This simple step will stop phantom energy from flowing. Conserving energy will help the environment. It will also save your family money.

Analyze The toothbrush in the picture above is turned off. How can you tell that it is still using energy?

....

....

Materials

ice cubes   3 plastic cups

newspaper

wool cloth

masking tape

clock

Which is the best way to slow the rate at which ice melts?

Ask a question.

Which insulator is better at slowing the rate at which ice melts?

State a hypothesis.

1. Write a **hypothesis** by circling one choice and finishing the sentence.

If cups containing identical ice cubes are wrapped in wool cloth or wrapped in newspaper, or unwrapped, then the ice cube

(a) *wrapped in wool cloth*

(b) *wrapped in newspaper*

(c) *unwrapped*

will take longest to melt because

....

....

Identify and control variables.

2. In this **experiment** you will measure the time it takes for each ice cube to melt. You will change only one **variable.** Everything else must remain the same. What should stay the same? List two examples.

....

....

3. Tell the one change you will make.

....

....

....

Design your test.

4. Draw how you will set up your test.

5. List your steps in the order you will do them.

Do your test.

☐ **6.** Follow the steps you wrote.

☐ **7. Record** your results in the table.

☐ **8.** Scientists repeat their tests to improve their accuracy. Repeat your test if time allows.

Collect and record your data.

☐ **9.** Fill in the chart.

Work Like a Scientist
Scientists work with other scientists. Communicate with other groups to compare the results of your investigation.

Interpret your data.

☐ **10.** Use your data to make a bar graph.

☐ 11. Look at your graph closely. Compare the effectiveness of the insulating materials.

_____

_____

_____

_____

☐ 12. Identify the evidence you used to answer the question.

_____

_____

_____

_____

_____

_____

Technology Tools
Your teacher may want you to use a computer (with the right software) or a graphing calculator to help collect, organize, analyze, and present your data. These tools can help you make tables, charts, and graphs.

First, look at the trend shown by your bar graph. Then, conclude which material was the best insulator.

State your conclusion.

13. Communicate your conclusion. Compare your **hypothesis** with your results. How did your results compare with others?

_____

_____

_____

_____

_____

Height and Potential Energy

Find out how the height of an object affects its potential energy. Use modeling clay to make three balls of the same size. Place a ball in a plastic bag and put it on the floor. Hold a thick book flat above the ball. Release the book so it lands on the clay. Remove the flattened ball from the bag and trace its outline on a sheet of paper. Repeat the procedure using the other balls of clay, but drop the book from different heights. Record your procedures and your observations. Draw conclusions based on your information.

Cooking up Science

Write a "scientific recipe" for a simple meal you like to eat. What types of energy are used to prepare the meal?

Science and Engineering Practices

1. Ask a question or define a problem.
2. Develop and use models.
3. Plan and carry out investigations.
4. Analyze and interpret data.
5. Use math and computational thinking.
6. Construct explanations or design solutions.
7. Engage in argument from evidence.
8. Obtain, evaluate, and communicate information.

Write a Poem

Write a poem about some forms of energy. Include some examples of each type of energy. Tell how they may be useful or dangerous. Here are some tips to help you write your poem:

- A poem often has words that repeat.
- The words can be recited in rhythm, and they often rhyme.

Design a Device

Work with a small group of classmates to design a device that converts energy from one form to another. Your device might convert light energy to heat energy. It might use electric energy to produce motion, light, or sound. An example might be an electric circuit that converts electrical energy into the motion energy of a vehicle. Here are some guidelines to help you as you work on your device:

- Brainstorm materials you will need to build your device.
- Determine whether the materials are available.
- After you design and build your device, test it to see whether it performs as planned.
- Refine your design and test it again.

Where is this coconut going?

Plants and Animals

Chapter 4

 Try It! How can flower parts be classified?

 STEM Activity Natural Humidifier

 Investigate It! What is inside an owl pellet?

You might not recognize it, but this floating seed is a coconut! Coconuts are hollow and have thick shells, called husks. Coconuts can float until they wash up on a shore. Then the seed can grow into a new coconut tree.

 Predict How do a coconut's hollow center and thick husk help it travel?

....

....

 What do living organisms need to survive?

How can flower parts be classified?

Flowering plants make seeds to reproduce.

☐ **1.** Carefully separate the different parts of 3 types of flowers. **Observe** how the parts are alike and different.

☐ **2.** Use the yarn circles to help **classify** the parts into groups. Label each group. **Record** the names of the groups.

petal

....

....

....

....

....

Materials

3 flowers

6 labels

hand lens

yarn circles

Inquiry Skill

Botanists make close observations of plant parts. Their observations show similarities and differences that they use to **classify** plants.

Explain Your Results

3. **UNLOCK THE BIG ?** **Observe** how other students **classified** their flower parts. Discuss with other groups. Tell another way you could have classified the flower parts.

....

....

....

....

Text features, such as headings, pictures, and captions, give you clues about what you will read.

Headings tell what the content that follows is about.

A **picture** shows something you will read about.

A **caption** tells specific information about the picture.

Parts of a Flower

Flowers are the organs that make seeds in flowering plants. Most flowers have four main parts. The parts are different shapes and sizes on different flowers. The part that you can see easily is the petal. Petals are often colorful. They protect the parts of the flower that make seeds. They attract bees, butterflies, birds, and other living things.

The wide green leaves below the petals are sepals. **Sepals** are the leaflike parts that cover and protect the flower bud before the flower opens.

The female part of the flower is the **pistil.** The pistil extends into the flower and contains the ovary, where egg cells are produced. The **stamen** is the male part of the flower. Stamens surround the pistil and produce pollen. The pollen contains sperm cells. Sperm cells in pollen combine with egg cells to make seeds.

2. **Text Feature Underline** the part of each sentence that explains the word highlighted in yellow.

3. **Infer** Which part of a flower might you be able to see before the flower is ready to bloom?

130

4. **Identify Outline** the female part of the flower. **Draw** a rectangle around the male part of the flower.

These are the top parts of the pistil.

— *anther*

The smaller stalks around the pistil are stamens. At the tips of the stamens are the anthers. The anthers make tiny grains of pollen.

The petals are often the most colorful part of the flower.

As the bud opens and the flower spreads its petals, the sepals are pushed apart.

PearsonRealize.com   131

picture of a pencil

yellow highlight

technology bar

Practice It!

Find the text features in the textbook pages shown above. Write a clue that each one gives you about the content.

Text feature	Clue

Natural Humidifier

Transpiration is the evaporation of water from plant leaves and stems. It is an important process for plants. As water evaporates from the leaves and stems, more water moves up the plant to all its parts, carrying with it new nutrients and minerals.
It is also important in cooling the plant.

Certain factors affect how much water evaporates from plant leaves. When the temperature around the plant increases, more water evaporates. More water also evaporates on windy days. If there is a lot of water in the soil, more water will evaporate. Transpiration is one way moisture is added to the air. Humidity increases when water is added to the air.

A city garden center has hired you to design a transpiration meter to estimate how much water a plant releases into the air in one day.

Identify the Problem

☑ **1.** What is your task? _____

_____

_____

☑ **2.** In what situation could this information be helpful? _____

_____

_____

Do Research

Look at a diagram of the water cycle.

☑ **3.** What are the main sources of water vapor that contribute to humidity in the atmosphere? _____

_____

☑ **4.** Which of these sources contributes more to the overall humidity? _____

_____

Look at a picture of a greenhouse.

☑ **5.** Do you think the amount of humidity in the air in the greenhouse is low or high? Explain.

_____

_____

Now think about water evaporating from a body of water.

☑ **6.** How do you know that high air temperatures cause more water to evaporate from plants? _____

_____

☑ **7.** How do you know that high winds increase the amount of water that evaporates from plants? _____

_____

_____

Go to the materials station(s). **Examine** each material and think about how it may or may not be useful in your design. Leave the materials where they are.

Develop Possible Solutions

☑ **8. Describe** two ways you could combine some of the materials to build a transpiration meter. _____

_____

_____

Choose One Solution

☑ **9. Describe** your transpiration meter and how you will build it.

_____

_____

_____

☑ **10. List** the materials that you will need. _____

_____

_____

_____

☑ **11.** If you are only testing part of a plant, **describe** how you will find out how much water
the entire plant releases into the air during transpiration. _____

_____

_____

_____

Design and Construct a Prototype

Gather your materials as well as a plant (or plant cutting). Using the plant, **build** your
transpiration meter. Determine a place in the classroom you can leave your setup.

☑ **12. Record** the measurements of your prototype. **Record** the air temperature. **Describe**
whether it is sunny or windy. If you are testing only part of a plant, count the total
number of leaves on your plant. Count the number of leaves tested by your meter.

_____

_____

_____

Test the Prototype

☐ **13.** Leave your plant undisturbed for 24 hours. Then, **examine** your meter and **estimate** the amount of water you collected. If you are testing only part of a plant, use your data to estimate how much water the whole plant releases in one day through transpiration. Show your work.

_____

_____

_____

Communicate Results

☐ **14.** Did your prototype work like you expected? Explain. _____

_____

_____

☐ **15.** **Compare your results** with those of your classmates. How do your results compare?

_____

_____

Evaluate and Redesign

☐ **16.** What were the problems with your design? _____

_____

☐ **17.** What changes could you make to your design to make it work better? _____

_____

_____

How are plants and animals classified?

plant

Which picture do you think shows a plant? Which shows an animal? Label each picture with your choice.

Inquiry Explore It!

What are some ways you can classify animals?

☐ **1.** Look at the Animal Cards.

☐ **2.** Think of a way to **classify** the animals. **Record** your system.

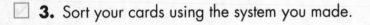

☐ **3.** Sort your cards using the system you made.

Explain Your Results

4. What systems did other groups use to **classify** the animals?

5. Interpret Data How were the different systems useful?

Materials

Animal Cards

Animals

I will know how to classify plants and animals.

Words to Know

classify
vertebrates
invertebrates

Classifying Organisms

Scientists sort all living things, such as plants and animals, into different groups. To arrange or sort objects or living things according to their properties or characteristics is to **classify.**

Scientists ask questions about the organism they want to classify. They look closely at its appearance. They think about where it lives and how it gets its food. All organisms in the same group have some common characteristics. The smallest two groups are genus and species. A genus is a group of closely related living things. Black-footed cats and house cats are classified in the *Felis* genus. They share characteristics such as sharp claws and hunting behaviors. A species is a group of similar organisms that can mate and produce offspring that can also produce offspring. All house cats are classified in the same species.

The species name of the house cat is domesticus.

The species name of the black-footed cat is nigripes.

1. ◎ **Text Features** In the graphic organizer, write the content clues that the text features give you.

Text feature	Clue
Picture	living things
Caption	

2. **Apply** The word *domesticus* is Latin for "of the house." What does this name tell you about the animal?

lives in a house

Classifying Plants

Scientists use several characteristics to classify plants. Two of these characteristics are how plants transport nutrients and how they reproduce.

Water and Nutrient Transportation

Some plants have tubelike structures that connect their leaves, stems, and roots. These structures transport water and nutrients to all parts of the plant. They also add support to the stems and leaves. The added support helps the plant grow larger. Plants with tubelike structures are called vascular plants. Ferns, wildflowers, and many other plants are classified as vascular plants. Plants that pass water and nutrients from cell to cell are called nonvascular plants. Mosses are classified as nonvascular plants.

3. **CHALLENGE** Why do mosses grow low to the ground?

They dont have tublike structure for them to have support

Tubelike structure
If you look at a very thin slice of bamboo stem with a microscope, you can see the tubelike structures.

4. **Observe** Tell what you notice about the bamboo's tubelike structures. _They are in groups_

5. **Explain** How do the bamboo leaves at the top of the plant get the water they need from the bamboo roots?

It helps the plants get there water and nutrients.

bamboo

122

Reproduction

Plants have different ways of reproducing. Plants with flowers or cones produce seeds. A seed has many cells. It has a young plant and stored food inside a protective covering. Other plants produce spores. Each spore is one cell surrounded by a protective cell wall. A spore needs a moist, shady place where it can get nutrients and begin to grow.

Flowers and Seeds

Flowering plants are vascular plants. Daffodils are flowering plants. They produce seeds.

6. **Exemplify** List three other types of flowering plants.

lillies, lavender, lilacs

daffodils

Cones and Seeds

Plants with cones are vascular plants called conifers. The long-leaf pine and red cedar are conifers. They make seeds and have cones instead of flowers.

pine cones

Vascular Plants with Spores

Some vascular plants form spores. Fern spores form in cases on the underside of leaves. They look like brown dots or streaks.

ferns

Nonvascular Plants with Spores

Mosses are nonvascular plants. They make spores. Their spores form in cases at the tips of short stalks. Each spore case holds hundreds of spores.

7. **Conclude** Why do you think a moss produces many spores?

There will still be more moss reproducing.

moss

Classifying Animals

Like plants, animals are classified based on their similarities and differences. One way scientists classify animals is by physical characteristics. Some animals have backbones while others do not have backbones.

Animals with Backbones

Animals that have backbones are called **vertebrates.** There are five groups of vertebrates. These groups are fish, amphibians, reptiles, birds, and mammals.

Fish

Fish are usually covered with scales. They all live in water. Fish breathe mostly with gills. They are cold-blooded, so their body temperature depends on the temperature of their surroundings. Most fish lay eggs.

red drum fish

barred tiger salamander

southern crawfish frog

Amphibians

Amphibians are covered with a smooth skin. They can live both on land and in the water. They breathe with lungs or gills or both. They are cold-blooded. Amphibians hatch from eggs.

8. **Classify** A southern crawfish frog has lungs and hatches from an egg. Is this frog a fish or an amphibian? Explain.

It is an amphibian because it has lungs.

pine snake

Reptiles

Reptiles are covered with scales. Most reptiles live on land. Some can live in water. They have lungs and breathe air. Reptiles are cold-blooded. Most reptiles lay eggs.

Birds

Birds are covered with feathers. They usually live on land, but many birds spend much of their time on water. Birds have lungs and breathe air. They are warm-blooded, which means that their body controls their temperature. All birds lay eggs.

painted bunting

bobcat

Mammals

All mammals have hair or fur. Most mammals live on land, but some live in water. They have lungs and breathe air. Mammals are warm-blooded. Most mammals do not lay eggs. They make milk to feed their young.

9. **Analyze** An animal lives in the water, has scales, is cold-blooded, and lays eggs. What else do you need to know to classify its vertebrate group?

   If they breate gills or lungs.

Animals Without Backbones

Animals without backbones are called **invertebrates.** Most animals on Earth are invertebrates. Arthropods are the largest group of invertebrates. Insects, spiders, crabs, and shrimp are arthropods. Their legs and bodies are divided into sections. Their bodies are covered by a hard, lightweight outer skin, or exoskeleton. The exoskeleton protects their soft bodies. Other invertebrates, such as worms, have no protection for their soft bodies. Others, such as snails and clams, have a soft body inside a hard shell.

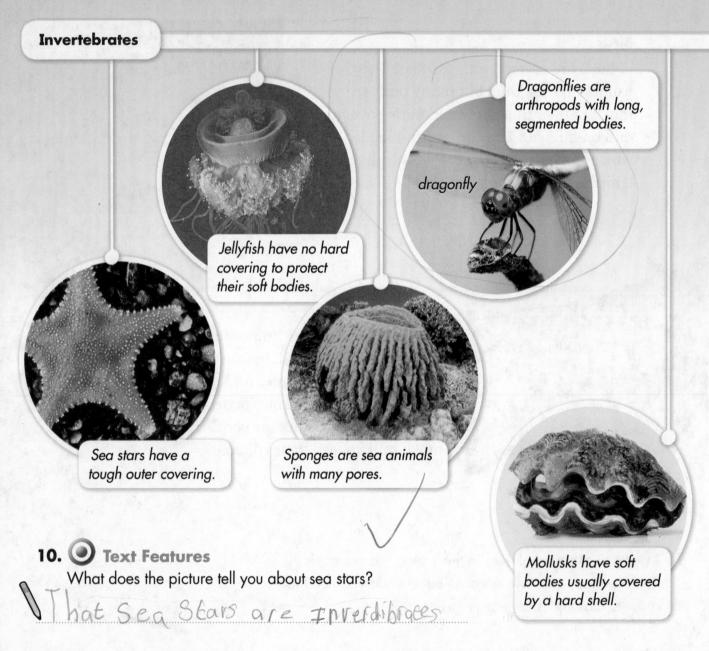

Invertebrates

Dragonflies are arthropods with long, segmented bodies.

dragonfly

Jellyfish have no hard covering to protect their soft bodies.

Sea stars have a tough outer covering.

Sponges are sea animals with many pores.

Mollusks have soft bodies usually covered by a hard shell.

10. Text Features

What does the picture tell you about sea stars?

That Sea Stars are Inverdibraces

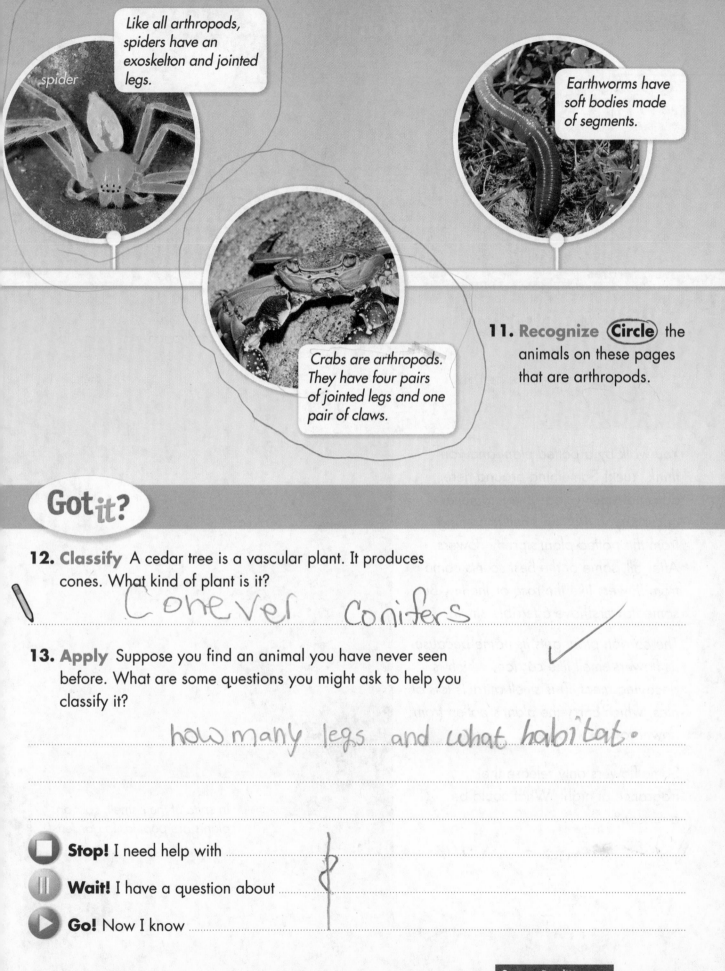

Like all arthropods, spiders have an exoskelton and jointed legs.

spider

Earthworms have soft bodies made of segments.

Crabs are arthropods. They have four pairs of jointed legs and one pair of claws.

11. Recognize (Circle) the animals on these pages that are arthropods.

Got it?

12. Classify A cedar tree is a vascular plant. It produces cones. What kind of plant is it?

Conever Conifers

13. Apply Suppose you find an animal you have never seen before. What are some questions you might ask to help you classify it?

how many legs and what habitat.

Stop! I need help with ....

Wait! I have a question about ....

Go! Now I know ....

How do plants reproduce?

Tell what you think will happen when these seeds blow away.

my PLANET DiaRY

FunFact

You walk by a potted plant and you think, Yuck! Something around here does not smell good! *It would never occur to you that the smell is coming from the potted plant's pretty flowers. After all, some of the best scents come from flowers like the rose or the lily. But some flowers have a terrible smell!*

The carrion plant gets its name because its flowers smell like carrion, which is decaying meat. This smell attracts lots of flies, which carry the plant's pollen from flower to stinky flower.

Some flowers only release their fragrance at night. What could be a reason?

Because they dont wuo
fogefo

In spite of their smell, carrion plants are popular in gardens!

UNLOCK THE BIG ?

I will know structures that help plants survive and reproduce.

Words to Know

sepal	pollination
pistil	fertilization
stamen	germinate

Plants That Make Seeds

An important function of plants is to reproduce, or make more of the same kind of plant. Scientists often classify plants by how they reproduce. In nature, most plants make seeds that can grow into new plants. Other plants reproduce by forming tiny cells that can grow into new plants. These cells are called spores. Ferns and mosses are examples of plants that use spores to reproduce.

The plants that make seeds are classified again by the parts they use to produce seeds. Some plants, such as pine trees, grow cones to make seeds. Other plants make seeds by growing flowers. In this lesson, you will learn how flowering plants reproduce.

1. **Compare** How is the way an avocado reproduces different from the way a fern reproduces?

....

....

....

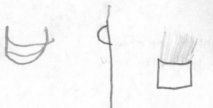

The hard pit in an avocado is actually an avocado seed. Roots and stems produced by the seed will grow into a tree.

Spore cases are on the underside of fern leaves. Each case contains tiny spores that may grow into a fern.

Parts of a Flower

Flowers are the organs that make seeds in flowering plants. Most flowers have four main parts. The parts are different shapes and sizes on different flowers. The part that you can see easily is the petal. Petals are often colorful. They protect the parts of the flower that make seeds. They attract bees, butterflies, birds, and other living things.

The wide green leaves below the petals are sepals. **Sepals** are the leaflike parts that cover and protect the flower bud before the flower opens.

The female part of the flower is the **pistil.** The pistil extends into the flower and contains the ovary, where egg cells are produced. The **stamen** is the male part of the flower. Stamens surround the pistil and produce pollen. The pollen contains sperm cells. Sperm cells in pollen combine with egg cells to make seeds.

2. ⊙ **Text Feature Underline** the part of each sentence that explains the word highlighted in yellow.

3. **Infer** Which part of a flower might you be able to see before the flower is ready to bloom?

Sepal

130

4. Identify Outline the female part of the flower. **Draw** a rectangle around the male part of the flower.

These are the top parts of the pistil.

anther

The smaller stalks around the pistil are stamens. At the tips of the stamens are the anthers. The anthers make tiny grains of pollen.

The petals are often the most colorful part of the flower.

As the bud opens and the flower spreads its petals, the sepals are pushed apart.

Pollen on the Move

In order for seeds to form, pollen has to get from a stamen to a pistil. Sometimes animals may help play a part in moving pollen.

Flowers make a sweet liquid called nectar. This is a tasty food for bats, bees, butterflies, and birds. Scent and color guide animals to the flower. As an animal feeds, pollen from the stamens rubs off onto its body. The pollen may then rub off onto the pistil of the next flower the animal visits. This movement of pollen from stamen to pistil is called **pollination.**

pollen

5. **Analyze** Look at the photos of the bees on these pages. How do a bee's features help pollinate plants?

Most trees and grasses rely on wind for pollination. These plants do not attract animals. They do not have sweet smells or big flowers with colorful petals. However, they produce huge amounts of pollen. The wind will carry at least a few pollen grains to the pistil of another plant.

6. **Infer** Some people are allergic to pollen. Why do you think their allergies are worse on windy days?

The pollen will fly around

After Pollination

Once a pollen grain lands on a pistil, a thin tube grows down through the pistil. This pollen tube reaches the thick bottom part of the pistil called the ovary. Sperm cells from the pollen travel down the pollen tube to the egg cells. The sperm cell and egg cell combine in a process called **fertilization.**

The flower changes after fertilization. The petals and stamens dry up and fall off. The fertilized egg inside the ovary develops into a seed. The ovary grows into a fruit, which protects the seed or seeds. When the fruit is ripe, the seeds are ready to grow into new plants.

7. **Explain** How are the seeds in this apple protected?

They are protected by the fruit.

Dandelion seeds spread with the wind—or by a person blowing on them.

The wing-shaped fruits of maple trees twirl through the air like propellers.

Seeds on the Move

Suppose that all the seeds on a tree fell to the ground nearby. Many of the seeds would start to grow. But the parent tree would take up most of the living space and resources that the seeds would need to grow properly. They would grow much better if they were scattered farther from the parent tree. That is why plants have adaptations that help them scatter their seeds. This scattering of plant seeds is also called seed dispersal. Some seeds are built to spread with the wind. Some can float. Some have tiny hooks that stick to an animal's fur or a person's clothes. Some animals, such as squirrels, gather and bury nuts and seeds to be eaten later. Some of those nuts and seeds will grow.

A seed that falls to the ground contains a small, young plant. Each seed needs water, oxygen, and the right temperature to **germinate,** or start to grow. Food stored in the seed gives the young plant enough energy to germinate. The pictures below show a germinating plant.

8. **Underline** a reason why seeds may not grow well near the parent tree.

9. ◎ **Text Features** How do the photographs and captions help you understand how seeds move?

The Seeds on a tree fell to the ground nearby.

leaf

seed coat

stem

root

Life Cycle of a Plant

A plant's life cycle includes all of the changes the plant goes through from fertilization to death. When a seed has the right conditions, it sprouts. The young roots grow downward because of gravity. The new stem looks like it is reaching for the sunlight as it pushes up through the seed coat. The seedling grows into an adult plant. The plant gets larger. Flowers start to grow. The color of the flowers is one of the traits that the plant gets from its parents.

Flowers that are pollinated produce fertilized eggs that develop into seeds. Fruit grows around the seeds. In time, the fruit and seeds separate from the parent plant. The new seeds germinate, and the cycle begins again.

After fertilization, an apple tree's flowers develop into seeds. Apples grow around the seeds.

10. Paraphrase Explain in your own words what a plant's life cycle is.

A Plant life cycle includes all Of the Plant goes through fertilization so death.

Got it?

11. UNLOCK THE BIG ? Identify What are the functions of the pistil and stamen in flowering plants?

The new Stem looks like it is reaching for the sunlight as it pushes up through the seed coat.

12. Infer Why is reproduction important to the survival of a plant species?

When the seed has the right conditions.

⬛ **Stop!** I need help with ....

⏸ **Wait!** I have a question about ....

▶ **Go!** Now I know ....

How do plants make food?

Tell what plant parts you can see in this photo.

Inquiry ▸ Explore It!

How can plants react to light?

☑ **1.** Set a shoebox on one end, as shown in the picture.
The hole in the box's other end should be on the left.
Place a sprouted bean plant on the left side of the box.

☑ **2.** Tape an index card inside the box.
The hole in the index card should be on the right.

☑ **3.** Cover the box. Place the box in bright light.

☑ **4.** **Predict** what may happen.
Observe the plant every day for 5 days.

Explain Your Results

5. Discuss how the plant's growth changed.

6. **Infer** You observed how the stem grew.
What is one function of this plant structure?

Materials

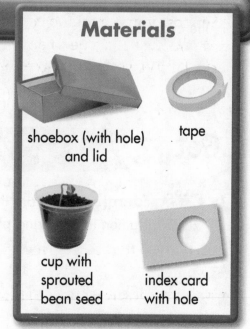

shoebox (with hole) and lid

tape

cup with sprouted bean seed

index card with hole

*Water your plant as needed.
Do not overwater.*

UNLOCK
THE BIG
?

I will know the roles of roots, leaves, and stems in making food.

Words to Know

photosynthesis
chlorophyll

Needs of Plants

Suppose you are taking care of plants in a garden. You make sure that they get plenty of sunlight and water. Sunlight and water are two things that plants need to live, grow, and reproduce. Plants also need carbon dioxide from the air and nutrients from the soil.

The amounts of sunlight and water that plants need can be different. Some plants need different amounts of sunlight. For example, petunias and irises are flowering plants. Petunias need direct sunlight to grow well. However, irises can grow well in partly shaded areas that receive indirect sunlight. Some plants need only a little water. For example, a cactus is able to grow in the desert where little rain falls.

1. Infer How might you be able to tell if a plant in a garden needs more water?

If it looks dry, or

2. Apply These children are caring for plants in a garden. What kinds of information do they need to know about the plants?

How much water it needs. How much Sunlight it needs. How much nutrients it needs.

How Plants Make Food

Unlike animals, plants make their own food. Most plants have three special parts: roots, leaves, and stems. Each part plays a role in making food for a plant. Most plants make food in their leaves. Plants must take in a gas called carbon dioxide, water, nutrients, and sunlight to make food.

Photosynthesis

The food plants make is sugar. The process in which plants make sugar is called **photosynthesis.** In photosynthesis, plants use carbon dioxide that their leaves absorb from the air, and water and nutrients that their roots absorb from the soil. The water and the nutrients travel through tubes in the stems to the leaves. The plants use sunlight energy to change these ingredients into food that the plant can use. Oxygen, the waste product of photosynthesis, passes into the air through the openings in leaves. Tubes in the stem carry sugar to other parts of the plant. The stems, roots, and leaves of a plant all store extra sugar.

3. [CHALLENGE] Why do you think it is helpful for the widest part of a leaf to face the sky?

so it can gather sunlight

4. ◉ **Text Features** What content clues does the picture give you?

It Shows what plant parts look alike.

Leaves absorb energy from sunlight and take in carbon dioxide.

Stems hold the leaves up to the sunlight. Water moves through stems to the leaves.

Roots take in the water and nutrients needed to make food.

Chlorophyll

Plant cells contain tiny structures called chloroplasts. Photosynthesis usually takes place in the chloroplasts of leaf cells. When you look at a chloroplast through a microscope, you see stacks of dark green disks connected by threadlike materials.

Chloroplasts contain chlorophyll. **Chlorophyll** is the substance in plants that makes their parts green and captures energy from sunlight. Plants use this energy and nutrients from the soil during photosynthesis to change water and carbon dioxide into sugar and oxygen.

5. **Underline** the sentence that tells where photosynthesis usually takes place.

6. Mark an ✗ on a tubelike structure in the diagram that brings water to the cells for photosynthesis.

Cross Section of a Leaf

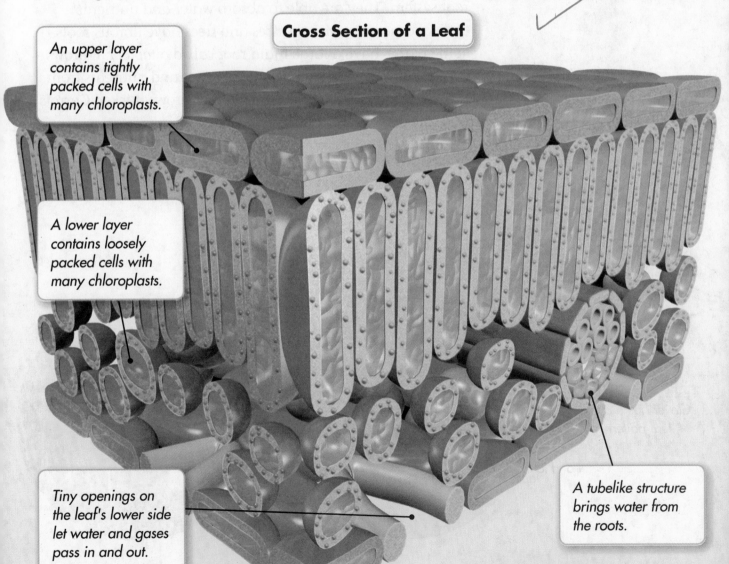

An upper layer contains tightly packed cells with many chloroplasts.

A lower layer contains loosely packed cells with many chloroplasts.

Tiny openings on the leaf's lower side let water and gases pass in and out.

A tubelike structure brings water from the roots.

Leaves, Stems, and Roots

The shape and positioning of leaves helps them catch the sunlight they need to make food. Most leaves are flat on top to catch as much sunlight as possible. Leaves are usually spread out along stems in ways that catch the most sunlight. Some leaves grow opposite each other, like a mirror image. Some leaves grow in a staggered, zig-zag pattern. Some leaves grow in a circle around the same point on the stem.

Stems also grow toward light. The woody stems of trees and bushes are hard and rigid. A waxy covering protects the stems and prevents them from drying out. The stems of many other plants are soft and flexible. These stems are usually green and carry out photosynthesis just like leaves do.

Roots grow away from the stem in search of water and nutrients. Gravity causes roots to grow down. In some plants the roots spread out in many directions, forming a fibrous root system. They are able to absorb water and nutrients from a large area. Most grasses and trees have fibrous roots. Some plants have a large main root called a *taproot*. It grows straight down. The taproot absorbs water and nutrients from the soil. As it stores food for the plant, it grows thicker. Carrots and radishes are taproots.

7. **Analyze** Why do you think there are different kinds of leaves, stems, and roots?

....

....

Ash trees have an opposite leaf pattern.

Grape vines have a zig-zag leaf pattern.

Clover has a circle leaf pattern.

taproots

fibrous roots

Plants Without Roots

Some plants do not have true underground roots.
Yet they are able to get what they need to make
their own food. These air plants, as they are called,
absorb moisture directly from the air. They take the
nutrients they need from dust in the air. Spanish
moss is an air plant that grows in many parts of
the southern United States.

8. Mark an ✗ on the Spanish moss in the picture.

9. **Infer** The leaves of Spanish moss are long and thin.
   They are covered with cuplike scales. How might the
   structure of the leaves help the plant survive?

....

....

*Spanish moss wraps its scaly
stems around tree branches.*

Got it?

10. **Explain** How do water and nutrients get from the soil into
    a plant's leaves?

....

....

11. **Summarize** What is the function of leaves in a plant's
    ability to make food?

....

....

🔲 **Stop!** I need help with ....

⏸ **Wait!** I have a question about ....

▶ **Go!** Now I know ....

What are adaptations?

Envision It!

bald eagle

Tell how you think the feet of each bird shown above help it survive in its habitat.

Inquiry **Explore It!**

How can some fish float?

Some fish have swim bladders that help them float. Inherited behaviors allow a fish to use its swim bladder to help get food and stay safe.

☐ **1.** Tape the mouth of a balloon around one end of a straw. Put the balloon inside a bottle.

☐ **2.** Put the bottle in a tub of water. Tip the bottle until all the air escapes. **Observe** what happens. **Record.**

☐ **3.** Blow into the straw to inflate the balloon. Observe. Record.

Explain Your Results

4. Think about your **model. Infer** how a fish uses its swim bladder to help get food and stay safe.

....

....

....

Materials

tape

balloon

straw

plastic bottle

plastic tub of water

bottle = model of fish

balloon = model of swim bladder

mallard duck

I will know how physical features and behaviors help organisms interact with their environments.

Word to Know

adaptation

Adaptations

Animals and plants inherit characteristics from their parents. These special features and behaviors help them survive. An **adaptation** is a physical feature or behavior that helps an organism survive in its environment. An environment is everything that surrounds a living thing. Organisms with useful adaptations for their environment are more likely than other organisms to get the resources they need to survive. If they survive, they are more likely to reproduce and pass their adaptations to their young.

Plants and animals in different areas often have different adaptations. A plant or animal adapted to one ecosystem may not survive in a different ecosystem. Hares that live in snowy environments have different adaptations from hares that live in a desert. So, a hare from a snowy environment might not survive in a desert.

1. ◉ **Text Features** Complete the chart below to identify some text features on this page.

Feature	Clue
heading	The heading tells that the paragraphs are about adaptations.
picture	*It is showing that the hare is blending in with the snow.*

snowshoe hare

2. **Explain** How do you think the snowshoe hare in the picture is adapted to live in an environment that has a lot of snow?

The snowshoe hare blends in the snow so it can not be eatan by prey.

Animal Adaptations

Animals have many adaptations that help them survive in their environments. Some adaptations, such as sharp beaks, teeth, or claws, may help them get food. Other adaptations, such as stingers, quills, smelly sprays, or bitter-tasting flesh, protect some animals from being eaten by predators. Bright colors, like those of the monarch butterfly, may warn predators that the animal is poisonous.

Some adaptations for moving help an animal protect itself. For example, fins enable a fish to swim away from its enemies. Birds' wings help them quickly move if they need to get away from predators or cold weather.

Hibernation, or a state of rest, is a behavior that helps some animals survive low temperatures. Some animals that hibernate include bats, chipmunks, and marmots.

3. **Describe** Write a caption about an adaptation this tiger has. Include how you think the adaptation helps the tiger survive.

The sharp Teeth help them get food.

4. **Classify** Read about the animals on this page. (Circle) the names of the animals with adaptations for getting food. **Underline** the names of the animals with adaptations for protection.

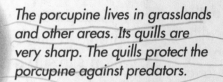

The porcupine lives in grasslands and other areas. Its quills are very sharp. The quills protect the porcupine against predators.

This poison-dart frog lives in a South American rain forest. Its bright color warns predators that it is poisonous.

This flying gecko lives in the jungle forest. It has flaps of skin that help it to glide away from predators.

This red-tailed hawk hunts in forests and fields. It has a sharp, curved beak that can hold and tear prey it finds.

Chameleons live in deserts and tropical areas. Their long tongues stretch to catch insects.

5. **Observe and Compare** Look at the animals on these pages. Describe to a partner how each is adapted to its environment. Tell how their physical characteristics are alike.

At-Home Lab

Cactus-Stem Model
Cut a sheet of paper into two pieces. Color both sides of one piece with a crayon. A crayon is waxy, like the stem of a cactus. Place both pieces in a bowl of water. Record what happens to each piece and communicate the results to your class.

Plant Adaptations

Like animals, plants have many adaptations that help them survive in their environments. Some adaptations, such as cactus thorns, protect plants from harm. Other adaptations help plants reproduce. These adaptations may help plants pollinate or spread their seeds.

Adaptations such as harmful oils and thorns may protect a plant from being eaten. Other adaptations allow plants to survive in extreme conditions. For example, sundew plants that live in nutrient-poor soil have a sticky substance that attracts insects. These insects provide nutrients to the plant.

6. **Apply** The hairs on a stinging nettle release a chemical that irritates skin. Explain how this adaptation might help the plant.

You would not want to irritate your skin

This burdock bush has seeds with spikes that stick to furry animals that brush against them.

Cactus plants live in deserts where there is little rain. They have tiny needle-like leaves and a thick waxy coating on their stem that keeps them from drying out.

Some flowering plants depend on insects or other animals to pollinate their flowers. This is how they make new plants. The flower of a bee orchid looks like a bee. This adaptation helps the orchid attract insects.

bee orchid

7. **Illustrate** Draw another plant you know. Describe an adaptation the plant has and how it helps the plant.

It has tedols

Got it?

8. **Describe** How is a cactus adapted to its habitat?

Catus adapted to its habitat because they have tiny needles like leaves and thick waxy coating on their stem that keeps them dry out.

9. **Analyze** How is a <u>duck</u> adapted to help it survive in its environment?

A Duck is adapted to help them survive in its environment ~~meny~~ is byusing it feet to swim faster.

⬛ **Stop!** I need help with ....

⏸ **Wait!** I have a question about ....

▶ **Go!** Now I know ....

Lesson 5

What plant and animal characteristics are inherited?

Tell why you think peacocks have inherited showy tails.

Inquiry **Explore It!**

How can some characteristics be affected by the environment?

Many characteristics are inherited. Some are affected by the environment. *A Cards* show living things as they often appear. *B Cards* show how the living things may appear depending on the environment. *C Cards* tell what factors affected the living things.

☐ **1. Observe** the living thing on an *A Card*. Match it with a *B Card*.

☐ **2.** Find the matching *C Card*.

☐ **3.** Repeat for each *A Card*. Compare your matches with others. Explain any differences.

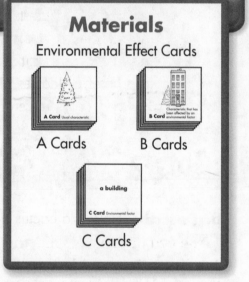

Materials

Environmental Effect Cards

A Cards   B Cards

C Cards

A Card Usual characteristic

B Card Characteristic that has been affected by an environmental factor

a building

C Card Environmental factor

Explain Your Results

4. Communicate Pick an *A Card*. Explain how the characteristic was affected by the environment.

....

....

148

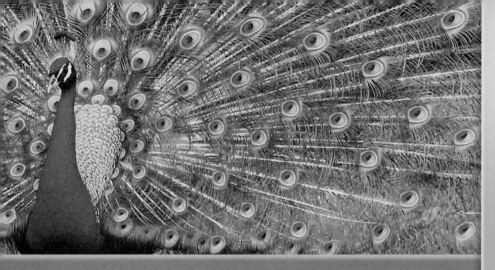

UNLOCK THE BIG ?

I will know that plants and animals inherit characteristics that may help them survive and reproduce.

Words to Know

characteristics
inherit
advantage

Characteristics of Living Things

In the middle of the nineteenth century, a monk named Gregor Mendel was hard at work in his garden. He noticed that his pea plants were not all exactly alike. All of the pea plants had stems, leaves, flowers, pods, and peas. But they also had some differences in characteristics. **Characteristics** are the qualities an organism has. Some of the plants were tall while others were short. Some had purple flowers while others had white ones. The pods might be green or yellow. The peas themselves might be smooth or wrinkled.

The pea plants were like their parents because of characteristics passed on to them. But Mendel found that the offspring did not always look exactly like their parents. Sometimes they received different characteristics. Some offspring even had different characteristics than other plants with the same parents. Mendel asked himself why. Many years later, his work became the basis for the scientific study of heredity, or the passing of characteristics from parents to offspring.

pea plant

1. **Underline** the different characteristics Mendel's pea plants showed.

2. **Infer** What characteristics will all pea plants have?

   leaf, Stems, Peaspods

Inherited Characteristics

Animals and plants inherit their characteristics from their parents and look very much like them. In science, to **inherit** is to receive characteristics from an organism's parents. Animals and plants will pass these traits on to their own offspring.

Plants

The prickly pear cactus has sharp spines. Look at its paddle-shaped pads. These are flattened stems that act like leaves. They have a waxy coating to help the plant hold in moisture. Notice that the pads have two kinds of sharp spines. Some spines are long. Other spines are short but break off easily. The cactus looks the way it does because it has inherited these traits.

3. **Conclude** What characteristic helps the prickly pear cactus survive in a dry environment?

It helps them because waxy coating so they are moistures.

Animals

You are not likely to mistake a zebra for any other animal. They look like horses, but they are not horses. Zebras have black and white stripes. Their manes are short and stand up on their necks. These are inherited characteristics. They are shared by all zebras.

4. **Analyze** How is a zebra's pattern like a fingerprint?

The general coat pattern is shared by zebras of the same kind. The pattern of each individual zebra is different.

5. **Text Features** Find five text features on these pages. Tell a partner the clues they give you.

Did you look twice at the fish in the photo? Something does not look quite right. The peacock flounder has both eyes on one side of its body! This flat fish is unusual in another way too. The peacock flounder can change its color and pattern to match its background. This allows it to surprise the animals it eats as they swim by. It also hides itself from animals that would eat it. This fish looks and acts the way it does because it has inherited these traits.

6. **⊙ Summarize** List three characteristics that the peacock flounder inherited.

o They can change color
They have flat eyes
They can eat whik swim

Human Beings

People also inherit many characteristics from their parents. A person's parents may be very tall, and so that person may grow to be very tall also. However, this is not always the case. Sometimes a child may grow up to be taller or shorter than his or her parents. Height is not the only inherited characteristic. Some characteristics, such as hair and eye color, are also inherited.

7. **Give an Example**
Write a characteristic you may have inherited from your parents.

My moms nose eyes
My dads head and eyes

Lightning Lab

Dimpled Cheeks
Do you get dimples in your cheeks when you smile? Some people have inherited this characteristic, and some people have not. Take a survey of your classmates. Make a chart to show your data.

Parents, Offspring, and Advantages

You know that baby animals look somewhat like their parents. Cats give birth to kittens, and lions give birth to lion cubs. Sometimes, offspring from the same parents can look different from each other. They may have different characteristics than other organisms of the same type. It may be easier or more difficult for the offspring with different characteristics to compete. Competition occurs when two or more living things need the same resources in order to survive.

8. CHALLENGE Trees get energy from sunlight. How might competition affect the height of a tree?

They are competing for the sunlight.

One example that shows competition is in giraffes. Male giraffes use their long necks to fight with other males. The winner of the fight is more attractive to the female giraffe. This male reproduces. The longer and stronger a male giraffe's neck is, the better chance he has to pass these characteristics on to offspring. Over time, giraffes inherit longer and stronger necks.

9. **Infer** How did giraffes' necks get so long?

So they could fight other mammals.

male giraffes competing

In England, peppered moths used to survive by using their light color as camouflage on the lichens growing on trees. As coal use increased in England, the lichens began to die off. Birds that eat peppered moths could see them more easily against the dark color of the trees. Moths that inherited a darker color could blend in better against the trees. These moths survived and had offspring who were also darker in color. Over time, the common color of the peppered moth shifted from light to dark. The darker color gave those individual organisms an advantage over the lighter colored moths. An **advantage** is a characteristic that can help an individual compete.

10. ◉ **Summarize** Describe how the dark moths' coloring gives them an advantage over the light-colored moths.

The white ones stick out and the black ones dont

Got it?

11. **Apply** What is one characteristic that might give a hawk an advantage over other hawks?

If they have sharp talents or bigger wings.

12. **UNLOCK THE BIG ?** Think about what you learned in this lesson. Describe why offspring usually look like their parents.

They inherted traits

■ **Stop!** I need help with

‖ **Wait!** I have a question about

▶ **Go!** Now I know

How do animals respond to the environment?

Envision It!

Tell how these monkeys are responding to their environment.

MY PLANET DIARY

//// MISCONCEPTION ////

A common misconception about bats is that they are blind. Some bats use something called echolocation to locate prey, such as insects. Echolocation uses sound energy. Bats make a sound and then use specialized sense receptors to hear the echo as it bounces off an object, such as a delicious mosquito. This information is then processed by the bat's brain to determine how far away and in what direction the insect is flying. Because bats can find prey in the dark, many people have assumed they were blind. But all types of bats have eyes that can see.

How can some bats get information from their environments?

By using echo location

UNLOCK THE BIG ?

I will know how animals respond to their environments and get what they need.

Words to Know

stimulus
instinct

Animal Behaviors

Have you ever tried to touch a turtle? If so, you may have seen a typical behavior of turtles. When a turtle feels threatened, it may pull its head inside its shell. This behavior protects the turtle from other animals.

Behaviors are the ways that animals act. Every behavior is caused by a stimulus. A **stimulus** is something that causes a reaction in a living thing. Some behaviors are responses to stimuli in the environment. When a turtle pulls its head inside its shell, it is reacting to something it has heard, seen, or smelled in its environment. Other behaviors are responses to stimuli inside an animal. For example, hunger is a stimulus that causes animals to look for food and eat.

The box turtle is hiding in its shell.

1. **Apply** Give an example of a stimulus that might cause a turtle to pull its head into its shell.

   The turtle hide
   is then predoter.

Animal Instincts

Animals inherit physical characteristics, such as wings or fur, from their parents. They can also inherit behaviors. An **instinct** is a behavior that is inherited. Instincts help animals meet their needs and respond to stimuli in their environments.

Sea stars, for example, have an important instinct that helps them respond to changes in temperature. Sea stars live along the coast. During low tide, the water gets shallower in these areas. There is less water for sunlight to pass through, so the ocean floor gets warmer. Sea stars prepare for the warmer temperatures of low tide by sucking in cold water during high tide. The cooler water inside the animal keeps it from getting too hot.

sea star

2. Paraphrase Explain in your own words what an instinct is.

a behavior that was inherited

Do the math!

Division

Animals often travel great distances. Some geese travel from Hudson Bay in Canada to central Wisconsin. The distance is about 1,400 km. About how many hours of flying would it take geese to migrate on this route if they fly 50 km per hour? To find out, divide the distance by the speed:

$$\frac{1400 \text{ km}}{50 \text{ km/hr}} = 28 \text{ hours}$$

Use the formula to solve these problems.

1. A peregrine falcon travels from Maine to Argentina. The distance is about 8,100 km. About how many hours of flying would the falcon's trip be if it flew at 45 km/hr?

2. A flock of pelicans travels from Washington to California's Channel Islands. The distance is about 1,469 km. About how many hours of flying would it take the pelicans to migrate at 43 km/hr?

Examples of Instinctive Behaviors

	**Migration** Migration is movement between habitats. Some animals are born with the instinct to migrate when seasons change. Birds' eyes are specialized sense receptors used to gather information for navigation. Their brains then process that information to help them find their way. Flocks of Canada geese migrate from Canada and the northern United States as far south as Mexico to escape cold winters and to find food.
	**Protection** Animals have different ways of protecting themselves. The porcupine is born with quills. The quills are hairs with sharp edges. When the porcupine is threatened, it will turn its back and raise the quills toward its enemy. The porcupine's muscles force the quills to stand straight up.
 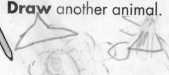	**Hibernation** Some mammals, reptiles, and amphibians hibernate. Hibernation is a state of inactivity that occurs when outside temperatures are cold. Some hibernating animals conserve energy by slowing down their body functions. Marmots hibernate in burrows through the winter.
Draw another animal.	3. [CHALLENGE] Write about the animal and its instincts. The peperd moths instincts are that they survive by using its cambefh camoefloge

4. ⊙ **Text Features** Tell why a chart is a good way to organize the information on this page.

A good way to organize the information on this page is to tell how animals inhert to other animals

At-Home Lab

Migrating Animals
Identify an animal in your area that migrates. Describe the path of the animal's migration.

Learned Behavior

Not all behaviors happen by instinct. Some behaviors develop as a result of training or changes in experience. Young animals learn many things as they interact with the environment. A dog that attacks a skunk may get sprayed with a bad-smelling liquid. The dog may learn to keep away from skunks.

Human babies learn many things by observing their parents. Young animals do too. Lion cubs learn to hunt by watching older lions. A pride, or group of lions, often hunts together. Zebras are common prey for lions. A herd of zebras keeps safe from attack by staying together. When a zebra is separated from the herd, the lions will chase it toward a group of lions that is hiding. The lions will then pounce on their prey. A lion cub learns to pounce on its prey by pouncing on its mother's twitching tail. Learning the pouncing behavior helps the lion cub survive and get the food it needs.

5. Identify <u>Underline</u> the sentence that tells how the lion cub learns to hunt its prey.

6. Exemplify Name two behaviors that a human baby might learn from her parents.

Learning and Instinct Combined

Some behaviors are partly instinctive and partly learned. The white-crowned sparrow inherits the ability to recognize the song its species sings. But knowing how to sing the song is not inherited. Sparrows must learn the song from their parents. Scientists have found that young sparrows that are separated from their parents never learn to sing the complete song.

Humans inherit the ability to learn much more than animals can learn. For example, humans inherit the ability to learn language. But we are not born knowing English, Spanish, or Chinese. We must learn the words used in our language.

7. **Draw Conclusions** If this adult sparrow cannot complete its song, what can you conclude?

....

....

Got it?

8. **Identify** **Underline** the behavior that is a response to a stimulus in the environment.

   A thirsty elephant looks for water.

   A fish moves to deeper water as the temperature of a lake changes.

9. **Classify** Humans sometimes build fires to keep warm. Is this an instinctive behavior or a learned behavior? Explain how you know.

....

....

⬜ **Stop!** I need help with ....

⏸ **Wait!** I have a question about ....

▶ **Go!** Now I know ....

What is inside an owl pellet?

Follow a Procedure

☐ **1.** Place an owl pellet on a sheet of paper.
Measure its length.

☐ **2.** **Observe** the pellet. Separate the contents of the pellet.

Materials

safety goggles

owl pellet

forceps

wooden probe

hand lens

sheet of paper   metric ruler

Inquiry Skill
You **infer** when you explain your observations.

Be careful! **Wear safety goggles. Wash your hands when finished.**

3. Fill in the chart to **classify** the contents of the pellet.

4. Record your observations below.

Owl Pellet Observations					
	Pellet Length	**Skulls**	**Other Bones**	**Teeth**	**Fur or Feathers?** (describe)
Pellet contents					

Analyze and Conclude

5. Draw a Conclusion   What can you **infer** about the diet of the owl?

....

....

....

....

6. **UNLOCK THE BIG ?**   How does examining an owl pellet help you learn about the ecosystem of an owl?

....

....

....

....

....

Wildlife Biologist

If you like animals, you might like to be a wildlife biologist. Wildlife biologists study animals and their habitats. They want to know how the animals live and how they behave.

At the International Crane Foundation (ICF) near Baraboo, Wisconsin, biologists study cranes in captivity and in the wild. With the information the biologists gather, they hope to increase the number of these endangered birds.

One important job the biologists have is to teach cranes raised in captivity to migrate. Cranes raised in captivity do not learn migration routes from their parents. So biologists teach the cranes how to migrate. Biologists fly small aircraft and train the cranes to follow them.

If you think wildlife biology is for you, plan to take science classes in high school. You might volunteer to work with animals in a local habitat. You will need a college degree in biology or a related science.

APPLY
THE BIG
?

How does a captive environment affect the cranes' ability to survive?

It affects the cranes because they don't know how to migrate.

stimulus

estímulo

instinct

instinto

something that causes a
reaction in a living thing

Write an example.

....
....
....
....

algo que provoca una
reacción en un ser vivo

a behavior that is inherited

Write a sentence using this
word.

....
....
....
....

conducta que se hereda

Study Guide

What do living organisms need to survive?

Life Science

Lesson 1

How are plants and animals classified?

- Scientists classify plants and animals into groups.
- Vertebrates are animals that have a backbone.
- Invertebrates are animals without a backbone.

Lesson 2

How do plants reproduce?

- Plant seeds form when pollen cells fertilize egg cells in the pistil.
- Seeds begin to germinate, or grow, when they have the water, oxygen, and temperature they need.

Lesson 3

How do plants make food?

- Plants make sugar through a process called photosynthesis.
- Chlorophyll is a green substance in plants that captures energy from sunlight for photosynthesis.

Lesson 4

What are adaptations?

- Adaptations help organisms survive in their environments.
- Some adaptations help animals get food or protect themselves.
- Some adaptations help plants survive or reproduce.

Lesson 5

What plant and animal characteristics are inherited?

- Organisms inherit some characteristics from their parents.
- Some characteristics may give an individual an advantage over other individuals.

Lesson 6

How do animals respond to the environment?

- Animal behaviors are a response to stimuli in the environment or stimuli within the animal.
- Animals inherit instinctive behaviors. Other behaviors are learned.

SavvasRealize.com

Chapter Review

REVIEW THE BIG ? What do living organisms need to survive?

Lesson 1

How are plants and animals classified?

1. **Summarize** What are two characteristics scientists might use to classify a plant?

....

....

....

....

....

Lesson 2

How do plants reproduce?

2. **Vocabulary** The part of a flower that makes pollen is a(n)
   A. pistil.
   B. stamen.
   C. sepal.
   D. ovary.

Lesson 3

How do plants make food?

3. **Describe** What are the roles of a plant's roots, stems, and leaves in the process of making food?

....

....

....

....

....

....

Lesson 4

What are adaptations?

4. **Explain** How do the wings of an eagle help the eagle survive?

It helps them survive because if a predator is near they can fly away.

....

....

....

....

STEM

Plant Engineering

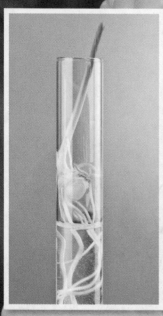

Some corn we eat today is a result of selective breeding and genetic engineering.

For centuries, people selectively bred plants with traits valuable to humans. People still selectively breed plants. What is selective breeding? It is when a few organisms with desired traits serve as parents of offspring. When scientists and farmers selectively breed plants, they want to make better plants. Genetic engineering is another way to change plants. Genetic engineering is the changing of the structure of an organism's genes to change inherited traits.

Why do companies change the genes of a plant? They change the genes of a plant for many reasons. For example, the genes of some corn are altered to resist insects that kill corn plants. Genetic engineering may also cause problems. Seeds of plants with newly changed genes may spread to other areas and affect ecosystems.

Predict How could seeds with changed genes help NASA scientists prepare for human life on the moon or Mars?

....

....

What do armadillos eat?

Ecosystems

 Try It! How can you estimate how many animals live in an ecosystem?

STEM Activity Home, Sweet Home!

Investigate It! How do earthworms meet their needs in a model of an ecosystem?

Life Science

Apply It! Do mealworms prefer damp or dry places?

Nine-banded armadillos live in brush, woods, scrub, and grasslands. The armadillo is a medium-sized, insect-eating mammal.

 Predict What things do you think an armadillo needs to survive?

....

....

THE BIG ? How do living things interact with their environments?

How can you estimate how many animals live in an ecosystem?

Scientists can figure out how many animals live in a large area by counting how many animals there are in small parts of the area and then **estimating.** The more small parts that they check, the better their estimate usually is.

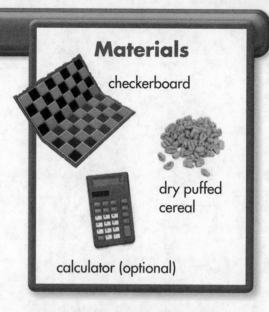

Materials

checkerboard

dry puffed cereal

calculator (optional)

☐ **1.** Scatter two handfuls of cereal on a checkerboard. Guess how many pieces are on the board.

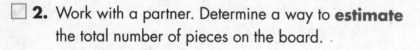

☐ **2.** Work with a partner. Determine a way to **estimate** the total number of pieces on the board.

Write your estimate. ....
Hint: Start with a small area.

☐ **3.** Count all the pieces of cereal on the board. ....

> **Inquiry Skill** Sometimes you can use math to help you make a good **estimate.**

Explain Your Results

4. Which was easiest: guessing, **estimating,** or counting?

....

Which was most accurate? ....

5. Infer How do you think you could make your estimate more accurate?

....

6. **UNLOCK THE BIG ?** **Infer** Why do you think scientists might want to know how many animals live in an ecosystem?

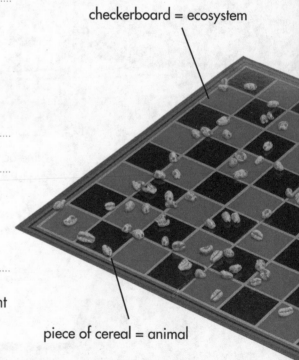

checkerboard = ecosystem

piece of cereal = animal

....

....

....

◉ Main Idea and Details

- The **main idea** is the most important idea in a reading selection.
- Supporting **details** tell more about the main idea.

The Desert Ecosystem

Plants can live in a hot, dry desert. Long roots that grow close to the surface allow a cactus to take in as much rainwater as possible during a single storm. The roots of a large saguaro cactus may grow to 15 meters in length. The stem of a cactus expands to fill with the rainwater it collects.

Practice It!

Complete the graphic organizer below to show the main idea and details in the example paragraph.

Main Idea

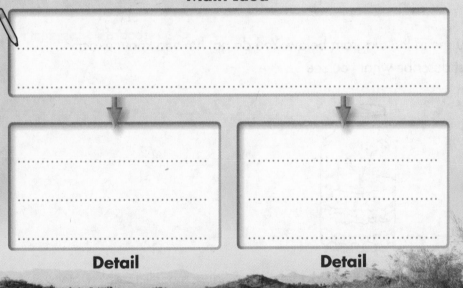

Detail   Detail

Home, Sweet Home!

A terrarium is a small, closed environment. Plants can survive in a terrarium for a long time with little attention. In fact, plants can grow in a terrarium for years without being watered. For this reason, the amount of water added to a terrarium as it is being made is very important. If there is too much water, the plants will rot. If there is too little, the plants will wilt.

The local nature museum has asked you to design a terrarium and determine the correct amount of water.

Identify the Problem

☐ **1.** What is your task? _____

_____

Do Research

Examine a terrarium.

☐ **2. Describe** each layer you see in the diagram below. You do not have to know exactly what each material is. Just describe what you see.

☐ **3. Examine** a diagram of the water cycle. **Explain** how a terrarium models Earth's water cycle. _____

_____

_____

_____

Go to the materials station(s). Pick up the materials one at a time. Think about how each may or may not be useful in your design. Leave the materials where they are.

☐ **4.** What are your design constraints? _____

_____

_____

Develop Possible Solutions

☐ **5. List** two different ways you could combine some of the materials to make a terrarium.

_____

_____

_____

_____

_____

Choose One Solution

☐ **6. Describe** your terrarium and how you will make it. _____

_____

_____

_____

_____

☐ **7. List** the materials that you will need. _____

_____

☐ **8.** How will you determine the correct amount of water for your terrarium? _____

_____

Design and Construct a Prototype

☐ **9. Draw and label** a diagram of your terrarium.

Gather your materials and a ruler. **Build** your terrarium. **Record** the mass of the different materials and the thickness of each layer. Remember to measure the amount of water you plan to add.

☐ **10. Record** the design details of your prototype. _____

_____

_____

_____

Test the Prototype

Test your terrarium. Close it and leave it for 24 hours. After 24 hours, **examine** your terrarium.

☐ **11. Record** your observations. _____

_____

_____

_____

12. After one week, **examine** your terrarium and **record** your observations. _____

_____

_____

_____

Communicate Results

13. How much water in centimeters is in the bottom of your terrarium? _____

_____

14. How well do you think the layers in your design worked? Explain. _____

_____

_____

_____

Evaluate and Redesign

15. Describe any changes you would make to your terrarium. How could you make it wetter? Drier? _____

_____

_____

_____

What are ecosystems?

Envision It!

Tell how the organisms in this picture interact.

MY PLANET DIARY

Let's Blog!

by Emma
Middleburg, FL

Today we went to the Alligator Farm in St. Augustine. We saw American alligators. One alligator was an albino. Did you know they feed them rodents called Cavia? The worker that fed them said they only need 80 pounds of food a year. I was surprised when she walked among the alligators in the exhibit as she fed them. One of them kept hissing at her. I would have been scared.

Although we saw many crocodiles and alligators, my favorite was the albino alligator. It was all white. I learned that the parents of albino alligators don't always have to be albino themselves. We rarely see these in the wild because they can't camouflage themselves from their predators.

It was an exciting day and a great way to spend the afternoon learning.

Write a response to Emma's blog. Talk about an animal you have seen or read about.

I will know the parts of ecosystems and some examples of ecosystems. I will know how specific structures of organisms help them live in their habitats.

Words to Know

ecosystem   population
habitat

Parts of an Ecosystem

An **ecosystem** is all the living and nonliving things in an environment and the many ways they interact. An ecosystem may be large like the ocean or small like a park. Animals and plants are living parts of an ecosystem. These organisms interact with each other and with the nonliving parts of the system. The nonliving parts of an ecosystem include air, water, soil, sunlight, and landforms.

1. ◎ **Main Idea and Details** Complete the graphic organizer below. Write details about ecosystems.

Main Idea

There are many parts of an ecosystem.

Tithmayrbealiv

Detail

They have nonliving parts that include air, water, soil, sunlight and landforms

Detail

2. **Infer** The seahorse can interact with its ocean ecosystem by holding on to the coral. Why do you think the seahorse might hold on to the coral?

It holed on so it does not blow away

Kinds of Ecosystems

There are several different ecosystems in North America, such as tundra, rain forest, desert, grassland, and forest. Many factors, such as climate and soil, make ecosystems different. Some ecosystems are cold and dry, while others are warm and wet. Some ecosystems have sandy soil while others have fertile soil. The kinds of plants and animals that live in an area depend on the climate and soil. Organisms can survive only in environments in which their needs are met. In any environment, some kinds of plants and animals survive better than others.

For example, you may think that nothing can live in a desert ecosystem, but deserts have many organisms living there. Cacti and lizards live in deserts. Sandy soil is used as a hiding place for the desert horned lizard. The lizard can quickly become invisible by throwing sand over its body.

3. ◎ **Main Idea and Details** Read the first paragraph again. **Underline** the main idea. Circle the details.

4. CHALLENGE How might a grassland change if very little precipitation falls on the area for several years?

Because they have alot of rain so they can fine more

Wetlands

In wetlands, the ground is covered with water for at least part of the year. Water lilies and cypress trees grow in some wetlands. Different kinds of animals, such as insects, raccoons, and alligators, live in wetlands too.

raccoon

Tundra

1 A tundra is a cold region. The ground beneath the surface is frozen all year. Some grasses can grow, but trees cannot. Arctic foxes, caribou, and other animals thrive in these areas.

caribou

Rain Forests

2 Not all rain forests are tropical. The mild and rainy climate of the Pacific Northwest supports temperate rain forests. They are home to organisms such as spotted owls, banana slugs, and Douglas fir trees.

northern spotted owl

Desert

3 The driest ecosystem is a desert. Some plants and animals have adapted to the limited water supply. Cacti, coyotes, and lizards are desert organisms.

4

Grassland

Grasslands, as their name suggests, are covered with grasses. They receive a medium amount of rain. Grasshoppers, prairie chickens, and bison are animals that live in grasslands in North America.

grasshopper

desert horned lizard

Living Things Within Their Ecosystems

Habitat

The area or place where an organism lives in an ecosystem is its **habitat.** You can think of a habitat as an "address." The habitat of the lion is open grassland with shrubs, trees, and water. A habitat contains all the living and nonliving things that an organism needs to survive.

Population

Look at the picture on this page. It shows a savannah ecosystem in Africa. A savannah is a kind of grassland. There are many populations found in this savannah. A **population** is all the members of one species that live within an area of an ecosystem. For example, the wildebeests that live in the African plains form a population. A population may be large or small.

5. **Apply** Find another population in the picture and draw an ✗ on each member of that population.

6. **Identify** Write the names of two other populations that you think could be part of the ecosystem shown here.

A Rhino

giraffe

a habitat within a savannah ecosystem

wildebeest

zebra

Structures for Survival

Many organisms such as the platypus have special structures that help them survive in their habitats. These structures may include wings that allow them to fly, webbed feet that help them swim, and fur that keeps them warm. Different organisms in an ecosystem may have similar structures that help them live there. For example, many organisms that live in the ocean have fins that help them move easily through water.

7. **Infer** What kind of ecosystem might this animal live in? Explain how you know.

   Riverss Because they have webbed feet.

Got it?

8. **Identify** What kind of habitat do you think an animal with long, thick fur would most likely live in?

   AT Bdtrabos

9. **Explain** What structures might monkeys have that help them to live in trees?

   The long hands help them survive.

■ **Stop!** I need help with ....

❙❙ **Wait!** I have a question about ....

▶ **Go!** Now I know ....

How do living things affect the environment?

Tell how humans have affected this deer's environment.

Inquiry Explore It!

What happens when one part of an ecosystem is removed?

In this model of an ecosystem, you will find out what can happen to animals when a resource decreases.

☑ **1. Make a Model** Lay out blue paper squares. Lay two red squares of paper to overlap each blue square.

☑ **2.** Roll the dot cube. Remove that number of water holes.

☑ **3.** Roll the cube five times.
After each roll, match animals with water holes.

☑ **4.** No more than two animals can be at a water hole. Remove extra animals. **Record** information on the Water Holes and Animals Chart.

Explain Your Results

5. Infer What might happen to animals when there is a long drought?

....

....

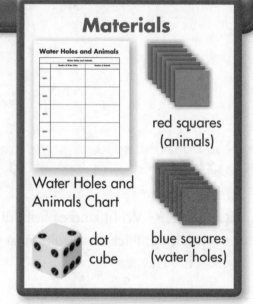

Materials

Water Holes and Animals Chart

red squares (animals)

dot cube

blue squares (water holes)

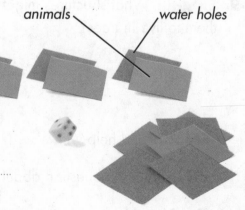

animals — water holes

I will know the effect of a sudden change of one group of organisms on another group.

Word to Know

competition

Changes to the Environment

The environment is like a balance. One side holds what lives in the environment. The other side holds resources that the environment provides. If the environment provides enough resources to support life, the balance is level.

Change often tips the balance. For example, tree seeds may sprout on a log and start to grow. The young trees need light and space to grow. The young trees are in competition. **Competition** occurs when two or more living things need the same resources in order to survive. Some trees get enough light. As their branches grow, they shade nearby plants. The environment changes. Other young trees may not get enough light to survive.

1. **Identify** In the paragraphs on this page **underline** what young trees are competing for against other living things.

2. **Examine** How can the fallen tree in this picture change a forest habitat?

It more of a house for bugs to live in.

Plants Cause Change

Changes can help some living things and harm others. For example, a plant called purple loosestrife was brought to the United States. No animals eat this plant. It is spreading to new places. That is great for the loosestrife! However, there is less space for other plants to grow. Some kinds of plants are completely pushed out of the environment.

A plant called kudzu was originally brought to the United States from Japan. At first, kudzu was thought to be beneficial to the environment. Kudzu was used in gardens for its beauty and in many open spaces as a cover over soil to prevent erosion. The plant, however, grows very well in the southeastern United States. Because the vines grow so well, they destroy forests by blocking trees' sunlight.

3. **Summarize** How has kudzu both helped and harmed habitats?

....

....

....

....

....

....

kudzu

Animals Cause Change

Some animals change the environment to improve their habitat. Beavers, for example, need deep water. If the stream where they live is too shallow, the beavers build a pond. They cut down trees with their teeth. They use the wood to build a dam across the stream. The blocked water forms a pond behind the dam.

The change helps plants and animals that need to live in still water. Also, the trees the beavers cut down no longer shade the ground below. Small plants and shrubs that benefit from direct sunlight grow in their place.

The change harms plants and animals whose homes are flooded. Trees needed to make the dam are lost. The pond also takes homes away from plants and animals that prefer the flowing water of streams.

A beaver can cut down over 200 trees per year!

4. **Conclude** This habitat was once a grassy meadow. How has this beaver dam changed it?

The Bevers dam makes the pond.

A beaver can add over 5 feet of length to its dam per day.

The Recycling Plan
Sometimes people harm the environment by throwing out a lot of trash. To help the environment, organize a recycling plan for your classroom. Share your ideas with other classes.

5. Visualize This bridge was built in and over an aquatic ecosystem. Discuss how this bridge affected the plants and animals living in the area.

There trees would die. So the animals that live in there would die.

Humans Cause Sudden Change

People often change the environment to meet their needs. Some changes people make cause sudden changes in the environment. When they build a new group of homes, they may cut down a small forest in days to make room for houses. Some people may build birdhouses in their backyards. This provides shelter and food for certain kinds of birds in the area. But most birds and other animals must move away to find new homes all of a sudden.

Some people use chemicals to kill organisms such as beetles and other insects that eat crops or plants around their homes. These chemicals quickly decrease the number of these organisms. Birds that feed on these organisms might have less to eat and may move away or die.

6. Explain How did this birdhouse affect the environment?

It affect the evirsnment So there would be no food or shelter

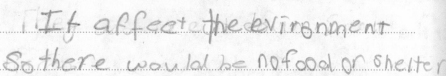

Got it?

7. Describe How do beavers and humans modify their environments?

Bevers bulid dams and humans bulid Cities

8. UNLOCK THE BIG ? Think about what you learned in this lesson. Are changes to the environment always harmful?

Some are harmful and other are not would die.

⬜ **Stop!** I need help with ....

⏸ **Wait!** I have a question about ....

▶ **Go!** Now I know ....

Lesson 3

What are natural resources?

Tell what resources are available in this picture.

Inquiry **Explore It!**

How can you collect the sun's energy?

☐ **1.** Line the bowl with foil. If needed, use loops of tape to hold the foil on the bowl.

☐ **2.** Tilt the bowl so the sun shines into it. Use clay to hold the bowl in place.

Put one thermometer near the bowl.

Use clay to prop up one thermometer.

☐ **3. Measure** and **record** the temperatures at the start, after 1 minute, and after 3 minutes.

Materials

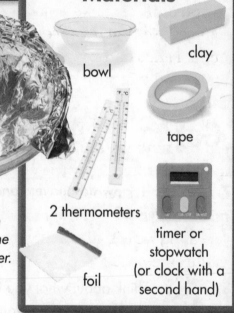

bowl

clay

tape

2 thermometers

foil

timer or stopwatch (or clock with a second hand)

Explain Your Results

4. Compare the effects of sunlight on the 2 thermometers.

....

....

5. Infer What made the temperatures different?

....

Data Table		
Time	Temperature (°C)	
	Near Bowl	In Bowl
At start		
After 1 min		
After 3 min		

194

I will know that people need resources and that some resources can be replaced in nature and some cannot.

Words to Know

renewable resource
nonrenewable resource

Natural Resources

Are you wearing jeans? Are you holding a pencil? Did you drink some water today? You're using natural resources! Natural resources are supplies found in nature. Plants and animals are natural resources. So are nonliving things such as air, water, soil, minerals, and sunlight.

All living things depend on natural resources. Plants need air, sunlight, soil, and water to live. People need air and water too. They use plant and animal resources for food. Earth's resources also provide the raw materials and energy that we use to make the products we need. Everything we eat, use, or buy has been made from or is a natural resource.

Products Consumed per Person in 2005		
	Gasoline (L)	**Paper products** (kg)
The average person in the world used...	186.9	55.83
The average person in the U.S. used...	1,772.6	302.97
This country used the most per person:	United States 1,772.6	Luxembourg 340.16

Sources: U.S. Energy Information Administration; Food & Agriculture Organization of the United Nations

1. **Apply** Look around your classroom. What resources do you need during the school day?

Water
whiteboard
Pencil

2. **Analyze** What natural resources are used to create the products listed in the chart?

Petroluem

Renewable Resources

Earth has two types of natural resources, renewable and nonrenewable. **Renewable resources** are resources that can be replaced. Plants and animals are examples of renewable resources. So is the oxygen in the air we breathe. These resources are renewable as along as they are replaced as fast as they are used.

Water

Water is one of our most important renewable resources. All living things need water to survive. Humans also use water for things such as cooking and bathing.

Earth constantly recycles its water through precipitation and evaporation. This makes water a renewable resource. But only one percent of Earth's water is drinkable. The rest is either salt water in the oceans or frozen in glaciers and polar ice caps. Also, not all people live near water sources. Gathering drinkable water and keeping it safe for people to use takes time and more resources.

 Draw Conclusions

What conclusions might you draw about the amount of drinkable water on Earth?

....

....

....

....

....

Solar and Wind Energy

People use energy to run machines, heat and cool homes, and help grow food. Solar energy is a renewable resource. Energy from the sun can be used to heat buildings. Solar cells can change energy from the sun into electrical energy.

Wind is another source of renewable energy. Windmills can be used to run machinery and to produce electricity.

Solar and wind energy do not cause pollution. Sunlight will not run out for billions of years. But neither solar nor wind energy are available all the time. Some people think windmills are noisy or ugly. Systems to collect solar energy are expensive to make. Factories that make certain kinds of solar cells also produce dangerous wastes.

4. **Identify Underline** the advantages of renewable energy.

   (Circle) the disadvantages of renewable energy.

Do the math!

Read a Circle Graph

The circle graph shows how an average family of four in the United States uses water each day. The average household uses about 1,049 liters of water per day.

Daily Water Use, Family of Four

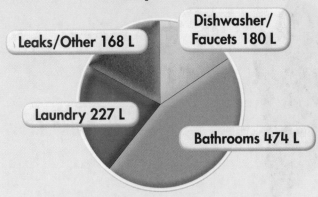

Leaks/Other 168 L
Dishwasher/Faucets 180 L
Laundry 227 L
Bathrooms 474 L

Source: American Water Works Association

1. How much water does the average U.S. family use in bathrooms each week?
   A. 3,318 L
   B. 1,176 L
   C. 7,343 L
   D. 1,260 L

2. In a family of four, about how much water does each person use per day?
   A. 4,196 L
   B. 2,620 L
   C. 262 L
   D. 26.2 L

Nonrenewable Resources

All minerals are nonrenewable resources. **Nonrenewable resources** are resources that exist in limited amounts or are used faster than they can be replaced in nature. People use minerals and other nonrenewable resources to make products and to provide energy.

Fossil Fuels

Oil is the common name for petroleum. Oil and coal are nonrenewable resources. They are fuels, which means that they are burned to provide energy. Oil is also used to make various products.

Coal and oil are called fossil fuels because they were made from organisms that lived long ago. After these organisms died, their remains and the unused stored energy slowly became buried under thick layers of sediments. Over millions of years, pressure, heat, and decaying action changed the remains into coal, oil, and natural gas.

Ores

Mineral resources are often found in ores. An ore is a rock rich in valuable minerals. Fossil fuels and ores are removed from below Earth's surface. But ores are removed for the minerals they contain, not for burning as fuel.

People use mineral resources in different ways. For example, iron ore contains the metal iron. Often the iron is mixed with other materials to make steel. Steel is used to make things ranging from skyscrapers to paper clips.

Oil and gas drilling platform

5. Compare and Contrast How are ores and fossil fuels alike? How are they different?

Fossel fuels are mostly energy and ores are removed so they dont contain fuelz Fossel fuels and ore are alike because they are removed from below earth surface

iron ore

How Resources Can Last Longer

People use natural resources to make products they use in their daily lives. As people use more and more resources, fewer nonrenewable resources will be available in the future. Conservation means using what you need as efficiently as possible. You can reduce unnecessary resource use in many ways. For example, to travel short distances, you can walk or ride a bike. You can drink from a reusable container instead of buying bottled water and throwing the bottle away.

Recycling is saving or using materials again instead of treating them as waste. Some products and materials are easier to recycle than others.

6. **Apply** Think about the resources you used today. How might you conserve them in the future?

I chosse lights because, you don't want to waste light energy.

Got it?

7. **Analyze** How might nonrenewable resources be used to collect renewable resources?

By a truk might cut down trees but then can be used by the resourses.

8. **UNLOCK ESSENTIAL ?** Think about what you learned in this lesson. How do Earth's resources change?

Earth changes by descrising resourses.

○ **Stop!** I need help with ....

○ **Wait!** I have a question about ....

▷ **Go!** Now I know ....

What are fossils?

Compare the tracks. **Tell** what you can conclude about the animals that made them.

my planet Diary

DISCOVERY

Woolly mammoths disappeared from Earth about 10,000 years ago. Scientists have learned about mammoths by studying their bones and other remains. In 2007, however, scientists got an amazing opportunity to learn what mammoths were like.

That year, reindeer herders in northern Russia discovered the frozen body of a baby mammoth. The mammoth had been frozen underground for about 40,000 years. Except for missing toenails and hair, the month-old mammoth was in nearly perfect condition. Even the food in its stomach was preserved!

What do you think scientists might learn by studying the baby mammoth?

....

....

....

The baby mammoth has been named Lyuba.

I will know that a fossil is the remains or mark of a living thing from long ago. I will know the ways a fossil can form.

Words to Know

fossil

extinct

Fossil Clues

Some plants and animals that lived millions of years ago have left clues about their lives. A line of footprints preserved in rock can show how an animal walked. The skeleton of a small animal can help scientists understand what the animal looked like.

Skeletons and footprints are examples of fossils. A **fossil** is the remains or mark of an animal or plant that lived long ago. Scientists can study fossils to learn about species that are extinct. An **extinct** species no longer exists. More than one million species currently live on Earth, but many more have become extinct. In fact, most types of organisms that have lived on Earth no longer exist.

1. ◉ **Main Idea and Details** Read the first paragraph again. **Underline** the main idea.

2. **Explain** Read the caption below. What is one thing scientists might learn by examining a trilobite fossil?

....

....

....

Trilobites are now extinct. These animals had hard shells and lived in the sea hundreds of millions of years ago.

How Fossils Form

Fossils form in different ways. Most fossils form when a plant or animal dies and becomes buried under layers of sediments. Sediments are bits of rock, sand, shell, and other material. Over time, the sediments harden into rock and preserve the shape of the buried plant or animal. The diagram below shows this process.

Usually only the hard parts of animals, such as bones and shells, become fossils. The soft parts decay or may be eaten by other animals. Once the remains of an animal are buried, different things can happen. Sometimes the buried remains break down and disappear, leaving an empty space in the sedimentary rock. A space in rock in the shape of a living thing is called a *mold fossil*. Later, minerals from the surrounding rock might fill the mold fossil. Over time, these minerals harden into the shape of the mold. This type of fossil is called a *cast fossil*. Dinosaur "bones" that come from cast fossils are not bones at all! They are hardened minerals.

3. Fill in the Blanks Complete the captions in the diagram below. Fill in each blank with the correct word.

Most fossils are found within sedimentary rock, or rock that forms in layers.

An animal dies and sinks to the bottom of a lake or shallow sea. The .... parts of its body decay.

Sand, mud, and other .... settle on top of the animal's remains.

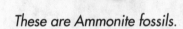

4. Identify Draw an ✗ on the mold fossils. Circle the cast fossil.

5. Infer Many dinosaurs once roamed Earth, but fossils do not exist for all of them. Look at the diagram. What might be some reasons why not all dinosaurs left fossils?

....

....

....

These are Ammonite fossils.

More layers of sediments form. The sediments

harden into .... ,

preserving the shape of the animal's parts.

Over time the rock layers above the fossil wear away. The fossil appears at or near Earth's surface.

This fly has been preserved in amber.

The skull of this saber-toothed cat was preserved in a tar pit.

Other Types of Fossils

Casts and molds are called *body fossils* because they are formed from the body parts of living things. There are several other types of body fossils. Sometimes, the whole body of an animal may be preserved in a fossil. For example, insects can become trapped in sticky tree sap. The sap surrounds the insect and hardens over time. The hardened sap is called amber. Amber preserves all of an insect's remains—both the hard parts and the soft parts.

Parts of an animal's body, such as teeth or bones, make up another type of body fossil. The bones of some animals were preserved in tar pits. Tar pits are oily pools that exist on Earth's surface. Animals that fell into tar pits became trapped. The soft parts of their bodies broke down, but their bones remained. Fossils of these animals are actual bone and not hardened minerals.

7. **Contrast** How are the fossils of the saber-toothed cat different from cast fossils?

6. CHALLENGE What do you think scientists can learn from an insect preserved in amber?

Trace Fossils

Most fossils show what the parts of a plant or animal looked like. *Trace fossils* give clues about a living thing's activities. Footprints, or tracks, are a kind of trace fossil. Preserved burrows, nests, and eggshells are also trace fossils. Studying trace fossils can help scientists answer questions about where an animal lived, what it ate, and how fast it moved.

8. **Identify** Draw an ✗ on the photo of a trace fossil.

Lightning Lab

Tell-Tale Footprints
Take several steps on a long piece of paper. Have a partner trace your feet with each step. Then do the same for your partner. Compare the footprints. Why are they different? Write a short paragraph explaining what scientists can learn by studying different fossil footprints.

Got it?

9. **Infer** Explain how a mold fossil of a footprint would form.

....

....

10. **Conclude** Suppose you are a scientist studying saber-toothed cats. Would you be more excited to find cast fossils or fossils from a tar pit? Explain your answer.

....

....

....

⬜ **Stop!** I need help with ....

⏸ **Wait!** I have a question about ....

▶ **Go!** Now I know ....

What can fossils tell us?

Tell what clues this fossil gives about what this dinosaur ate.

MY PLANET DIARY

//// MISCONCEPTION ////

Dinosaurs were a group of reptiles that lived on Earth for about 150 million years. That period has been called the Age of the Dinosaurs. A common misconception is that all of the large reptiles alive at that time were dinosaurs. In fact, Earth was home to many other kinds of reptiles during the Age of the Dinosaurs.

Pterosaurs, for example, were a group of flying reptiles. They did not have feathers, but flew on wings made of skin. The largest pterosaur had wings measuring more than 30 feet from tip to tip!

Pterodactyls are sometimes called "flying dinosaurs." In fact, the pterodactyl was a kind of pterosaur.

Pterosaurs and dinosaurs shared a common ancestor. But scientists have used fossils to identify important differences between the two. Dinosaurs, for example, had a different hip structure than pterosaurs. Like dinosaurs, pterosaurs became extinct about 65 million years ago.

Write one way in which dinosaurs and pterosaurs were alike and one way in which they were different.

....

....

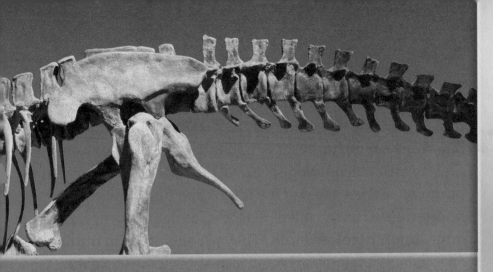

I will know how scientists use fossils to learn about the past.

Word to Know

paleontologist

Windows to the Past

Scientists study fossils to learn about plants, animals, and environments of the past. A scientist who studies fossils is called a **paleontologist.**

Some fossils show us what extinct organisms looked like and how they lived. For example, paleontologists have found skulls from dinosaurs called sauropods. Sauropods were a group of dinosaurs that had small heads, long necks, and enormous bodies. They ate plants and may have used their long necks to reach tall trees.

Because of their size, these dinosaurs needed huge amounts of food. However, their small heads meant that they could only take small bites. How did they get enough to eat? Paleontologists studied the dinosaurs' skulls and the shape of their teeth. They concluded that some sauropods may have swallowed their food without chewing it. Doing this allowed the dinosaurs to get food to their stomachs more quickly and take more bites.

This illustration shows what one kind of sauropod may have looked like.

1. **Recall** What did paleontologists conclude about sauropods by studying their skulls and teeth?

....

....

....

....

....

....

paleontologist

This illustration shows what one kind of hadrosaur might have looked like.

Fossils and Living Organisms

One way paleontologists learn about extinct plants and animals is by comparing them with plants and animals that exist today. For example, fossils show that some dinosaurs called hadrosaurs had large, hollow crests on their heads. Paleontologists have different ideas about the purposes of these crests. One idea came from comparing hadrosaurs to birds called peacocks. Male peacocks have large, brightly colored tails. They use their tails to attract mates. Paleontologists hypothesize that hadrosaurs may have used their crests in the same way.

Fossils can also show how plants and animals have changed over time. Many living things today are related to plants and animals of the past. Fossils show that some extinct plant species looked a lot like modern plants. For example, compare the pictures of the horsetail fossil and the modern horsetail plant. Some horsetail plants of the past grew to the size of trees. Modern horsetail plants are much smaller. This suggests that the plants changed slowly over time.

3. **Hypothesize** What is another possible use of the hadrosaur's hollow crest?

....

....

....

....

....

2. **Compare** Tell how the horsetail fossil and the modern horsetail plant are alike.

Then

Now

Fossils and the Environment

Fossils also show that Earth's environment has changed. For example, scientists in Kansas have found the remains of sea animals called ammonites. Ammonites are related to modern squids, but they died out 65 million years ago. In South Dakota, scientists have discovered fossils of giant sea turtles. These turtles lived about 70 million years ago but are now extinct. What do these discoveries tell us? They show that areas of present-day states such as Kansas and South Dakota were once covered with water!

4. **Describe** How has the environment of Kansas changed?

....

....

....

5. ◉ **Main Idea and Details** What details support the idea that Earth's environment has changed?

....

....

....

....

....

Then

Now

ammonite

Geologic Time Scale

Present

Cenozoic Era
In the last 65 million years, dogs, cats, and humans appeared.

65 million years ago

Mesozoic Era
The Mesozoic Era, also called the Age of the Dinosaurs, was the time of hadrosaurs and Tyrannosaurus rex. Most dinosaurs became extinct at the end of this period.

248 million years ago

Paleozoic Era
Fish, simple plants, insects, and early land animals lived during this time.

544 million years ago

Precambrian
Some rocks from the late Precambrian time have fossils of jellyfish.

Fossil Age

Scientists determine the age of fossils in two ways. Many fossils are located within layers of rock. Older layers of rock are under newer layers of rock. Scientists can conclude that fossils found in deeper or lower layers are older than those found in layers above. Differences in rock layers and patterns of rock formations can also show changes over time due to earth forces, such as earthquakes.

Another way scientists can determine the age of fossils is by examining how quickly certain materials in the fossils change. These materials change at steady rates after a plant or animal dies. Scientists can measure these materials in a fossil to determine how long ago the organism died.

Geologic Time Scale

Scientists have used information about the ages of fossils and rocks to make a timeline of the history of Earth. This timeline is called the geologic time scale. When they draw the scale, scientists place the earliest time span at the bottom. They put the most recent time span at the top. This matches the way rock layers of different ages are arranged. The time scale helps scientists show when different animals existed.

6. **Infer** What era are the sea turtle fossils of South Dakota from?

7. ⊙ **Draw Conclusions** Suppose that you found two different fossils in two different layers of rock. How could you tell which fossil was older?

Scientists divide Earth's history into time spans of millions of years. These time spans are labeled on the geologic time scale.

Fossil Fuels

Did you know that fuels from natural sources, such as coal and oil, are a kind of fossil? Most of these "fossil fuels" come from the remains of organisms that lived millions of years ago. It took millions of years for the remains to become coal or oil. People use fossil fuels as resources. For example, at power plants, fossil fuels are use to produce the electricity that powers homes and businesses. Therefore, once fossil fuels are used, they will not renew at a rate in which humans would be able to use them again.

The use of fossils fuels affects the environment in many ways. For example, when burned, coal can pollute the air. If there is an oil spill, the oil can pollute the water and harm animals that live there.

8. [CHALLENGE] What might happen if people use up all the fossil fuels currently available? Explain your answer.

....

....

Got it?

9. ◎ **Draw Conclusions** A scientist finds the fossil of a sea creature on top of a mountain range. What can the scientist conclude about the land around the fossil?

....

10. **Summarize** What can paleontologists learn from studying fossils?

....

....

....

⬛ **Stop!** I need help with ....

⏸ **Wait!** I have a question about ....

▶ **Go!** Now I know ....

How do earthworms meet their needs in a model of an ecosystem?

Follow a Procedure

☑ **1.** Obtain an earthworm bottle from your teacher.
Use a spoon to add a thin layer of sand. Add 6 worms.

Be careful! Earthworms are living organisms. Handle with care.

Materials

spoon

safety goggles

foil

earthworm bottle

plastic cup with sand

black paper

rubber band

6 earthworms

masking tape

☑ **2.** Tape black paper around the bottle. Cover the top with foil fastened with a rubber band. Wait 24 hours.

Inquiry Skill
Scientists make careful observations and record data accurately. They use their data to help make **inferences.**

3. Remove the paper and foil. **Observe** the sand, dirt, and earthworms. **Record** your observations.

Earthworm Observations	
Day	**Observations**
Day 1 (24 hours after making ecosystem)	
Day 2	
Day 3	
Day 4	

4. Replace the paper and the foil. Observe daily for 3 more days. Record your observations.

Be careful! **Wash your hands when finished.**

Analyze and Conclude

5. Explain your **observations.**

....

....

6. Infer Do the earthworms get what they need from the ecosystem? Tell how you know.

....

....

7. UNLOCK THE BIG ? What does the model ecosystem show about how living things interact in their environments?

....

....

Rachel Carson

In the 1950s, people used a chemical called DDT to poison harmful insects. Farmers sprayed it on their fields. In cities and towns, it was used on the plants in parks.

Rachel Carson was a scientist and a writer. She began to notice that every spring there were fewer and fewer songbirds. She wondered what was happening to the bird populations. After making careful observations, Carson learned that DDT was building up on land and in lakes and streams. The chemical had entered the food chains and webs of many ecosystems.

Carson wanted to warn as many people as possible about the dangers of using DDT. In 1962, she wrote a book titled *Silent Spring*. Because of her book, laws forbidding the use of DDT were passed. Society has been more aware of the delicate balance of ecosystems ever since.

REVIEW THE BIG ? How do you think the interaction of DDT in the environment affected the birds?

....

....

....

....

....

Vocabulary Smart Cards

- ecosystem
- habitat
- population
- competition
- renewable resource
- nonrenewable resource
- fossil
- extinct
- paleontologist

Play a Game!

Cut out the Vocabulary Smart Cards.

Work with a partner. Choose a Vocabulary Smart Card.

Say as many words as you can think of that describe that vocabulary word.

Have your partner guess the word.

215

competition

competencia

ecosystem

ecosistema

renewable resource

recurso renovable

habitat

hábitat

nonrenewable resource

recurso no renovable

population

población

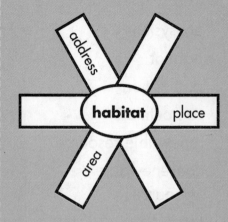

all the living and nonliving things in an environment and the many ways they interact

What is the prefix for this word and what does it mean?

....

todos los seres vivos y las cosas sin vida que hay en un medio ambiente y las múltiples interacciones entre ellos

---

occurs when two or more living things need the same resources in order to survive

Write a sentence using the verb form of this word.

....

....

situación en la que dos o más seres vivos necesitan los mismos recursos para sobrevivir

---

area or place where an organism lives in an ecosystem

Use a dictionary. Find as many synonyms for this word as you can.

....

....

área o lugar de un ecosistema donde vive un organismo

---

resource that can be replaced

Write an example.

....

....

....

recurso que se puede reemplazar

---

all the members of one species that live within an area of an ecosystem

Write another definition for this word.

....

....

....

todos los miembros de una especie que viven en un área de un ecosistema

---

resource that exists in limited amounts or is used faster than it can be replaced in nature

What is the prefix of this word?

....

recurso que existe en cantidades limitadas o que se usa más rápido de lo que le toma la naturaleza reponerlo

---

Make a Word Wheel!

Choose a vocabulary word and write it in the center of the Word Wheel graphic organizer. Write synonyms or related words on the wheel spokes.

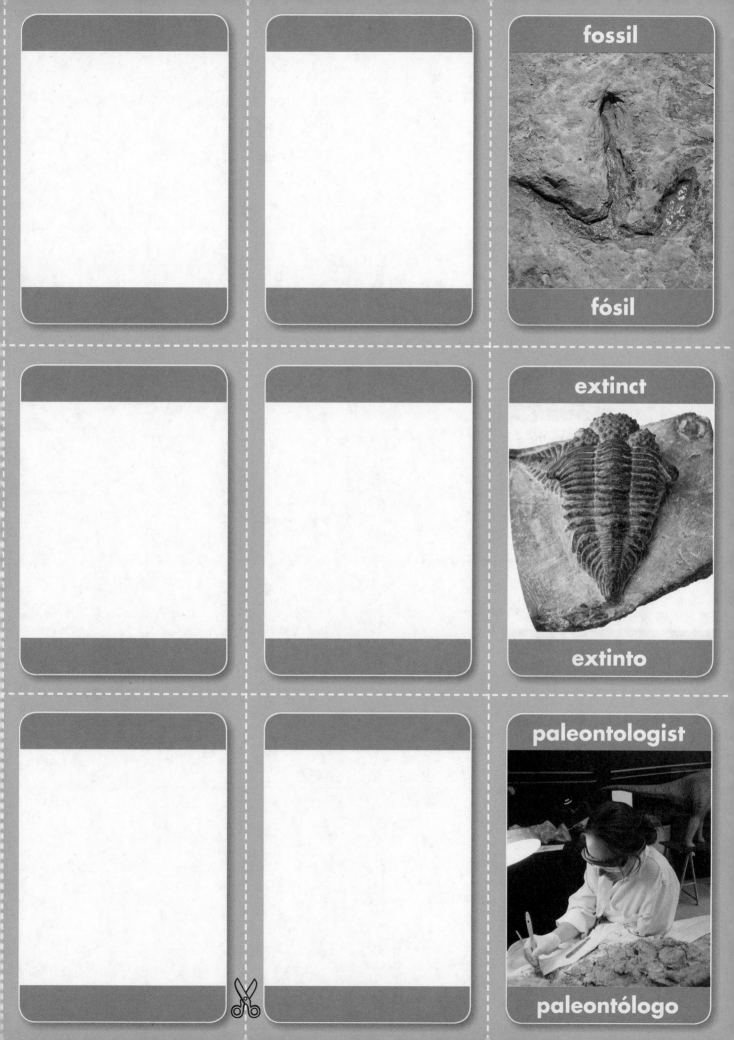

fossil

fósil

extinct

extinto

paleontologist

paleontólogo

remains or mark of an animal or plant that lived long ago

Draw an example.

restos o marca de un ser vivo que existió hace mucho tiempo

no longer existing as a species

Write a sentence using the word.

ya no existe más como especie

a scientist who studies fossils

What is the suffix of this word and what does it mean?

científico que estudia los fósiles

Chapter 5
Study Guide
 How do living things interact with their environments?

 Life Science

Lesson 1

What are ecosystems?

- An ecosystem is all the living and nonliving things in an environment.
- There are many ecosystems including desert, tundra, and forest.
- Special structures help many organisms survive in their habitats.

Lesson 2

How do living things affect the environment?

- Living things compete with each other for food and space.
- Some animals change the environment to improve their habitat.
- Changes in the environment help some living things and harm others.

Lesson 3

What are natural resources?

- Renewable resources can be replaced in nature.
- Nonrenewable resources exist in limited supply or are used faster than they can be replaced.

Lesson 4

What are fossils?

- A fossil is the remains or mark of an animal or plant that lived long ago.
- Most fossils form when a plant or animal dies and becomes buried under layers of sediments.

Lesson 5

What can fossils tell us?

- Paleontologists study fossils to learn about extinct organisms.
- Fossils can show how plants, animals, and Earth's environment have changed over time.

Chapter Review

How do living things interact with their environments?

Lesson 1

What are ecosystems?

1. **Vocabulary** A group of organisms of the same kind living in an area is a(n)_____.
   A. community.
   B. population.
   C. ecosystem.
   D. habitat.

2. **Explain** How do the fins of a sunfish help it survive in water?

   ....

   ....

3. **Define** What makes up an ecosystem?

   ....

   ....

   ....

   ....

   ....

Lesson 2

How do living things affect the environment?

4. **Communicate** People build roads in new areas. How does this activity affect the living things in that environment?

   ....

   ....

   ....

   ....

   ....

   ....

Lesson 3

What are natural resources?

5. **Classify** Classify the following resources as renewable or nonrenewable resources.
   petroleum, solar energy, soil, water, wind, minerals

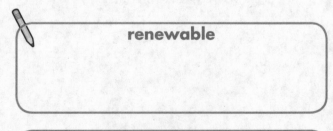

renewable

nonrenewable

Lesson 4

What are fossils?

6. **Explain** Tell how this mold fossil of an ammonite may have formed.

Lesson 5

What can fossils tell us?

7. **Conclude** Horseshoe crabs are called "living fossils" because they have changed little in 300 million years. How do paleontologists know this?

horseshoe crab

8. **APPLY THE BIG ?** **How do living things interact with their environments?**

Think about an ecosystem near where you live. How do the organisms there interact?

Read each question and choose the best answer.

1 **How does a habitat function within an ecosystem? Use the graphic organizer for an example of one kind of ecosystem.**

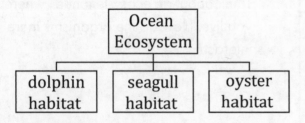

A A habitat is a type of ecosystem.

B Ecosystems only have one type of habitat.

C Habitats are smaller areas within an ecosystem.

D Habitats have only one type of living thing for each ecosystem.

2 **How many populations can live within one ecosystem?**

A no set number

B only a few

C up to 20

D one per ecosystem

3 **Which of these things might trees compete for in an environment?**

A ecosystems

B consumers

C populations

D resources

4 **Which of the following is a nonrenewable resource?**

A phosphate

B water

C oxygen

D trees

5 **What is a trace fossil?**

A a fossil that is a form of a living thing, which was filled in by minerals

B a fossil, such as a footprint or nest, that shows how an animal lived

C a fossil preserved by another substance, such as tree sap

D All fossils are trace fossils.

6 **What might a paleontologist conclude about a dinosaur that left fossil footprints of webbed feet?**

A The dinosaur ran fast.

B The dinosaur ate plants.

C The dinosaur was large.

D The dinosaur could swim.

Denver Zoo

You can visit a zoo to learn about many types of animals. Animals that live in different habitats in the wild can all be seen in one place. At the Denver Zoo, you can see Komodo dragons in the Tropical Discovery exhibit. You might see a rhinoceros at the Pachyderm Habitat. These animals live far apart in nature, but you can see them in one day at the zoo!

Animals must find their own food in the wild. At the zoo, zookeepers give the animals the food they need. A zoo needs many types of food because the different animals in the zoo eat many different types of food. This food includes fruits, vegetables, meats, fish, and insects.

Suppose a zoo gets a new type of animal. What might the zookeepers need to know about the animal?

....

....

Materials

small plastic tub

2 sponges   water

plastic spoon

plastic cup
of sand

10 mealworms and food

Inquiry Skill
Experiments have a
variable you change and a
variable you observe.

Do mealworms prefer damp or dry places?

A mealworm can sense whether the environment is damp or dry. Sometimes conditions change. You will **experiment** to find out how the environment affects mealworms' behavior.

Ask a question.

Do mealworms prefer to live in a damp place or a dry place?

State a hypothesis.

1. Write a **hypothesis** by circling one choice and finishing the sentence.
   If mealworms can move to a damp place or a dry place, then they will move to a place that is (a) *damp* or (b) *dry* because

....

....

....

Identify and control variables.

2. In this experiment you will observe where the mealworms move. You must change only one variable. Everything else must remain the same. What should stay the same? List two examples.

....

....

3. Tell the one change you will make.

....

....

....

Design your test.

4. Draw how you will set up your test.

5. List your steps in the order you will do them.

Do your test.

☑ **6.** Follow the steps you wrote.

Be careful! They are alive! Handle with care!
Wash your hands after handling mealworms.

☑ **7.** Make sure to **record** your **observations** in the table.

Collect and record your data.

☐ **8.** Fill in the chart.

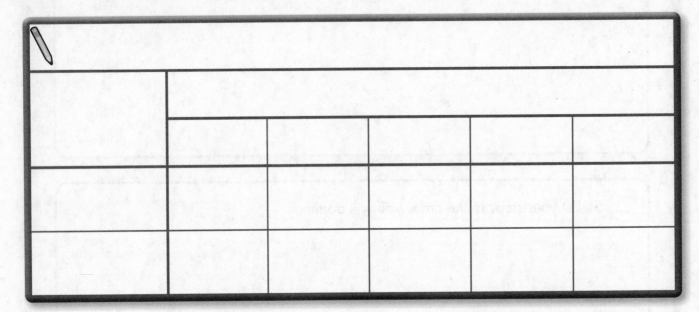

Check to see if your data are reasonable. You started with 10 mealworms. Each day add up the total number of mealworms. Make sure the total is 10.

Work Like a Scientist

Scientists work with other scientists. Compare your observations with other groups. Seek reasons that might explain any differences.

Interpret your data.

☑ **9.** Use your data to make bar graphs.

10. Compare what you see in the 2 graphs.

....

....

....

....

....

State your conclusion.

11. Communicate your conclusion. Compare your hypothesis with your results. Share your results with others.

....

....

....

....

Technology Tools

Your teacher may want you to use a computer (with the right software) or a graphing calculator to help collect, organize, analyze, and present your data. These tools can help you make tables, charts, and graphs.

Build a Model of an Ecosystem

Choose one type of ecosystem you have read about. Use a cardboard box, clay, construction paper, foam, or other materials to build a model of your ecosystem. Include labeled models of living and nonliving things. Write about the adaptations of the plants and animals in your ecosystem.

Write a Biography

Choose an animal found in your state, and write a biography for the animal. Be sure to include these things:

- the type of animal
- the animal's ecosystem and habitat
- the adaptations that help the animal survive in its environment
- ways the animal responds to changes in its environment

Science and Engineering Practices

1. Ask a question or define a problem.
2. Develop and use models.
3. Plan and carry out investigations.
4. Analyze and interpret data.
5. Use math and computational thinking.
6. Construct explanations or design solutions.
7. Engage in argument from evidence.
8. Obtain, evaluate, and communicate information.

Research Animal Instincts

Animals can inherit instinctive behaviors, such as migration, protection, or hibernation. Research a local animal that participates in one of these behaviors and gather information about how the animal responds to stimuli in its environment. Share your information with the class in a brief presentation. Your presentation should include:

- the name of the animal and a description of the instinctive behavior.

- animal structures involved in performing the behavior.

Make a Presentation

Like beavers, humans build dams that change the flow of rivers. Research some dams in your state to find out more about how dams change environments. Find or draw pictures of one dam to show in a presentation to your class. Write captions for the pictures, explaining how the dam affects the environment. Share your findings in your presentation.

How can magma form steps?

Earth's Resources

Try It! How can rocks and minerals be classified?

STEM Activity Hold Back the Water

Lesson 1 How are minerals classified?

Lesson 2 How are rocks classified?

Lesson 3 What are weathering and erosion?

Lesson 4 How can Earth's surface change rapidly?

Lesson 5 Where is Earth's water?

Lesson 6 What is the water cycle?

Investigate It! How does the steepness of a stream affect how fast it flows?

Earth Science

Apply It! What affects how soil erodes?

Giant's Causeway is a formation of about 40,000 stone pillars in Northern Ireland. The tops of the pillars form a path of stepping stones to the sea. Cooling magma from an ancient volcano formed Giant's Causeway between 50 and 60 million years ago.

Predict What forces might have shaped this formation?

....

....

THE BIG ? How do Earth's resources change?

How can rocks and minerals be classified?

Minerals are the building blocks for rocks.

☐ **1. Observe** the rocks and minerals.

☐ **2. Classify** the rocks and minerals into groups.
Use texture, color, and hardness.
Draw a picture and label the groups.

☐ **3.** Sort the rocks and minerals in other ways.

Materials

rocks and minerals

hand lens

Inquiry Skill
Observing objects carefully can help you **classify** them.

This group of rocks and minerals is	This group of rocks and minerals is ....
This group of rocks and minerals is	This group of rocks and minerals is ....

Explain Your Results

4. **UNLOCK THE BIG ?** List the property or properties you used to help **classify** the rocks and minerals.

....

....

◉ Draw Conclusions

- A **conclusion** is a decision you reach after you think about observations and data that you know or have gathered.
- The conclusion should make sense and be supported by the facts.

Quartz

Amethyst is the purple form of the mineral quartz. Citrines are also quartz, but they range in color from yellow to orange. A green form of quartz is known as prasiolite. Pure quartz, called rock crystal, is clear and colorless. All of these forms of quartz are used in rings, necklaces, and other jewelry.

Practice It!

Complete the graphic organizer. Read the three facts about quartz from the paragraph above. Then write a conclusion.

Facts	Conclusion
Amethyst is purple quartz.	
Citrine is yellow or orange quartz.	
Pure quartz is clear and colorless.	

Hold Back the Water

Water is an agent of erosion. As water flows over or past a surface, it erodes it or wears the surface away. Erosion produces beautiful landforms such as the Grand Canyon. However, water erosion also causes a lot of damage and can be a threat to homes and other property.

Humans try to control erosion by reinforcing the surface being eroded. This is the purpose of a bank reinforcement—to make the bank of a river or the shore of a lake or ocean more resistant to wearing away.

Your local government has hired you to design and test a reinforcement for a river bank. You will evaluate the effectiveness of your design by how much the reinforcement reduced riverbank erosion.

Identify the Problem

☐ **1.** What problem will your reinforcement help solve? _____

_____

☐ **2.** Why is there a need to solve this problem? _____

_____

Do Research

Examine pictures of bank reinforcements.

☐ **3.** What do the bank reinforcements have in common? _____

_____

☐ **4.** How are the bank reinforcements different? _____

_____

_____

_____

_____

5. What do you think are important characteristics for bank reinforcements? _____

_____

_____

Go to the materials station(s). Pick up each material one at a time. Think about how it may or may not be useful in your design. Leave the materials where they are.

6. What are your design constraints? _____

_____

_____

_____

Develop Possible Solutions

7. List two ways you could use the materials to build a bank reinforcement. _____

_____

_____

Choose One Solution

8. Describe your bank reinforcement and how you will build it. _____

_____

_____

_____

9. List the materials that you will need. _____

_____

10. Why did you choose these materials? _____

_____

_____

Design and Construct a Prototype

☐ **11.** Begin by running three trials on the unreinforced bank. **Build** a straight stream in your stream table. Rebuild your bank after each trial. Devise a way to collect the water that flows through your table. Pour the same amount of water through the table three different times. Collect the water and filter it through a coffee filter placed in a sieve. **Record** your observations of how the water eroded the bank.

Trial	Amount of water poured into the stream	Amount of water collected at the end of the stream	Observations
1			
2			
3			

Gather the materials you need for your bank reinforcement plus a ruler. **Build** your bank reinforcement in the stream table. **Measure and record** the dimensions of your bank reinforcement.

☐ **12.** **Record** the design details of your prototype. _____

_____

_____

Test the Prototype

☐ **13.** **Test** your design. Run three trials as you did before. Use the same amount of water as you did with the unreinforced stream bank.

Trial	Amount of water poured into the stream	Amount of water collected at the end of the stream	Observations
1			
2			
3			

Communicate Results

☑ **14. Compare** these observations to the observations without your bank reinforcement.

Describe the differences. _____

_____

_____

_____

☐ **15.** Did your bank reinforcement have the desired effect? Rate your design on a scale of 1 to 3 where 1 — poor results, 2 — good results, and 3 — great results. Explain why you give your bank reinforcement this rating. _____

_____

_____

_____

Evaluate and Redesign

☐ **16.** What changes could you make to your design to make it work better? _____

_____

_____

_____

☐ **17.** What other factors would need to be considered to make a bank reinforcement in a real river? _____

_____

_____

How are minerals classified?

One of these minerals is gold. Write which one you think is gold and which is "fool's gold."

my planet DiaRY

//// MISCONCEPTION ////

You may have seen or heard people talk about minerals in food. Does that mean you are eating rocks? No! In this case, the word mineral refers to small amounts of chemicals, called elements, that are found in the foods you eat. These elements also make up certain minerals that are found in rocks in Earth's crust.

For example, iron helps your blood cells carry oxygen throughout your body. Foods containing iron include red meat and leafy green vegetables. Iron is also found in many minerals. But the iron in food is in a different form than the iron in minerals. You would not be able to digest the iron in a mineral.

How do you think iron and other minerals get into vegetables?

....

....

....

....

Words to Know

mineral   streak
luster   cleavage
hardness

Mineral Crystals

The salt you sprinkle on your food is a mineral. The metal fork you use when you eat is made from minerals. The ceramic plate you put food on is made from minerals. **Minerals** are natural, nonliving solid crystals that make up rocks. Scientists have identified more than 4,000 kinds of minerals. But most of Earth's rocks are made up of only a small number of them. These are often called the "rock-forming" minerals.

All around the world, each mineral has the same chemical composition. A grain of the mineral quartz from a beach in Australia has the same chemicals in it as a chunk of quartz chipped from a mountain in California.

Pure quartz is clear. Different impurities give quartz its color.

1. **Analyze** What is the relationship between minerals and rocks?

....

....

2. ◎ **Compare and Contrast** How are the two examples of quartz described above alike? How are they different?

....

....

....

hardest

Mohs Scale for Hardness

| 10 diamond | 9 corundum | 8 topaz | 7 quartz | 6 feldspar |

Properties of Minerals

Most rocks are made of different combinations of minerals. Each type of rock always has a similar combination of minerals. Granite always contains quartz and feldspar crystals. Some rocks have only one or two minerals. White marble is made only of the mineral calcite.

How can you tell minerals apart? Scientists identify minerals by testing their properties. These include color, luster, hardness, streak, cleavage, and crystal shape.

Color and Luster

It is easy to see the color of a mineral. But the same mineral can be different colors. So color alone is usually not enough to identify a mineral. Scientists must look at other properties, such as luster. **Luster** is the way the surface of a mineral reflects light. A glassy luster is shiny, like glass. A metallic luster looks like polished metal. A soft shine can be described as a waxy, silky, or pearly luster. Some minerals have a greasy or a dull, chalky luster.

Satin spar gypsum has a silky luster.

3. **Classify** Look at the Mohs Scale for Hardness at the top of these pages. Write adjectives on the scale describing the luster of the mineral samples shown in the scale.

Calcite has a pearly luster. It can be colorless, white, or other pale colors.

Galena has a metallic luster.

softest

| 5 apatite | 4 fluorite | 3 calcite | 2 gypsum | 1 talc |

Hardness

Scientists may also measure a mineral's hardness. **Hardness** is how easily the surface of a mineral can be scratched. The Mohs Scale shown above ranks minerals by hardness. Talc is the softest mineral. It has a hardness of 1. Diamonds are the hardest minerals.

A mineral can scratch other minerals with lower Mohs rankings. For example, fluorite has a hardness of 4. It can scratch all minerals with a hardness of less than 4, such as gypsum.

Streak

The same mineral can be different colors. But all samples of a certain mineral will leave the same streak. **Streak** is the color of the powder that a mineral leaves when it is scratched across a special plate. Some minerals, such as gold, leave streaks that match their colors. But sometimes the streak is a different color than the mineral itself. For example, hematite can be silver or red. But its streak is always red.

Cinnabar has a bright red streak.

Pyrite, or fool's gold, has a green-black streak.

Orpiment has a pale yellow streak.

4. Analyze Look again at the *Envision It!* at the start of this lesson. What could you do to help tell the difference between gold and fool's gold?

....

....

....

....

....

Lightning Lab

Texture and Effervescence

Work with an adult. Find 8 rocks. Classify them by texture. Then put a few drops of vinegar on each. Observe if bubbles form. Classify the rock based on effervescence.

Shape and Cleavage

Each mineral has crystals that are a particular shape. These crystal shapes can be helpful when trying to identify a mineral crystal. Crystals are classified by these shapes and the angles that they form. For example, fluorite has cube-shaped crystals. Corundum crystals look more like hexagons. The shape of a mineral is not always easy to see. Scientists must sometimes use magnifiers or microscopes to see a crystal's shape.

Most minerals will break in definite patterns. Minerals that break along smooth, flat surfaces have **cleavage.** For example, mica has perfect cleavage. It breaks into thin, shiny layers that are flat and smooth. Some minerals do not have any cleavage. Quartz often breaks into pieces with smooth surfaces that look like the inside of a seashell. Still other minerals splinter, like pieces of wood.

5. CHALLENGE Draw the three directions of cleavage on the halite sample below.

Mica breaks into thin flakes that are flat and smooth.

Magnetite crystals often form shapes called octahedrons.

6. **Classify** If you have a small mineral sample, why might testing for cleavage be one of the last things you do?

....

....

....

....

....

Halite has cleavage in three directions. Halite is the mineral form of table salt.

Other Mineral Properties

There are many other ways to identify certain minerals. Two minerals, pyrrhotite and magnetite, are attracted by magnets. Sometimes magnetite can actually be a magnet. Some minerals, such as gold, silver, and copper, can be shaped or cut. Scientists can use chemical tests to identify some minerals. For example, if you drop vinegar on calcite, bubbling will occur.

You can use other senses to identify minerals. Not all minerals feel the same when you touch them. Some minerals can be identified by their smell or taste.

7. **⬤ Draw Conclusions** Which of your senses might you use most often when identifying minerals?

The magnetite in this lodestone attracts objects that contain iron.

Got it?

8. **UNLOCK THE BIG ?** **Explain** How can minerals be classified?

9. **Infer** Which property might you test by rubbing one mineral directly against another?

⬛ **Stop!** I need help with

⏸ **Wait!** I have a question about

▶ **Go!** Now I know

Lesson 2

How are rocks classified?

Envision It!

Tell what you think will happen to this lava when it hits the water.

Inquiry Explore It!

What can you learn from rock layers?

☐ **1. Make a model** of rock layers. Fill a small cup with sand. Slowly pour the sand into a large cup.

☐ **2.** Put a paper clip in the sand so it touches the side of the cup. The paper clip represents a fossil animal.

☐ **3.** Slowly add layers of other materials to the cup. To make a model of more fossil animals, put a rubber band and crayon piece in two of the layers.

Explain Your Results

4. Infer Suppose you found 2 fossils in 2 different layers of rock. Would the older one be in the upper or lower layer of rock? Explain.

....

....

....

....

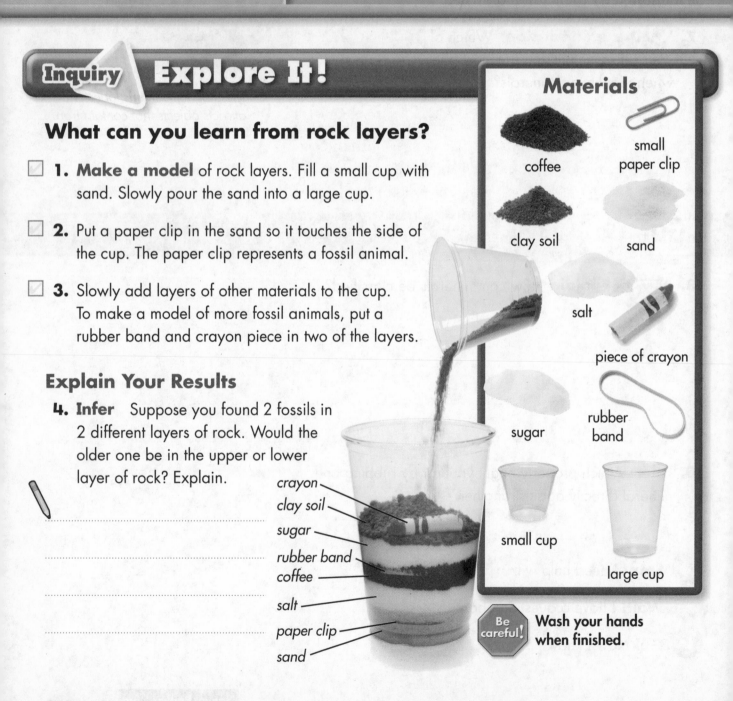

crayon
clay soil
sugar
rubber band
coffee
salt
paper clip
sand

Materials

coffee

small paper clip

clay soil

sand

salt

piece of crayon

sugar

rubber band

small cup

large cup

Be careful! Wash your hands when finished.

I will know the three categories of rocks and how they are formed.

Words to Know

igneous   metamorphic
sedimentary

Classifying Rocks

Earth's crust is made of rocks. Huge boulders are rocks. So are single grains of sand. The bits of rock that make up silt and clay can be too small to see without a microscope.

Rocks are nonliving, but they can change form both above and below Earth's surface. It can take millions of years for some rocks to form. Other rocks can form very quickly. One important way scientists classify rocks is based on how they are formed. The changes that form rocks produce three main kinds: igneous, sedimentary, and metamorphic rocks.

1.  **Draw Conclusions** Use these two facts from the text above to draw a conclusion.

Facts

Huge boulders are rocks.

The bits of rock that make up silt and clay can be too small to see without a microscope.

Conclusion

....
....
....
....

Igneous Rocks

Some rocks form from other rocks that have melted. Rock below Earth's crust can be so hot that it is partially melted. This melted, or molten, rock is called magma. Rocks that form from molten rock are called **igneous** rocks. Igneous rocks may form above or below Earth's surface.

Magma Cooling Quickly

If you have seen pictures of a volcano erupting, you have seen magma exploding onto Earth's surface. After it reaches the surface, the molten rock is called lava. Sometimes lava oozes from a volcano like a red-hot river. Or, it may fly from a volcano in hot, gooey globs. Either way, the lava on the surface cools quickly. It may harden into solid igneous rock in just a few minutes to days.

As the lava cools, mineral crystals form. But when lava cools quickly, there is not much time for crystals to form. Any crystals that do form are very small. Pumice is an igneous rock that forms when air quickly cools lava.

Water can also cool lava. Basalt is an igneous rock that often forms under the ocean. The ocean water quickly cools the lava.

2. **Analyze** *Igneous* comes from the Latin word *ignis,* meaning "fire." Study the photo of a lava flow on these pages. Why is *igneous* a good name for this type of rock?

....

....

Pumice forms from lava that has lots of trapped gas bubbles. Crystals do not have time to form in pumice.

Granite has large crystals of quartz, feldspar, and mica. Its crystals are easy to see.

Obsidian is volcanic glass. It has no crystals.

Magma Cooling Slowly

When magma slowly rises toward Earth's surface, it fills in cracks and melts the surrounding rock or forces it aside to make space. The magma cools slowly. As it hardens, crystals of minerals form in the rocks. These crystals are large. The longer it takes magma to cool, the larger mineral crystals can get. The cooling and hardening of magma into igneous rock below Earth's surface is a very slow process. It can take more than a million years!

Basalt is one of the most common igneous rocks. It often has small, fine crystals.

Gabbro is similar in makeup to basalt, but has larger crystals.

Pegmatite contains the same minerals as granite. It often has very large crystals.

3. ◎ **Draw Conclusions** If you needed a microscope to see an igneous rock's crystals, what would that tell you about how the rock cooled?

....

....

....

....

....

4. **Classify** Study the photos and captions of igneous rocks on these pages. (Circle) the rocks that cooled quickly. Draw an ✗ on the rocks that cooled slowly.

Sedimentary Rocks

Look at the sandstone cliffs shown on these pages. What do you notice? The cliffs may look like a stack of pancakes or sheets of paper. These layers show that the cliff is made of sedimentary rock. **Sedimentary** rocks form when layers of sediments settle on top of one another and harden. Sediments are made up of soil, shells, bits of rock, and dead plant and animal matter.

Water, wind, ice, and gravity make and move sediments from one place to another. Over time, sediments settle in layers on land or on the bottom of oceans, rivers, and lakes. Newer layers press the older layers together. The weight of the layers, sticky clay minerals in the sediment, and natural chemicals hold the particles together.

Scientists classify sedimentary rocks according to the materials in the sediment. Some sedimentary rock forms from materials that were once living things. Limestone, for example, is often made of hard skeletons and shells of sea animals that lived long ago. Sandstone is another type of sedimentary rock. It is usually made up of bits of quartz that are each about the size of a grain of sand. A third kind of sedimentary rock is made of very tiny particles. These particles usually settle at the bottom of lakes or oceans. Shale and mudstone are two examples of this kind of rock.

Conglomerate can form from rounded rocks that are the size of pebbles or larger.

Limestone often forms from tiny bits of skeletons and shells.

Sandstone can form from quartz sands.

248

5. ⊙ **Compare and Contrast** Look at the sedimentary rock samples on the previous page. How are conglomerate and sandstone alike? How are they different?

....

....

....

....

....

The layers of sedimentary rock are easy to see in these sandstone cliffs.

6. Identify Label a layer of sedimentary rock in the cliff on these pages.

Metamorphic Rocks

High temperatures deep inside Earth can change rocks. The rock is also under pressure from the weight of the rocks above it. These forces can cause rocks to change form completely. Rocks that have changed as a result of heat and pressure are known as **metamorphic** rocks.

As metamorphic rocks form, they can change in several ways. Heat and pressure may cause the mineral crystals in the rock to change. Sometimes the chemicals in the rock form new types of minerals. For example, the mineral graphite is made entirely of carbon. Enough heat and pressure can turn graphite into diamond.

Metamorphic rocks can form from sedimentary, igneous, and other metamorphic rocks. Limestone, a sedimentary rock, can become the metamorphic rock marble. The igneous rock granite can become the metamorphic rock gneiss. The next page shows how rock that has already been changed sometimes goes through even more changes.

7. Identify Based on the text, draw an arrow on the page to show a possible direction of the pressure that formed this metamorphic rock cliff.

Lightning Lab

Rock Model
Make a loose "brick" from different-colored layers of clay. What type of rock have you modeled? Now put the brick between two sheets of plastic wrap and press down hard with the heel of your hand to flatten it. Peel off the wrap. What type of rock have you modeled?

Sedimentary

Shale

Metamorphic

Slate

Metamorphic

Phyllite

Metamorphic

Schist

Shale

Tiny clay sediments settle on the bottom of oceans and lakes, forming shale. Shale is a soft sedimentary rock that often contains fossils. Shale that is exposed to heat and pressure can turn into much harder rock called slate.

Slate

Slate does not usually have fossils because the heat and pressure destroy them. The minerals in slate are arranged so that it splits easily into layers. Heat and pressure can change slate into other metamorphic rocks, such as a rock called phyllite.

Phyllite

Layers of the minerals mica and chlorite give phyllite a silky look. More heat and pressure can change phyllite into yet another kind of metamorphic rock! It can become a rock called schist.

Schist

Schist has larger grains than phyllite or shale. You might expect the cycle to end here, but it does not. Deep within Earth, schist and other rocks get hot enough to melt. If the melted schist cools, it can become new igneous rock!

8. **Summarize** How can shale become schist?

....

....

....

9. ◉ **Compare and Contrast** What feature do these four rocks have in common?

....

....

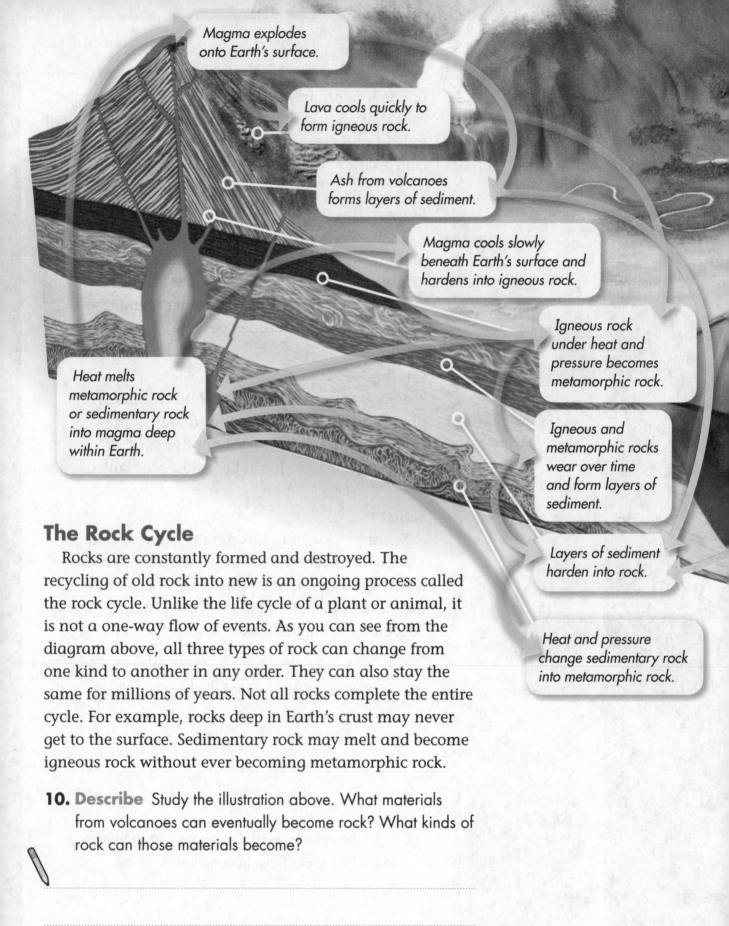

Magma explodes onto Earth's surface.

Lava cools quickly to form igneous rock.

Ash from volcanoes forms layers of sediment.

Magma cools slowly beneath Earth's surface and hardens into igneous rock.

Igneous rock under heat and pressure becomes metamorphic rock.

Heat melts metamorphic rock or sedimentary rock into magma deep within Earth.

Igneous and metamorphic rocks wear over time and form layers of sediment.

Layers of sediment harden into rock.

Heat and pressure change sedimentary rock into metamorphic rock.

The Rock Cycle

Rocks are constantly formed and destroyed. The recycling of old rock into new is an ongoing process called the rock cycle. Unlike the life cycle of a plant or animal, it is not a one-way flow of events. As you can see from the diagram above, all three types of rock can change from one kind to another in any order. They can also stay the same for millions of years. Not all rocks complete the entire cycle. For example, rocks deep in Earth's crust may never get to the surface. Sedimentary rock may melt and become igneous rock without ever becoming metamorphic rock.

10. Describe Study the illustration above. What materials from volcanoes can eventually become rock? What kinds of rock can those materials become?

....

....

....

11. Explain Complete the caption on the diagram.

Some ....
rock wears away to form new layers of sediment.

12. [CHALLENGE] Can magma ever directly become sedimentary rock? Why or why not?

Got it?

13. Describe What kind of rock is being formed in the *Envision It!* photo at the start of this lesson?

14. Recognize What forces can form the particles that make up sedimentary rock?

⏹ **Stop!** I need help with ....

⏸ **Wait!** I have a question about ....

▶ **Go!** Now I know ....

What are weathering and erosion?

Envision It!

Tell what you think is shaping this beach.

Inquiry Explore It!

How does a rock wear away?

☐ **1.** Shake chalk and rocks in a jar for 1 minute. Look for changes in the chalk. Shake for 3 more minutes. **Observe.**

☐ **2.** Empty the jar. Fill it half full with water. Repeat Step 1 using the rocks and 4 new chalk pieces.

Put on lid!

8 rocks
4 pieces
of chalk

Materials

plastic jar

8 small rocks

8 pieces of chalk

water   timer or stopwatch

Explain Your Results

3. How did the chalk change after being shaken with rocks for 1 minute? for 3 more minutes?

....

....

4. Infer Compared with shaking the chalk with only rocks, what effect did shaking with both rocks and water have on the chalk?

....

....

I will know how weathering, erosion, and deposition can change Earth's surface.

Words to Know

landform   erosion
weathering

Earth's Surface

The outer surface of Earth is a layer of rock called the crust. The crust covers all of Earth. In places such as the ocean, the crust is underwater.

A **landform** is a natural land feature on Earth's surface. A mountain is an example of a landform. Landforms can be different sizes and shapes. Plains are flat landforms on high or low ground, and plateaus are flat landforms on high ground. Along coasts, landforms such as peninsulas extend into the water. Valleys and canyons are also landforms. Some landforms, like mountains and valleys, can be found underwater. Maps are used to locate different features on land and underwater.

Some landforms take shape quickly, while others form over a long time. A mountain may take millions of years to form. But rocks rolling down the side of that mountain can change it in a hurry. Think of what happens to the large amounts of soil that a flood carries from one place to another.

1. **Describe** What landforms are near where you live?

....

....

....

....

....

Earth's crust is miles thick, but if Earth were the size of a peach, the crust would only be as thick as the peach's skin.

SavvasRealize.com   255

Weathering

Earth's landforms change constantly. Water, ice, temperature changes, wind, chemicals, and living things can all cause changes. Often, these changes occur over a long time.

Rocks in Earth's crust are slowly broken into smaller pieces in a process called **weathering.** There are two types of weathering, chemical weathering and physical weathering.

Chemical Weathering

During chemical weathering, chemicals cause rocks to change into different materials and break down. For example, rainwater mixes with carbon dioxide in the air to form a weak acid. When it rains, the acid combines with the rock material to form a new chemical. Gradually the new chemical breaks down the rock.

Animals and plants give off chemicals that can cause weathering. Sometimes the activities of people also add chemicals to the environment.

Water and warm temperatures are important for chemical weathering. Warmer areas or areas with a lot of rain have more chemical weathering than drier or colder areas.

2. **Analyze** Circle the evidence of weathering in this picture.

Physical Weathering

In physical weathering, rocks are broken into smaller pieces of the same kind of rock. Water is one cause of physical weathering. Flowing water can carry particles of rock, soil, and sand. The particles scrape against larger rocks. The rocks gradually become smaller and smaller. The force of waves pounding against rocks on a shore can also cause rock to break down. Wind can carry small particles that can weather rocks.

Ice can also cause physical weathering. Water can seep into cracks in rocks. If this water freezes, it forms ice. Ice in rock takes up more space than the water does. The ice can make the cracks in the rock deeper. The rock may eventually split.

Temperature changes to a rock's surface may also cause weathering. When a rock's surface gets hotter, it expands, or grows larger. When it gets colder, the surface contracts, or gets smaller. Some scientists think that many temperature changes can weaken the surface of rock.

Living things can cause weathering too. Plants can sprout in a crack in a rock. As these plants and their roots get bigger, they can cause the rock to split.

3. CHALLENGE How can water cause both chemical and physical weathering?

....

....

....

Water contributed to the weathering of these rocks.

Soil in Motion
Work with an adult. Let a hose run slowly in one spot in bare soil. Observe what happens. Let the water run more quickly. How does the flow of the water affect erosion?

5. [CHALLENGE] Read the text on these pages and study the photo below. Based on the erosion and deposition patterns, which way do you think the river flows? Draw an arrow to indicate direction.

Erosion carved this canyon along the Colorado River in Utah.

Erosion

You know that rainfall affects the kinds of living things found in an area. Do you also know that rainfall can shape landforms by washing away soil and carrying it to a new place? Water, gravity, wind, and ice can all move bits of weathered rock. The process of carrying away weathered bits of rock is called **erosion.**

Moving water erodes, or carries away, materials from the land. As water moves faster, it can carry along heavier pieces of rock. Moving water can slowly carve grooves into the land as it carries away weathered material. Over a very long time, these grooves may become deep canyons.

Waves constantly change the shape of a shoreline. They pound against the shore, breaking off pieces of rock. The waves carry away the pieces. Landforms, such as beaches, can form along the eroded shoreline.

In colder parts of Earth, moving ice erodes landforms. Glaciers are huge sheets of ice. Most glaciers move very slowly as gravity pulls them downhill. As glaciers move, they wear away bits of rock and soil.

4. ◎ **Draw Conclusions** What does a muddy river tell you about erosion?

....

....

Deposition

As parts of Earth's surface are broken down, other parts are built up. The forces that carry away bits of weathered rock during erosion must drop them somewhere else. This laying down of pieces of rock is called deposition.

As moving water slows, the larger pebbles in the water settle to the bottom first. Then smaller sand-sized pebbles sink. Finally, the smallest bits of silt and clay sink too. Rivers deposit large amounts of materials where they flow into the ocean. The deposited material forms an area called a delta.

In deserts and near beaches, wind moves grains of sand into mounds called sand dunes. Winds may move a sand dune or change its size and shape. The size and shape of a sand dune also depend on the amount of sand and the number of plants in an area.

6. Analyze Underline the sentence that explains what deposition is.

sand dunes

delta

Got it?

7. Explain Describe how a canyon forms.

....

....

8. Think about what you read in this lesson. Explain how Earth's surface changes slowly.

....

....

....

 Stop! I need help with ....

 Wait! I have a question about ....

 Go! Now I know ....

How can Earth's surface change rapidly?

Envision It!

Tell how the shape of the land is changing.

my PLANET DIARY

Science Stats

Most earthquakes occur at points where two plates, or two large pieces of Earth's surface, meet. But faults, or cracks in rock where Earth's crust can move, can form anywhere in Earth's crust and mantle. The Wabash Valley Fault System is a series of underground faults along the southern border of Illinois and Indiana. Movement along the faults caused medium-sized earthquakes in 1968, 2002, and 2008. The 2008 earthquake was felt in 16 states and in places more than 720 kilometers away.

Scientists cannot predict earthquakes. However, they can study patterns in Earth's crust to try to find out where earthquakes have occurred and how severe they were. By examining Earth's crust, scientists found evidence that the region has had earthquakes for at least 20,000 years.

How might people in the Wabash Valley Fault System prepare for earthquakes?

....

....

....

....

....

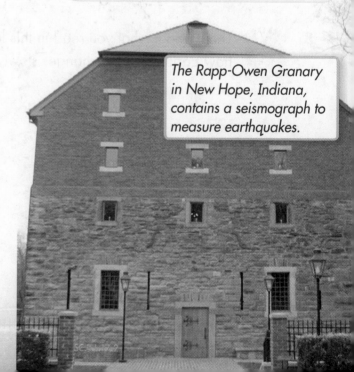

The Rapp-Owen Granary in New Hope, Indiana, contains a seismograph to measure earthquakes.

Word to Know

fault

Earth's Moving Plates

Earth's outer crust rests on top of another layer called the mantle. The crust and the top of the mantle are divided into very large pieces called plates. The plates move all the time. This movement can cause rapid changes in Earth's surface. Volcanoes and earthquakes often occur in bands along or near places where continental plates and ocean plates come together. Some mountain ranges and features on the ocean floor, such as deep trenches and tall ridges, also occur in patterns because of the movement of plates. Major mountain chains, for example, often form near the edges of continents or inside continents because of plate movements.

1. ⊙ **Draw Conclusions** Suppose that an area experiences frequent earthquakes. What might you conclude about that area?

....

....

....

....

Iceland has many volcanoes and earthquakes, because it is on top of two plates that are moving away from each other. The land on the left is part of the North American plate. The land on the right is part of the Eurasian plate.

3. Predict Ash and other particles from an eruption may fill the sky and block sunlight. How might this change Earth's temperature?

Volcanoes

A volcano is a landform that forms at an opening in Earth's crust where magma reaches the surface. Magma is very hot, partly melted rock.

When a volcano erupts, the magma reaches the surface and is called lava. Lava is still very hot, perhaps more than 1,100°C (2,000°F). The temperature and the kind of rock that makes up the magma determine the type of eruption. Sometimes the pressure builds up so that the gases in the magma explode. Hot rocks, gases, ash, and other particles burst from the openings, called vents. Sometimes magma oozes upward and flows from the volcano.

Lava and ash can spread over a wide area. Nearby forests or cities may be covered. The volcano and surrounding area may be reshaped. An eruption can also cause floods, landslides, and tsunamis, which are huge ocean waves.

2. ⊙**Draw Conclusions** Look at the pictures of the Kilauea Volcano. Tell how the volcano's eruptions have changed the surrounding area.

The Kilauea Volcano in Hawaii erupts frequently.

Earthquakes

Earthquakes occur along a fault. A **fault** is a break or crack in rocks where Earth's crust can move suddenly. Sometimes rocks along a fault get stuck. The plates continue their slow movement. This puts stress on the rocks. If the stress becomes strong enough, the rocks can break. Then the plates move suddenly. The sudden movement that causes Earth's crust to shake is an earthquake. The place underground where the earthquake begins is the focus. The point on Earth's surface that is directly above the focus is the epicenter.

Most earthquakes are small. But a few earthquakes are powerful enough to damage buildings, roads, and bridges. The damage is often greatest near the epicenter. Like volcanoes, earthquakes can cause a variety of natural hazards, including tsunamis and landslides. People cannot stop these hazards from occurring, but they can take steps to reduce their impacts. For example, scientists send out alerts when a tsunami forms. This can save many lives by giving people time to reach higher ground.

5. Infer Where would earthquakes that cause tsunamis probably happen?

....

....

....

....

....

....

4. Demonstrate (Circle) the area in the picture where the most damage would occur from the earthquake.

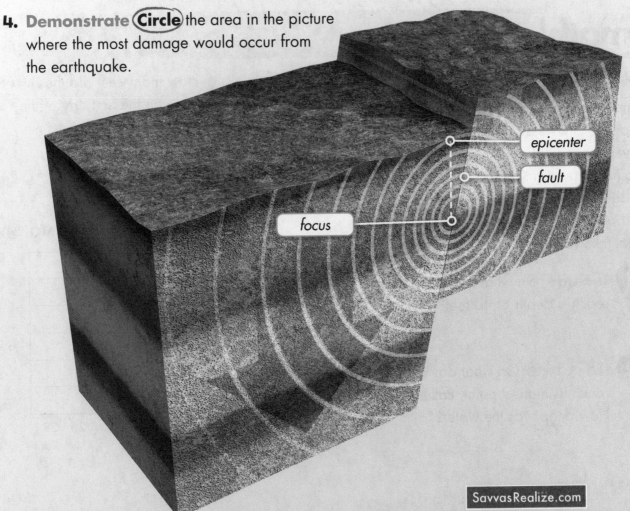

epicenter

fault

focus

Landslides and Floods

Heavy rains or earthquakes may loosen material on a steep slope. Gravity then pulls the loosened material downward. Bits of rock and soil may travel slowly downhill a little at a time. But sometimes they travel rapidly. The rapid downhill movement of a large amount of rock and soil is a landslide. Buildings, cars, trees, and other objects are sometimes carried along with the sliding soil.

Floods also can produce rapid changes. Fast moving water in flash floods can uproot trees, carry away big rocks, and change where rivers flow. Floods also can leave land covered with sand and mud. In 1993, huge amounts of rain caused the Mississippi and Missouri Rivers to overflow. Some areas were flooded for almost 200 days. The floods left thousands of acres covered with sand and mud.

6. Compare Underline two sentences that describe how the effects of landslides and floods are similar.

damage from landslide in Topanga Canyon, California

Do the math!

Read a Graph

The Missouri River flows through the city of Kansas City, Missouri. In early July 1993, the river flooded its banks after months of heavy rain. The river in Kansas City reaches flood stage when the water is 32 feet deep. The graph shows what happened in the weeks that followed, as the river continued to rise.

1 Identify On what day did the river reach a depth of 40 feet?

2 Determine On what day did the river reach its highest point, called the crest? How deep was the water?

3 Calculate How many feet did the river rise overall between the first day of the flood and the crest?

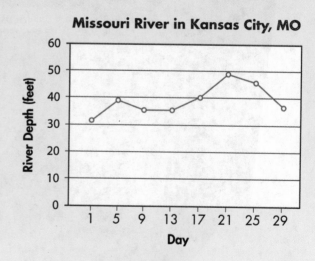

Missouri River in Kansas City, MO

264

Droughts

Sometimes an area experiences a period of weather that is much drier than usual. Periods of unusually low rain or snowfall are called droughts. A severe drought can change the surface of Earth by reducing the amount of water in rivers and lakes. Droughts can destroy farmland and kill trees and other plants. Droughts increase soil erosion too. In the 1930s, the United States experienced a severe drought. As crops died, high winds blew away the dry soil. Winds sometimes carried great, dark clouds of dust thousands of miles away.

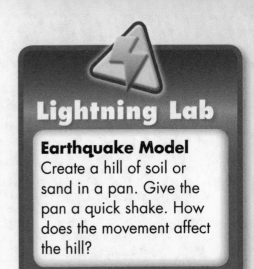

Lightning Lab

Earthquake Model
Create a hill of soil or sand in a pan. Give the pan a quick shake. How does the movement affect the hill?

7. **Infer** Why does drought increase the possibility of soil erosion?

....

....

....

Got it?

8. **Recognize** How can the actions around a fault cause an earthquake?

....

....

9. **UNLOCK THE BIG ?** Think about what you read in this lesson. Explain how Earth's surface changes rapidly.

....

....

⬜ **Stop!** I need help with ....

⏸ **Wait!** I have a question about ....

▶ **Go!** Now I know ....

Lesson 5

Where is Earth's water?

Where is this water and steam coming from?

Inquiry Explore It!

Where is Earth's water?

☐ **1.** Label 4 plastic cups as shown.

☐ **2.** Look at the chart. Find the amount of water shown for the atmosphere. Put that much water in the labeled cup.

Materials

plastic bottle (2L with cap) filled with water

4 clear plastic cups

masking tape

graduated cylinder

funnel

plastic dropper

Earth's Water	Amount
Atmosphere (fresh water)	about $\frac{1}{2}$ drop
Lakes, rivers, streams (fresh water)	about 4 drops
Groundwater (fresh water)	13 mL
Icecaps and glaciers (fresh water)	47 mL
Oceans and seas (salt water)	2139 mL

☐ **3.** Repeat for the next three places on the chart. **Measure** the water.

☐ **4.** Label the 2 L bottle "oceans and seas".

Explain Your Results

5. Use your **model.** Make an **inference** about the amount of fresh water available for human use.

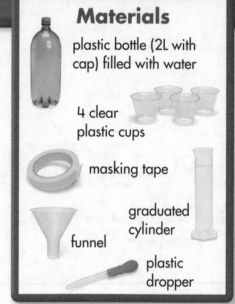

....

....

Word to Know

groundwater

Water on Earth

Think about a globe. When you look at a globe, you see much more blue water than green land. That is because almost $\frac{3}{4}$ of Earth's surface is covered with water.

Water exists as a solid, liquid, and gas. Ice is solid water. Some of Earth's water is frozen in glaciers and polar ice caps. You see liquid water in rivers, lakes, the ocean, and other bodies of water. When water gets hot enough, it turns into an invisible gas called water vapor. Some of the water near Earth's surface is water vapor in the air. The water vapor rises from water on Earth's surface and becomes part of the atmosphere.

1. **Clarify** Create a circle chart. Color the circle to show how much of Earth is covered with water and how much is covered with land. Label the parts of the circle.

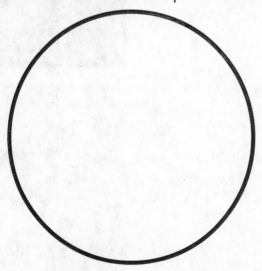

An iceberg is a large piece of floating ice. Icebergs form when pieces break off of glaciers.

Surface Water

Surface water is any water that is above the ground on Earth. You can see it, splash in it, or swim in it. The pictures to the right show different bodies of surface water. You can classify water bodies by the type of water they contain: salt water or fresh water.

Salt Water

"Water, water, everywhere, Nor any drop to drink." These lines in a famous poem describe a crew on an ocean ship that has run out of drinking water. Water is all around them. How could they run out of drinking water?

If you have ever tasted ocean water, you know the answer. It tastes very salty. However, taste is not the main problem. Ocean water is not healthy for drinking.

More than $\frac{97}{100}$ of Earth's water is salty water in the ocean and seas. Why is the ocean salty? Ocean water is a mixture of water and dissolved salts. These salts come mostly from rocks on land. As rivers flow over land, they dissolve salts from rocks. They carry the salts to the ocean.

Fresh Water

Only $\frac{3}{100}$ of Earth's water is fresh water. People need fresh water for drinking, cooking, growing crops, and many other activities. Most of Earth's fresh water is frozen in glaciers and ice caps. People cannot use that water. People depend on the small amount of fresh water available in rivers and lakes. People also get drinking water from underground.

2. ◎ **Compare and Contrast** Write how the ocean and a pond are alike and different.

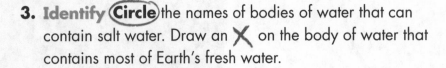

3. **Identify** Circle the names of bodies of water that can contain salt water. Draw an ✗ on the body of water that contains most of Earth's fresh water.

Ocean and Seas

The ocean is a large body of salt water. Seas are smaller areas of the ocean that are partly surrounded by land. Waves in the ocean cause the water to go up and down in place, but the water is not moving in the direction of the wave until it breaks against a shoreline, such as this beach.

Lakes and Ponds

Land surrounds lakes and ponds, which are smaller than the ocean. Lakes are generally larger than ponds. Almost all lakes and ponds contain fresh water, but a few lakes and ponds contain salt water.

Rivers

A river is flowing fresh water. Water in rivers moves downhill. Rivers flow into the ocean, lakes, and other rivers.

Glaciers and Ice Caps

A glacier is a large body of slowly moving ice. Glaciers form when more snow falls than melts in an area. The polar ice caps are large areas of ice at the North and South Poles.

Groundwater

When it rains, water falls into bodies of water and onto the ground. Some water that falls on the ground runs into bodies of water. This water is called runoff. But some water soaks into the ground. **Groundwater** is any water that is underground. Groundwater fills the spaces and cracks in underground soil and rock.

Think about all of the lakes, rivers, and ponds on Earth's surface. Although it is hard to imagine, there is more fresh liquid water underground than on Earth's surface. Groundwater is not trapped underground. It can flow slowly through most types of soil. In some places, groundwater may flow out of the ground and into a lake, pond, or river. A spring is a place where groundwater comes to the surface of the land. People also dig wells to reach water stored underground.

4. **Infer** Why do people dig wells to reach groundwater?

....

....

well

lake

groundwater

Clean Drinking Water

People need clean water for drinking, cooking, and other activities. But fresh water from under the ground and from surface water bodies is not always clean. For example, water in lakes and rivers can contain germs that could make people sick. Chemicals used to grow crops can wash into bodies of water. Fresh water must usually be cleaned before people can drink it.

In some places, people get drinking water from their own wells. They must filter the water to remove chemicals and dirt. Many cities have water treatment plants. In these plants, drinking water goes through a cleaning process that removes dirt and other materials and kills germs. The clean water then travels in pipes to people's homes and businesses.

water treatment plant

5. Name Write two things that are removed from water at a water treatment plant.

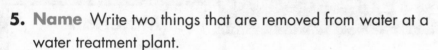

....

Got it?

6. Identify Name three places where Earth's fresh water is found. Which of these places has the most fresh water?

....

....

7. **UNLOCK THE BIG ?** Think about what you have learned about the amount of fresh water available for drinking. Why is it important to save water and keep it clean?

....

....

⬛ **Stop!** I need help with ....

⏸ **Wait!** I have a question about ....

▶ **Go!** Now I know ....

Lesson 6

What is the water cycle?

Draw arrows to show where the water goes when the sun's energy heats it.

Inquiry **Explore It!**

How can water move in the water cycle?

Materials

plastic cup with water

resealable plastic bag

tape

☐ **1.** Seal the cup in a resealable plastic bag without spilling the water. Tape the bag to a sunny window. **Predict** what will happen.

....

☐ **2. Observe** the bag after 2 days and after 3 days. **Record** what you observe each time.

....

....

....

....

Explain Your Results

3. Infer where water comes from when it rains.

....

....

Recycled Water

There is only a certain amount of water on Earth. Earth's water is constantly being recycled. Water moves from Earth's surface into the atmosphere. Water in the atmosphere falls back to Earth's surface.

Earth's water exists in three different phases: solid, liquid, and gas. Water changes phases as it is recycled. The sun's energy powers this process. The sun heats liquid water on Earth's surface. The water changes into a gas called water vapor. This process is called evaporation. Water vapor rises into the air and cools. As it cools, the water vapor changes into droplets of liquid water. This process is called condensation.

Clouds form when water droplets and ice crystals gather in the atmosphere. These droplets and crystals can combine and grow larger. Eventually they fall back to Earth. Any form of water that falls to Earth is called **precipitation.** Types of precipitation include rain, snow, sleet, and hail.

1. **Analyze** Look at the rain. Could the water falling as rain fall again in the future as snow? Explain.

....

....

....

The Water Cycle

The movement of water from Earth's surface to the atmosphere and back again is called the **water cycle.** This diagram shows the steps in the water cycle.

2. **Fill in the Blanks** Complete the captions in the diagram. Fill in each blank with the correct word.

Evaporation

Energy from the sun heats liquid water on

Earth's surface. The water changes to a gas

called ....

Storage

Precipitation falls into water bodies or onto land. Water that falls on land may soak into the ground and collect as groundwater. Some water runs off the land and collects in rivers, lakes, and the ocean.

3. **Underline** four places where water collects after it falls as precipitation.

Condensation

Water vapor cools and changes into droplets of liquid water. Water droplets and ice crystals gather in the air, forming ....

Precipitation

The water droplets and ice crystals combine and become larger. Eventually they become so heavy that gravity pulls them to Earth. Precipitation is any form of .... that falls to Earth.

Lightning Lab

Water Droplets

Suppose that you just took a hot shower at home. The mirror in your bathroom would probably be foggy. Work with a partner to explain why you see droplets of water on the mirror.

4. [CHALLENGE] Suppose hail falls on a warm day. What can you infer about the air temperature high in the atmosphere?

....

....

....

5. ⦿ **Draw Conclusions** Look at the pictures. Draw an ✕ on the type of weather you would expect if there was more evaporation than precipitation over a long period of time.

Water Cycle and Weather

You watch the local weather report. Will the weather be cloudy? Will there be rain? The answer to these questions depends partly on the water cycle. The water cycle is a main factor that causes daily weather conditions such as clouds and precipitation.

Weather is the result of how water, air, and temperature interact. For example, the temperature of air in the atmosphere affects the type of precipitation that falls. Water falls as rain when air in the atmosphere is above freezing. If the air near Earth's surface is colder than air higher up, rain may freeze as it falls. Sleet is rain that has frozen on its way to Earth.

Snow may form when the air in the atmosphere is very cold. Snow forms when water vapor changes directly into ice crystals. The crystals eventually grow large enough to fall out of the clouds. Hail can also develop at freezing temperatures. Hail forms when drops of water in clouds freeze and are coated with multiple layers of ice.

The pictures below show other types of weather that relate to the water cycle.

A thunderstorm can happen when warm, moist air rises quickly into much cooler air.

Long periods of rainfall or heavy storms can cause flooding.

A drought is a long period of dryness with little or no precipitation.

Water Cycle and Climate

Climate is the pattern of weather in a place over many years. Some places have a wet climate. Other places have a dry climate. Just as the water cycle affects daily weather conditions, it also affects climate.

For example, places near the ocean often receive a lot of precipitation. This weather pattern is caused by the water cycle. The sun's energy causes a lot of water to evaporate from the ocean. Wind carries the water vapor in the air over land. That land is likely to get more rainfall than a place that is not near a large body of water.

6. **Infer** Temperate rain forests can receive more than 250 centimeters (100 inches) of rain in a year. Tell why you think these forests receive so much rain.

Temperate rain forests grow along the northwestern coast of North America.

Got it?

7. **Explain** How does water move through the water cycle?

....

....

....

8. **Summarize** Why is the sun important to the water cycle?

....

....

⬛ **Stop!** I need help with ....

⏸ **Wait!** I have a question about ....

▶ **Go!** Now I know ....

How does the steepness of a stream affect how fast it flows?

Follow a Procedure

☐ 1. **Make a model** of a stream. Have one student hold a piece of tubing up. Set the stream angle to 10°. Place a cup at the low end of the stream.

☐ 2. **Measure** 50 mL of water into a graduated cylinder.

☐ 3. Attach a funnel to the top of the tubing. Start a timer as you pour the water into the tubing. Stop the timer when all the water has flowed into the cup. **Record** the time.

☐ 4. Change the stream angle to 25°, 40°, and 55° and repeat Steps 2 and 3.

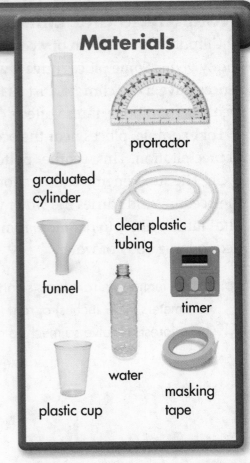

Materials

graduated cylinder

protractor

clear plastic tubing

funnel

timer

water

plastic cup

masking tape

Inquiry Skill
Recording data on a chart can help you make **inferences** based on the data.

Be careful! **Wipe up spills with paper towels!**

☐ **5. Record** your **data** below.

Observations of Model Stream	
Stream Angle (°)	**Flow Time** (seconds)
10	
25	
40	
55	

Analyze and Conclude

6. Communicate by summarizing your results.

....

....

....

....

7. **UNLOCK** **THE BIG** **?** **Infer** Where might you find a stream that flows at a 55° angle? Where might you find a stream that flows at a 15° angle?

....

....

....

The Galápagos Islands

The Galápagos Islands are a chain of islands located in the Pacific Ocean. This chain of islands is about 1,000 kilometers (600 miles) west of Ecuador, a country in South America. The chain has more than 100 islands in all. Some of the major islands have their own names.

The Galápagos Islands have not always existed. They were formed by volcanoes and are probably no more than five million years old.

How do volcanoes form islands? Volcanoes can erupt underwater as well as on land. Each time volcanoes erupt, more lava builds up. Eventually, volcanoes can build up above the surface of the ocean and form volcanic islands such as the islands that make up the Galápagos Islands.

Galápagos Islands

Can you think of another group of islands that was formed by volcanoes?

....

....

Vocabulary Smart Cards

mineral
luster
hardness
streak
cleavage
igneous
sedimentary
metamorphic
landform
weathering
erosion
fault
groundwater
precipitation
water cycle

Play a Game!

Work with a partner. Choose a Vocabulary Smart Card. Hold up the card with the word side facing your partner. Have your partner use the word in a sentence. Provide the definition if necessary.

Have your partner repeat with another Vocabulary Smart Card.

streak

surco

mineral

mineral

cleavage

fractura

luster

brillo

igneous

ígnea

hardness

dureza

natural, nonliving solid crystals that make up rocks

Draw an example. Label your drawing.

cristal natural, sólido y sin vidā del que se componen las rocas

---

color of the powder that a mineral leaves when it is scratched across a special plate

Draw an example.

color del polvo que sale de un mineral cuando se le rasga en una placa especial

---

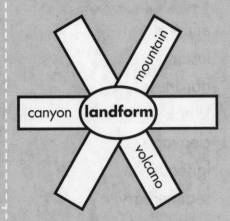

Make a Word Wheel!

Choose a vocabulary word and write it in the center of the Word Wheel graphic organizer. Write synonyms or related words on the wheel spokes.

---

the way the surface of a mineral reflects light

Write a sentence using this word.

....

....

....

....

reflejo de la luz en la superficie de un mineral

---

property of minerals to break along smooth, flat surfaces

Draw an example.

propiedad que les permite a los minerales romperse por superficies lisas y planas

---

how easily the surface of a mineral can be scratched

What is the suffix of this word?

....

....

....

facilidad con la que se puede rasgar la superficie de un mineral

---

rocks that form from molten rock

Write a sentence using this word.

....

....

....

....

rocas que se forman a partir de roca derretida

groundwater

agua subterránea

weathering
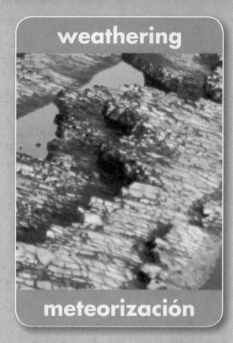
meteorización

sedimentary

sedimentaria

precipitation

precipitación

erosion

erosión

metamorphic

metamórfica

water cycle

ciclo del agua

fault

falla

landform

accidente geográfico

rocks that form when layers of sediments settle on top of one another and harden

What is the suffix of this word?

....

rocas que se forman cuando varias capas de sedimento se acumulan, una sobre otra, y se endurecen

process of rocks in Earth's crust slowly being broken into smaller pieces

Write a sentence using the verb form of this word.

....

....

proceso de las rocas de la corteza terrestre que se van rompiendo en trozos más pequeños

any water that is underground

Write a sentence using this word.

....

....

....

....

agua que está debajo del suelo

rocks that have changed as a result of heat and pressure

What is the prefix of this word and what does it mean?

....

....

....

rocas que han cambiado a causa del calor y la presión

process of carrying away weathered bits of rock

Draw an example.

proceso por el cual se transportan pedacitos de roca desgastada

any form of water that falls to Earth

Write a sentence using the verb form of this word.

....

....

....

cualquier forma de agua que cae a la Tierra

a natural land feature on Earth's surface

Draw an example. Label your drawing.

formación natural en la superficie terrestre

a break or crack in rocks where Earth's crust can move suddenly

Write a sentence using this word.

....

....

fisura o grieta en las rocas donde la corteza terrestre puede desplazarse en forma repentina

the movement of water from Earth's surface to the atmosphere and back again

Write a word related to this term.

....

....

recorrido de ida y vuelta que realiza el agua entre la atmósfera y la superficie de la Tierra

Lesson 1

How are minerals classified?

- Minerals are natural, nonliving crystals that make up rocks.
- Color, luster, hardness, streak, shape, and cleavage are some properties of minerals.

Lesson 2

How are rocks classified?

- Rocks are classified as igneous, sedimentary, or metamorphic, based on how they form.
- A cycle of heat, pressure, and chemical reactions can change rocks.

Lesson 3

What are weathering and erosion?

- Wind, water, ice, changes in temperature, and chemical changes can weather, or break down, rock.
- Erosion carries weathered rock away.

Lesson 4

How can Earth's surface change rapidly?

- Volcanic eruptions, earthquakes, landslides, and floods can cause Earth's surface to change rapidly.
- Earthquakes occur when Earth's plates move suddenly along faults.

Lesson 5

Where is Earth's water?

- Earth's fresh water exists as lakes, ponds, rivers, glaciers, and groundwater.
- Most of Earth's water is salt water in the ocean.

Lesson 6

What is the water cycle?

- The water cycle is the constant movement of water from Earth's surface to the atmosphere and back again.
- Evaporation, condensation, and precipitation are parts of the cycle.

Chapter Review

REVIEW
THE BIG
?

How do Earth's resources change?

How are minerals classified?

1. **Classify** The table shows five minerals and their Mohs ratings. List the minerals in order from softest to hardest.

Mineral	Mohs Rating
Augite	5.5
Cinnabar	2.5
Emerald	7.5
Magnetite	6
Sapphire	9

....

....

How are rocks classified?

2. **Identify** What causes sedimentary rock to turn into metamorphic rock?

....

....

3. **Vocabulary** What type of rock is formed from molten rock?
   A. shale
   B. igneous
   C. metamorphic
   D. magma

What are weathering and erosion?

4. ◉ **Draw Conclusions** Read the paragraph and fill in the graphic organizer.

Several processes work to shape Earth's surface. The process of weathering wears away rocks and particles. However, during another process, erosion, the weathered material is moved away. Various forces move the weathered material. Yet some of the same forces may work together to drop the rocks and particles in a new location. This process is called deposition.

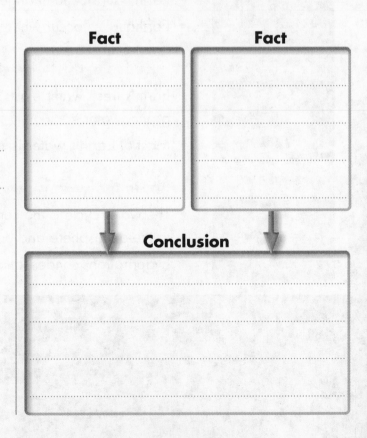

Fact

Fact

Conclusion

Lesson 4

How can Earth's surface change rapidly?

5. **Describe** How can a flood cause Earth's surface to change?

....

....

....

....

....

Lesson 5

Where is Earth's water?

6. **Write About It** Explain where fresh water and salt water exist on Earth's surface.

....

....

....

....

....

....

Lesson 6

What is the water cycle?

7. **Illustrate** Draw and label a diagram that shows the steps of the water cycle.

8. **APPLY THE BIG ?** **How do Earth's resources change?**

....

Think of a rocky cliff on a beach. What natural forces have shaped this landform? What forces continue to change it?

....

....

....

Benchmark Practice

Read each question and choose the best answer.

1 The chart below shows some mineral properties. Use the chart to identify the mineral sample.

Mineral	Hardness	Luster	Color	Streak
Galena	2.5	metallic	lead-gray	gray
Hematite	5–6	metallic or nonmetallic	silver-gray or red	reddish brown
Hornblende	5–6	silky	dark green to black	pale gray to gray
Magnetite	5.5–6	shiny, metallic	black	black

A mineral sample is black and has a rank of 6 on the Mohs Scale. It has a silky luster. This mineral is

A hornblende.

B hematite.

C galena.

D magnetite.

2 A rock with uneven layers of minerals is probably which kind of rock?

A an ore

B igneous

C sedimentary

D obsidian

3 Which of these landforms is probably the result of erosion caused by flowing water?

A a mountain

B a canyon

C a glacier

D a sand dune

4 The point on Earth above the focus of an earthquake is the

A fault.

B epicenter.

C volcano.

D plate.

5 What are two ways that water on Earth and the water cycle are related to weathering and erosion?

SavvasRealize.com

STEM

Robotic Fish

A robotic fish can swim like a real fish. It uses its back tail to swim through water like a real fish.

Have you ever seen fish swimming in a lake, river, or ocean? One of the fish may not be real! Scientists and engineers developed a robotic fish! A robotic fish can be used to detect and collect data on pollution. The robotic fish uses sensors to identify the pollutant and its cause. The cause can include chemical spills. This technology allows officials to learn more about the impact of pollution on lakes, rivers, or oceans. The robotic fish was built so it cannot get caught in nets easily. Also, the fish has internal tracking systems. These systems help it avoid collisions with boats. You might wonder if sharks can mistake these robotic fish for prey. The answer is no! The robot has an electromagnetic field. An electromagnetic field is a force that can be felt by other living things around the fish. It seems to make sharks and other predators uneasy.

Determine How could the robotic fish help detect oil spills?

Materials

gloves and masking tape

2 containers and soil

small paper cup and two books

small paper clip and foam cup

water

graduated cylinder (or measuring cup)

metric ruler

Inquiry Skill
A **hypothesis** is a statement that explains an observation. It can be tested by an experiment.

What affects how soil erodes?

Moving water can change the land. It can carry soil from one place to another.

Ask a question.

How does the amount of water that falls on soil affect the amount of soil erosion?

State a hypothesis.

1. Write a **hypothesis** by circling one choice and finishing the sentence.

If more water falls on soil, then (a) *more*, (b) *less*, (c) *about the same amount of* soil will be eroded because

....

....

Identify and control variables.

2. In an **experiment,** the **variable** you observe is called the **dependent variable** because it changes depending on the variable you change. In this experiment what is the dependent variable?

....

3. The variable you change is called the **independent variable** because you choose how to change it. It does NOT depend on anything except your choice. What is the independent variable?

....

4. In an experiment, there are factors that could be changed but must not be changed. These are called **controlled variables** because you control the experiment to make sure they do not change. List two controlled variables.

....

Design your test.

☐ **5.** Draw how you will set up your test.

☐ **6.** List your steps in the order you will do them.

Do your test.

☐ **7.** Follow the steps you wrote.

☐ **8.** Make sure to **measure** accurately. **Record** your results in a table.

☐ **9.** Scientists repeat their tests to improve their accuracy. Repeat your test if time allows.

Be careful! Wear safety goggles.

Work Like a Scientist

Scientists work with other scientists. They compare their methods and results. Talk with your classmates. Compare your methods and results.

Collect and record your data.

☐ **10.** Fill in the chart.

Interpret your data.

☐ **11.** Use your data to make circle graphs.

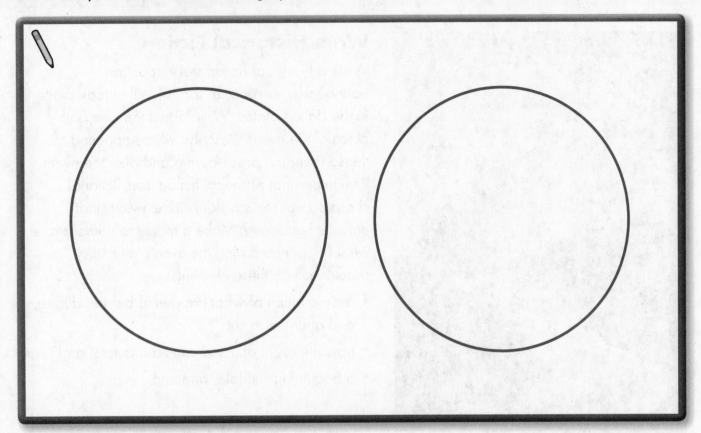

☐ **12.** Look at your graphs closely. Analyze how the amount of water that fell affected the amount of soil the water moved. Identify the evidence you used.

_____

_____

_____

State your conclusion.

13. Communicate your conclusion. Compare your **hypothesis** with your results. Compare your results with others.

_____

_____

_____

_____

Performance-Based Assessment

Write Historical Fiction

Write a historical fiction story about an earthquake, volcano, or landslide that took place in the United States. Write about the time and place of the event. Describe what happened to the surrounding areas during and after the event. Remember that historical fiction uses fictional characters but tells a story about events that actually happened. Make a model to demonstrate what happened during the event. Your story should include these elements:

- a description of what happened before, during, and after the event;
- how the event affected your characters; and
- a beginning, middle, and end.

Plan an Investigation

Design an investigation to identify a sampling of rocks and minerals. Identify which properties you will test and the tools you will use. Use the Science and Engineering Practices as your guide. Then conduct your experiment.

Science and Engineering Practices

1. Ask a question or define a problem.
2. Develop and use models.
3. Plan and carry out investigations.
4. Analyze and interpret data.
5. Use math and computational thinking.
6. Construct explanations or design solutions.
7. Engage in argument from evidence.
8. Obtain, evaluate, and communicate information.

Create a Booklet

Choose one way that Earth's surface changes rapidly (volcanoes, earthquakes, landslides, floods, or droughts). Research how people can predict the event and limit the impact of the event. For example, scientists might monitor the amount and size of earthquakes in a region. Engineers might design a building that can withstand an earthquake. Create a booklet that shares your research. Your booklet should

- identify the natural event you chose to research,
- explain how people can predict the event,
- describe how people can limit the impact of the event, and
- include illustrations.

Make a Map

Look at a map of your state. Identify landforms such as hills, mountains, plains, and valleys. Also, point out bodies of water, such as lakes, rivers, and oceans. Then, draw your own map that shows the geographic features of your local area.

- Label landforms.
- Label any bodies of water.
- Identify where your school is located.
- Include a key showing what different colors and symbols represent. For example, you may use blue as a color to represent a body of water. You may use a triangle to represent a hill or mountain.

Where is the scientist?

The Nature of Science

Try It! How do scientists make observations?

STEM Activity Time to Clean Green!

Lesson 1 What questions do scientists ask?

Lesson 2 How do scientists use tools?

Lesson 3 How do scientists answer questions?

Lesson 4 How do scientists draw conclusions?

Investigate It! What affects how many times a pendulum swings?

Scientists observe the natural world. Through observation they can learn about things such as what kinds of plants and animals live in an area. They can also learn how those plants and animals interact.

Predict What do you think these student scientists might ask about this environment? Why?

....

....

....

What is science?

How do scientists make observations?

☐ **1. Observe** a stapler or another object your teacher selects.

☐ **2.** Write 10 true statements about the object.

1. ....

2. ....

3. ....

4. ....

5. ....

6. ....

7. ....

8. ....

9. ....

10. ....

> **Inquiry Skill**
> Based on your careful
> **observations** you can
> make true statements.

☐ **3.** Work in a group. Put an ✕ by the true statements
that were written by more than one person.

Explain Your Results

4. UNLOCK THE BIG ? How did working in a group
help you make better **observations**?

....

....

....

....

....

Text Features

Text features, such as headings, labels, pictures, and captions, give you clues about what you will read.

A **picture** shows something you will read about.

A **caption** tells specific information about a picture.

Lightning Lab

Investigations

Scientists do investigations to help them find answers to their questions. An **investigation** is a careful way of looking for something. Scientists use process skills in science investigations. You already use many of these skills in your daily life whenever you answer questions or solve problems. You will use them in a more organized way as you do science activities.

Observe

Science often starts when a person observes something. For example, someone could visit a cave and observe the shapes of the cave walls. The person may then wonder how those shapes formed. Observations are made with the senses and with tools. Observations lead to questions that start an investigation. However, scientists continue making observations throughout an investigation.

Research

After scientists ask a question, they do research by studying reference materials. Reference materials include encyclopedias, books, magazines or journals, the Internet, and more. Scientists often write articles that appear in scientific journals. Other scientists read the articles. This helps scientists learn what others have already discovered.

When scientists use information from a reference material, they keep track of where the information came from. They write down the name of the book or article and the name of the person who wrote it. It is important for others to be able to find the reference material the scientists used.

3. **Underline** the information you would need to write down about an article in a scientific journal.

4. **Apply** Look at the cave photos on this page. What research might you want to do before exploring a cave?

A **heading** tells what the content that follows is about.

This scientist is studying cave formations.

Lightning Lab

Testing Observations
Working by yourself, explore the properties of different rocks. Write down your observations. Then work together as a class. Discuss the observations of others. Write down what you learned as a class that you did not discover on your own.

306

picture of a pencil

Practice It!

Find the text features in the textbook page shown above.
Write a clue that each one gives you about the content.

Feature	Clue
caption	tells me that a scientist is shown in the picture
picture of a pencil	
Lightning Lab	

Time to Clean Green!

People purchase many products to clean and disinfect their homes. These cleaners work well. But many of them include things that can be dangerous to your health and to the environment. For example:

- chlorine, found in cleaners that contain bleach, can react with other substances to produce deadly gases.

- phosphates in detergents can harm living things in rivers, streams, and oceans.

Also, many cleaners are made from petroleum. Using oil to make cleaners uses up a nonrenewable resource.

Some companies have developed "green" cleaners. Green brands promise to work just as well as the cleaners described above. They also promise to be nontoxic, biodegradable, and made from renewable (non petroleum-based) resources. Other people have looked to their own cupboards for ingredients that can be mixed into safe, effective cleaners.

You have just landed your dream job at a "green" cleaning company. Your first project is to modify the recipe of a green cleaner made with inexpensive household ingredients to make a cleaner that is effective on dried mud.

Identify the Problem

☐ **1.** What is your task? _____

_____

Do Research

Use a piece of chalk to divide your desk into four parts. Then use a paper towel to wipe a thin layer of mud into each of the four parts. (You should still be able to see your desk through the layer of mud!) Allow the mud to dry.

While the mud is drying, **examine** the labels of several household cleaners.

☐ **2.** What are the most important functions of a cleaner? _____

_____

3. What cautions are listed on these labels? Why are these cautions there?

_____

_____

Examine the labels of the materials you will use to make your cleaner.

4. What cautions are listed on these ingredients? _____

_____

_____

_____

Mix up your basic cleaning-solution recipe. Combine 1 cup of white vinegar and 1 cup of warm water in a beaker. Dip a paper towel into the mixture and test the cleaner on one section of your desk.

5. How well did the cleaner work? Explain. _____

_____

_____

6. What function does each ingredient in this cleaner serve? _____

_____

_____

7. How is this cleaner different from most cleaners you would buy in the store?

_____

Go to the materials station(s). Pick up each material one at a time. Think about how it may or may not be useful in your recipe. Leave the materials where they are.

8. What are your design constraints? _____

_____

Develop Possible Solutions

☑ **9. Describe** two different ways you could adjust, remove, or add ingredients to the vinegar and water recipe to make a better mud cleaner.

_____

_____

_____

_____

_____

Choose One Solution

☑ **10. Describe** how you will adjust, remove, or add ingredients to the recipe of the original cleaner to make a better green cleaner. _____

_____

_____

_____

_____

☑ **11.** Why did you choose these ingredients? _____

_____

Design and Construct a Prototype

Gather your materials, including a beaker or bowl and any measuring tools you will need. **Make** your cleaner.

☑ **12. Record** the details of your prototype. If anything unusual happened while you were making your cleaner, **record** your observations. _____

_____

_____

_____

Test the Prototype

Test your cleaner. Dip a paper towel into the cleaner and test it on a section of your desk.

☑ **13. Record** your observations. _____

_____

_____

_____

Communicate Results

☑ **14. Compare** your cleaner with the original vinegar/water recipe. _____

_____

_____

_____

Evaluate and Redesign

☑ **15. Describe** any changes you want to make to your recipe. **Record** your new recipe.

_____

_____

_____

_____

☑ **16. Make** your changes and test your revised cleaner. Did your revisions work as you expected? Explain. _____

_____

_____

_____

What questions do scientists ask?

Envision It!

Tell what questions scientists might ask about this rock structure.

my PLANET DiARY

Science Stats

The Paiute name for it is Paxa Uipi. You know it as the Grand Canyon. The Grand Canyon is located in the state of Arizona.

It is 446 kilometers long and ranges in width from 180 meters to nearly 29 kilometers. It is, on average, 1.6 kilometers deep. The canyon walls reveal layer after colorful layer of rock, nearly 40 of them. The oldest rock, at the bottom of the canyon, is the Vishnu schist. It is approximately 1.7 billion years old.

The Grand Canyon is clearly a wonder of the natural world. People from all over the world come to see this beautiful place.

Examine the statistics listed above. What questions might they make you want to ask about the Grand Canyon?

....

....

I will know what questions scientists ask. I will know how scientists find answers to their questions.

Words to Know

inquiry
investigation

Questions

Science includes **inquiry,** or the process of asking questions and searching for answers. Scientists ask questions about what they observe in the natural world. Someone looks at something carefully and asks about it. For example, a scientist studying Earth might think of a number of questions to ask. *How do islands form? What kinds of rock are on Earth's surface?*

Scientists first study what other scientists have already learned about the answers to their questions. Then scientists do experiments and make observations to find answers. They keep records of their observations and experiments. Keeping records can help them share what they learn with others.

2. **Ask Questions** What question do you think these scientists might be trying to answer?

....

....

....

1. ◎ **Text Features** Complete the chart to explain some of the features on this page.

Feature	Clue
heading	The heading tells that the paragraph is about questions.
picture	

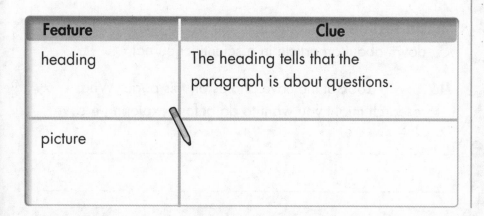

This scientist is studying cave formations.

Investigations

Scientists do investigations to help them find answers to their questions. An **investigation** is a careful way of looking for something. Scientists use process skills in science investigations. You already use many of these skills in your daily life whenever you answer questions or solve problems. You will use them in a more organized way as you do science activities.

Observe

Science often starts when a person observes something. For example, someone could visit a cave and observe the shapes of the cave walls. The person may then wonder how those shapes formed. Observations are made with the senses and with tools. Observations lead to questions that start an investigation. However, scientists continue making observations throughout an investigation.

Research

After scientists ask a question, they do research by studying reference materials. Reference materials include encyclopedias, books, magazines or journals, the Internet, and more. Scientists often write articles that appear in scientific journals. Other scientists read the articles. This helps scientists learn what others have already discovered.

When scientists use information from a reference material, they keep track of where the information came from. They write down the name of the book or article and the name of the person who wrote it. It is important for others to be able to find the reference material the scientists used.

3. **Underline** the information you would need to write down about an article in a scientific journal.

4. **Apply** Look at the cave photos on this page. What research might you want to do before exploring a cave?

_____

_____

Experiment

Scientists use their observations and research to come up with possible answers to their questions. Then they design and run tests to try to confirm those answers. These tests are called experiments. Scientists record their observations during experiments. The results of an experiment may match the earlier answer or provide a different answer. The results of their experiments are added to their earlier observations and research.

5. Apply What might you ask about the rock on this page? What experiment might you do to answer the question?

....

....

....

Got it?

6. Ask Questions What would you like to know about land features in your state? Write a question.

....

7. Judge Why might some reference materials be better than others?

....

8. Infer Why might scientists repeat experiments?

....

....

☐ **Stop!** I need help with ....

❚❚ **Wait!** I have a question about ....

▶ **Go!** Now I know ....

Lesson 2

How do scientists use tools?

Envision It!

Circle two tools that help you see things that are very small.

Inquiry ## Explore It!

How can tools help you observe?

☐ **1. Observe** a penny, a tissue, and a small rock using a hand lens.

☐ **2.** Use a microscope to observe the penny and the tissue.

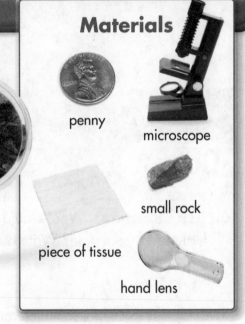

Materials

penny

microscope

small rock

piece of tissue

hand lens

Explain Your Results

3. Draw a Conclusion Which tool worked better for **observing** each object? Explain.

Be careful! Handle microscopes with care.

....

....

....

....

....

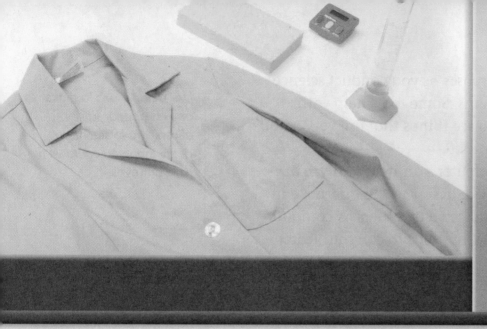

I will know how to use tools to do science. I will know how to do science safely.

Word to Know

tool

Tools

Scientists use many different kinds of tools. A **tool** is an object or device used to perform a task. The tool you use depends on the task. Tools can help you measure objects or gather information. You can measure volume, temperature, length, distance, mass, and more with the proper tools. Measurements give you exact observations that you can share with others. Scientists choose different tools based on how exact they need their measurements to be.

1. **Underline** two things that tools help you do.

2. **Infer** **Circle** the measurement that is more exact.
   about 5 cm
   5.3 cm

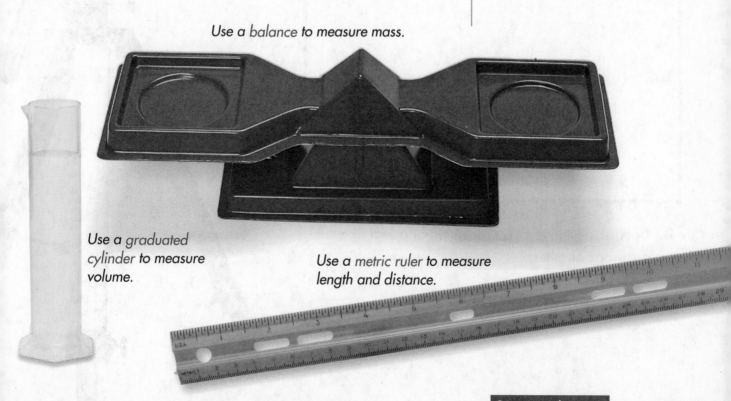

Use a balance to measure mass.

Use a graduated cylinder to measure volume.

Use a metric ruler to measure length and distance.

More Tools

Tools can serve many purposes as you conduct science experiments and investigations. Some tools help with observations, helping you to see things that are very small or very far away in more detail.

Other tools, such as a computer, can help analyze or visualize data. Computers with access to the Internet can help you find information collected by others. A computer can also help you create presentations to communicate your results to others.

Use a hand lens to make objects appear larger. This allows you to see more detail than you could with just your eyes.

3. Apply Use a hand lens to observe a leaf. Draw what you see.

Use a telescope to help you see objects that are far away.

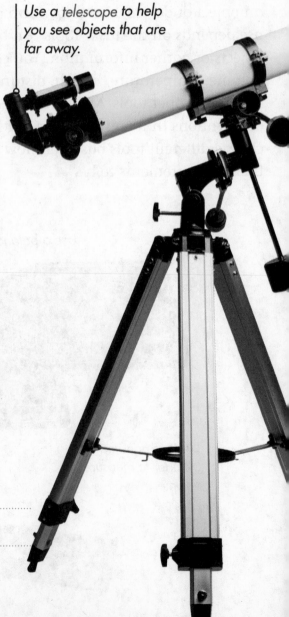

4. Compare How is your drawing of a leaf like the drawings of others?

....

....

Use a computer to analyze data.

5. Explain Tell another way you use a computer.

Microscopes use several lenses to make objects appear much larger. Use microscopes to see things in greater detail.

6. Apply Tell what you would look at with a microscope.

Use a *thermometer* to measure temperature.

Compare Observations

Scientists make observations many times to make sure their data are accurate. Data are the facts you collect as you observe. Scientists record their findings, and then compare their data with the observations of other scientists. Even though groups of scientists may use different tools to observe, their data should be similar.

Comparing your results with others is important. Sometimes there are errors in how observations are made. Sometimes the tool being used has a flaw. Sometimes a scientist misses an important detail.

7. Text Features Why do you think some of the words in the captions are purple?

8. Infer Why do you think people with long hair need to tie it back when they do a science experiment?

....

....

....

9. Identify Suppose you are doing an activity with vinegar and baking soda. (Circle) the safety rules that apply.

Safety

Scientists know that they must work safely when doing experiments and using tools. You need to be careful when you do science activities too. Always follow these safety rules.

Science Safety Rules

- Read the activity carefully before you start.

- Listen to the teacher's instructions. Ask questions about things you do not understand.

- Keep your work area neat and clean. Clean up spills right away.

- Never taste or smell any substance unless directed to do so by your teacher.

- Handle sharp items and other equipment carefully.

- Use chemicals carefully. Dispose of chemicals properly.

- Help keep plants and animals that you use safe.

- Tell your teacher if there is an accident or if you see anything that looks unsafe.

- Wash your hands well when you are finished.

- Wear safety goggles and gloves when necessary.

- Tie back long hair.

10. Explain What do these students need to do to be safe?

....

....

Following safety rules keeps you and others from getting hurt. Some chemicals can damage your skin or eyes. Safety goggles and gloves can protect you from these chemicals. If you are working with something that is sharp or moves quickly, safety goggles will protect your eyes. Gloves can protect your hands.

11. Write The students below are following safety rules. Explain how each student is protected.

Got it?

12. Summarize How can tools help you do science?

13. UNLOCK THE BIG ? **Judge** Why is it important for scientists to compare their observations with the observations of others?

⬜ **Stop!** I need help with

⏸ **Wait!** I have a question about

▶ **Go!** Now I know

How do scientists answer questions?

Envision It!

Tell what question you have about the starfish.

Inquiry **Explore It!**

What helps scientists answer questions?

Scientists try to find answers to questions by following certain principles. In an investigation, they change only one thing, measure how something else changes, and keep everything else the same. Think about these principles as you try to answer this question: How does temperature affect how much salt dissolves?

☑ **1.** To a cup of cold water, add 1 level spoonful of salt and stir until it dissolves. Repeat until the salt no longer dissolves. **Record** how many spoonfuls you added before it stopped dissolving.

☑ **2.** Repeat Step 1 but change from cold water to warm water.

Explain Your Results

3. Identify the one thing you changed.

....

4. Identify what you **measured.**

....

5. Identify one thing you made sure not to change.

....

Materials

plastic cup of very cold water
plastic cup of warm water

salt   spoon

Data Table

	Number of Spoonfuls of Salt
Cold Water	
Warm Water	

I will know some different scientific methods scientists use to answer questions.

Words to Know

scientific methods
hypothesis
evidence
three-dimensional
two-dimensional

Tell how you could find an answer to your question.

Scientific Methods

Scientists use scientific methods as they work. **Scientific methods** are organized ways to answer questions and solve problems. Scientific methods help scientists draw conclusions. Scientists do not always use the same methods. They do not follow the methods in rigid order. Scientists record their method so it can be repeated accurately. You will use scientific methods when you do experiments.

Scientific methods include experiments, observations, surveys, and sampling. In a survey, scientists ask people a number of questions and then analyze the answers. A survey might help scientists find the source of an illness, for example. Sampling is another way of collecting data. Scientists may take samples of a population. They might catch, test, and release birds to see if they are healthy.

1. **Underline** the definition of *scientific methods*.

2. **Evaluate** Cross out the statement that is not true.

   Surveys are one type of scientific method.

   The scientific method follows a rigid order.

   Scientists make careful observations.

3. **Ask Questions**
   Suppose the scientist in the picture below wants to see how petrels care for their young. What scientific methods can she use to answer her question?

   ....

   ....

This scientist studies the habits of petrels.

A Bouncing-Ball Experiment

Science begins with an observation. For example, you may notice that a ball bounces differently in different rooms. These two pages show a series of steps that can be used to design and conduct a bouncing-ball experiment.

Ask a question.

You might have a question about something you observe.

How high will the ball bounce on different surfaces?

State your hypothesis.

A **hypothesis** is a possible answer to your question. It often predicts an outcome of an experiment. Write it as an *If . . . then . . . because . . .* statement.

If I drop the ball, then it will bounce highest on the rubber mat, because the rubber mat is the most flexible.

Identify and control variables.

Variables are things that can change. For a fair test, choose just one variable to change. Keep the other variables the same.

In this experiment there are 3 types of variables. The *independent variable* is the thing that you change. In this experiment, the surface is the independent variable. The thing that you must measure or observe is the *dependent variable*. Here, the dependent variable is how high the ball bounces. *Controlled variables* are things you keep the same so they do not affect the dependent variable.

Test other surfaces. Bounce the ball off of wood, carpet, and a rubber mat.

4. **Identify** What are some of the controlled variables?

....

....

....

Test your hypothesis.

Make a plan to test your hypothesis. Collect materials and tools. Then follow your plan. Each time you test a surface is called a trial. Repeat each trial three times.

Collect and record your data.

Keep good records of what you do and find out. Use tables and pictures to help.

Interpret your data.

Organize your notes and records to make them clear. Make diagrams, charts, or graphs to help.

State your conclusion.

Your conclusion is a decision you make based on your data. Communicate what you found out. Tell whether your data supported your hypothesis.

The data did not support my hypothesis. The ball bounced highest when dropped onto the piece of wood.

Try it again.

Do the experiment a few more times. The results of one experiment might not be right. Be sure to do everything exactly the same each time.

5. **Generate** Write a new hypothesis about how high the ball will bounce on different surfaces.

....

....

....

....

....

6. **Text Features** Why are pictures shown with some of the steps?

....

....

....

....

7. **Predict** Tell how the outcome of the experiment might change when the experiment is repeated.

....

....

....

....

Creativity

Scientists have to be creative when designing experiments. They need to think of ways to control variables so trials are the same. They need to think of what might go wrong. Think about the bouncing ball experiment. What if the scientist only said to drop the ball from a table? Other scientists may not have tables that are the same height. Some scientists might push the ball off the table and others might just let it drop. These could lead to different results. Using a meterstick to measure the exact height eliminates the differences created by using a table.

8. CHALLENGE Sometimes tests like this are done by dropping the ball inside a clear plastic tube. How would that make the experiment better and how could it make it worse?

....

....

....

Observation and Evidence

Scientists make careful observations to find answers to their questions. Taking measurements is one way scientists can make observations. Scientists use evidence to decide whether their hypotheses are correct. Observations and facts gained from experiments are **evidence.**

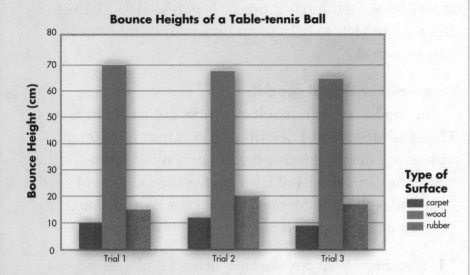

Bounce Heights of a Table-tennis Ball

Estimates and Measurements

Scientists often make estimates. They tell what they think an object's size, mass, or temperature will measure. Then they measure these factors in units. Scientists usually measure in metric units. The United States commonly uses non-metric units such as gallons, pounds, and inches.

Multiple Trials

A single trial may not give an accurate result. Because of this, scientists perform multiple trials during an experiment. When all the results are gathered together, patterns should develop. How many trials to perform depends on what you are trying to test. For example, the chart above shows results from three trials. Notice that all the heights in the trials are different. If you were testing the exact height a ball would bounce on a surface, you should complete several trials.

9. **Exemplify** What would you observe in the bouncing-ball experiment?

10. **Analyze** Do three trials give enough evidence to show which surface makes the ball bounce highest? Why or why not?

This is the largest moving model of Earth in the world.

Models

Sometimes scientists want to test things they cannot test on actual objects. For example, a scientist may want to know how strong winds affect an airplane. The scientist can test a model of the plane using a wind tunnel. Models are objects or ideas that represent other things. They may show how something is made or how it works. Scientists often use models to help them understand things in the natural world.

Three-dimensional models

The model of Earth at left is a three-dimensional model. **Three-dimensional** describes objects that have length, width, and height. Models are not exactly the same as the real thing. This model of Earth shows the location of Earth's land and water but does not show what is inside Earth, or features made by people.

11. Identify What are two other examples of three-dimensional models?

....

....

Two-dimensional models

Some models are two-dimensional. **Two-dimensional** describes something that has length and width but not height. Two-dimensional models are flat. A map is an example of a two-dimensional model.

12. Produce Draw a two-dimensional model of your classroom.

The World
Physical map

Explanations

After scientists design their experiments and run trials, they use evidence to explain the results. The explanation should answer the original question the experiment was designed to ask. The explanation will also tell whether the hypothesis was supported by data. An important thing to remember is that a hypothesis is a possible answer to the question. It is based on the best information you have at the time, but if your results do not support the hypothesis, an experiment is not a failure. It still gives information about the question.

13. **Summarize** What was the hypothesis in the bouncing-ball experiment? Did the data support the hypothesis?

At-Home Lab

Trial Testing
Test how high a table-tennis ball will bounce on concrete. Use the procedure from the bouncing-ball experiment. Record your data. Be sure to do multiple trials. Compare your data with others. Explain why the data might be different. Draw a conclusion.

Got it?

14. **Summarize** Name three methods scientists might use to investigate a question or problem.

15. Why do you think evidence is important in science?

Stop! I need help with

Wait! I have a question about

Go! Now I know

Lesson 4
How do scientists draw conclusions?

Envision It!

Tell what you think this scientist is writing down.

Inquiry Explore It!

How can data help you draw a conclusion?

☑ **1.** Put the paper clips in a cup. Dip a magnet into the cup. Pull it out. Count the paper clips it picked up. **Record** your **data.**

☑ **2.** Repeat your trials 2 more times. Record. Make a bar graph

Explain Your Results

3. Communicate Compare the **records** of your **data** with the records made by other groups.

....

4. Draw a Conclusion Based on the data you recorded, how many paper clips is your magnet able to pick up? How did the data help you draw your conclusion?

....

....

Materials

magnet

paper clips

plastic cup

Paper Clips Picked Up

Trial	Number
1	
2	
3	

Paper Clips Picked Up

Number of Paper Clips	Trial 1	Trial 2	Trial 3
30			
25			
20			
15			
10			
5			
0			

Trial

UNLOCK THE BIG ?

I will know how scientists keep records in order to share conclusions with other scientists.

Words to Know

procedure
inference

Record Procedures

The bouncing-ball experiment from the previous lesson identifies different variables to test the hypothesis. How can other scientists use the experiment to get their own results? How can you use the results to draw conclusions?

The scientist in the photo above is keeping records of underwater observations. Scientists must also carefully record how they performed experiments in procedures. A **procedure** is a set of step-by-step instructions for how to perform a test. When you write a procedure, be sure to be clear. This allows others to repeat the test to get similar results. When repeating an experiment, it is important to do a test exactly the same way each time.

1. **Analyze** What might happen if a procedure is not clearly written?

....

....

....

Question: A table-tennis ball will bounce highest on which surface?

Hypothesis: If I drop the ball, then it will bounce highest on the rubber mat, because the rubber mat is the most flexible.

Materials: table-tennis ball, piece of wood, rubber mat, piece of carpet, meterstick

Procedure:
1. Place the piece of wood on the floor. Hold the meterstick upright on the wood.

2. Drop the table-tennis ball from a height of 1 meter onto the wood. Be careful not to push or throw the ball down.

3. Record how high the ball bounces.

4. Repeat Steps 1–3 using the rubber mat.

5. Repeat Steps 1–3 using the piece of carpet.

6. Repeat the entire experiment two more times.

Keep Records

By keeping detailed and accurate records of observations, scientists are able to share their information with others. The more scientists repeat an experiment and get the same results, the more they can rely on the data. Conclusions based on reliable data are more likely to continue to be useful in the future. For example, think of the diver on the previous page. If the records of the dive are accurate, scientists can look for more or different information on future dives.

Scientists continue to repeat an experiment until they are sure of the results. If scientists repeat an experiment and get different results, they look for reasons why the experiment was different. Good records and procedures can be helpful in finding those reasons.

Organize Your Data

Scientists keep accurate records of their experiments. Often they organize their data in a table. The table below contains important information about the bouncing-ball experiment. The title explains what was tested. The table names the materials used and gives the test results. The table also shows that the experiment was done three times.

2. ◉ Text Features What information does the table give you?

....

....

....

3. Conclude Make a conclusion based on the data. Which surface caused the ball to bounce highest?

....

....

....

Bounce Heights of a Table-tennis Ball			
Material	Bounce Height (cm)		
	Trial 1	Trial 2	Trial 3
Carpet	10	12	9
Wood	70	68	65
Rubber	15	20	17

Presenting Data

There are many different formats for organizing and arranging your data. The table on the previous page is one format. Charts and graphs can also be helpful because they show information in a way that is easy to understand. However you format your data, it should be clearly labeled.

Bar graph

A bar graph uses rectangular bars to compare data. The bars may be vertical or horizontal. The bars often have different colors or shading for each variable.

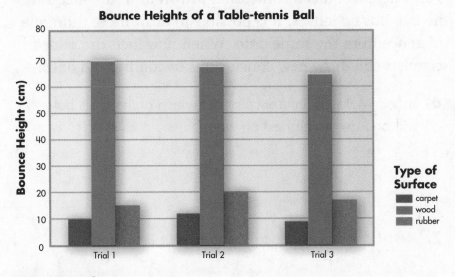

Bounce Heights of a Table-tennis Ball

4. Conclude In the bar graph shown here, what would happen if the color key was missing?

....

....

....

....

Line graph

Line graphs connect points of data on a graph with straight lines. Line graphs are often used to show patterns of data over time. For example, a line graph could show the amount of rainfall a place gets over two weeks. A graph may use different colored lines to compare different data.

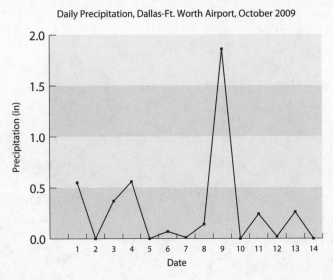

Daily Precipitation, Dallas-Ft. Worth Airport, October 2009

5. Express Data Work with a partner to write a 1–2 sentence explanation of the data in the line graph. Read your explanation.

....

....

....

....

....

Evidence and Inferences

Scientists base their explanations on evidence. Evidence includes any information you have and observations that you make. An observation from an experiment is a piece of evidence. Facts you already have, or research you have done, are also evidence.

Scientists use evidence to make inferences. An **inference** is a conclusion drawn from data and observations. For example, the statement *The tree has no leaves on it* is an observation. *The tree lost its leaves because the season is fall* is an inference. It is a conclusion drawn from the fact that the tree has no leaves. It is possible to draw more than one inference from the same data. When new facts are added, scientists can draw new conclusions or confirm old ones.

8. Infer Someone noticed that a tree had no leaves and inferred that it lost its leaves because the season was fall. Write another reasonable inference based on this observation.

6. Infer Make an inference about which of the balls below will bounce the highest on wood.

....

....

7. Justify What evidence supports your inference?

....

....

....

fabric ball

golf ball

table-tennis ball

Reasonable Answers

Scientists attempt to develop reasonable answers to the questions they pose. To do this, they use evidence from their observations and experiments. For the bouncing-ball experiment, you would use evidence gathered by doing the procedure from the previous pages. A reasonable answer should not favor one opinion over another unless it is supported by evidence.

Compare Results

Scientists often compare their methods or procedures with those of their peers. They also compare their results. By comparing methods and results, scientists can work to find results that can be retested.

In the bouncing-ball experiment, one group can compare their results with another group. The scientists determine whether the results are similar or different. They try to explain why the results are similar or different. Scientists often do this to think of new questions or better ways to perform a test.

9. **Decide** Why is it important to compare results with others?

....

....

....

....

Lightning Lab

Observations and Inferences

Examine a coin. List everything you can about the coin that is factual. Next, make some inferences about the coin or the country that minted it. Compare your lists of facts and inferences with those of your classmates.

plastic foam ball   rubber ball

Go Further

Once an experiment is complete, scientists use what they learn. The results of an experiment can become part of the background research other scientists use for future experiments. An experiment may lead to new questions to test. Scientists may also think of better ways to do a test.

10. Formulate Suppose you wanted to get a more precise measurement of how high the ball would bounce on wood. How would you change the experiment?

....

....

....

Think back to the bouncing-ball experiment. The original question was how high a ball would bounce on different surfaces. The hypothesis was that a rubber surface would make the ball bounce higher. The conclusion was a wood surface made the ball bounce higher. The completed experiment might raise questions about how other surfaces would affect the ball. Or it may raise questions about the ball itself. Does the ball bounce differently if it is hot or cold? How might it bounce compared to other balls?

11. Revise Suppose you wanted to perform three trials to test how high a ball bounced if it was at a cooler temperature. How might you organize your results? Complete the table below. Circle the independent variables in the completed table.

12. Predict This scientist is testing a pesticide on plants in a laboratory. When this experiment is complete, how might it lead to a new experiment?

....

....

....

....

Bounce Heights at Different Temperatures			

Interpret Data

Three different students tried the experiment with the table-tennis ball. They tested materials to see which caused the ball to bounce highest. The chart shows their results.

Bounce Heights of a Table-tennis Ball			
Material	**Bounce Height (cm)**		
	Student A	**Student B**	**Student C**
Carpet	7	12	6
Wood	70	73	65
Rubber	12	20	13

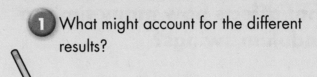

1 What might account for the different results?

....

....

....

2 What question were students trying to answer? What can they conclude?

....

....

....

....

Got it?

13. ◉ **Compare and Contrast** How is evidence different from an inference?

....

....

14. Evaluate Why is it important to do an experiment the same way each time?

....

⬛ **Stop!** I need help with ....

⏸ **Wait!** I have a question about ....

▶ **Go!** Now I know ....

What affects how many times a pendulum swings?

Follow a Procedure

☐ **1.** Set up a pendulum system.

☐ **2. Identify variables** that might change how many times the pendulum swings in 15 seconds. Use the materials you have. Make a list with other groups.

....

....

....

....

☐ **3.** Choose a variable to investigate. Which variable did you choose?

....

....

....

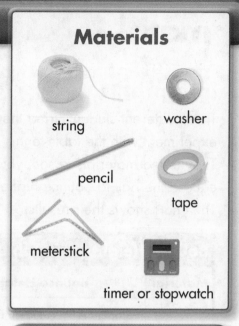

Materials

string

washer

pencil

tape

meterstick

timer or stopwatch

Inquiry Skill
Record your data on a chart. This can help you make **inferences** based on the data.

4. Swing the pendulum. **Measure** the number of swings in 15 seconds. **Record** on the chart.

5. Change the value of your variable. Repeat Step 4.

Observations of Pendulum Swings	
Variable: _____	Number of Swings in 15 seconds

Analyze and Conclude

6. Communicate Compare your results with other groups. Which variable had the greatest effect on the pendulum?

....

....

7. UNLOCK THE BIG ? **Infer** How did scientific methods help you during your investigation?

....

....

....

....

STEM

Healthcare Technology

Did you know your body has defense systems against germs? It does! These defenses include tears, saliva, skin, and blood. For example, the skin stops germs from entering the body. These defense systems help us resist germs and viruses in our environment.

What happens, though, if you get a cut? How can you help your body's defense systems? You could use a bandage to cover a cut! This helps your body defend itself. You could also get a shot to prevent infection! Bandages, needles, and shots are examples of healthcare technology. Doctors and nurses use this technology to help keep you safe from diseases.

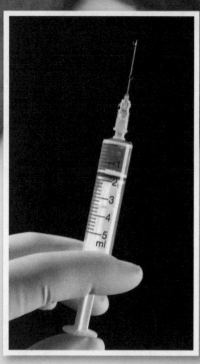

Vaccines help prevent the spread of viruses. One vaccine prevents the spread of diseases such as influenza, or the flu. A vaccine is a preparation of weakened germs that can keep people from getting sick.

Hypothesize How do bandages mimic the job of the skin?

....

....

....

....

Vocabulary Smart Cards

inquiry
investigation
tool
scientific methods
hypothesis
evidence
three-dimensional
two-dimensional
procedure
inference

Play a Game!

Cut out the Vocabulary Smart Cards.

Work with a partner. Choose a Vocabulary Smart Card.

Say as many words as you can think of that are related to that vocabulary word in some way.

Have your partner guess the word.

scientific methods

métodos científicos

inquiry

indagación

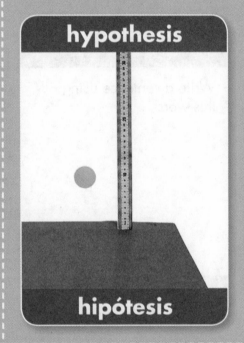

hypothesis

hipótesis

investigation

investigación

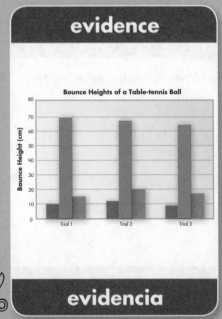

evidence

Bounce Heights of a Table-tennis Ball

evidencia

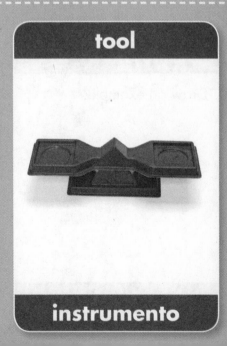

tool

instrumento

the process of asking questions and searching for answers

Write a sentence using the verb form of this word.

....

....

....

proceso que consiste en preguntar y buscar respuestas

---

organized ways to answer questions and solve problems

Write two examples.

....

....

....

maneras organizadas de responder a preguntas y resolver problemas

---

a careful way of looking for something

Write three related words.

....

....

....

....

manera cuidadosa de buscar algo

---

a possible answer to a question

Write a sentence using this word.

....

....

....

....

respuesta posible a una pregunta

---

an object or device used to perform a task

Draw an example.

objeto o herramienta que se usa para hacer un trabajo

---

observations and facts gained from experiments

Write a sentence using this term.

....

....

....

....

observaciones y datos obtenidos de experimentos

Interactive Vocabulary

Scientists use inquiry to find answers.

Inquiry: the process of asking questions and searching for answers

Make a Word Pyramid!

Choose a vocabulary word and write the definition in the base of the pyramid. Write a sentence in the middle of the pyramid. Draw a picture of an example, or of something related, at the top.

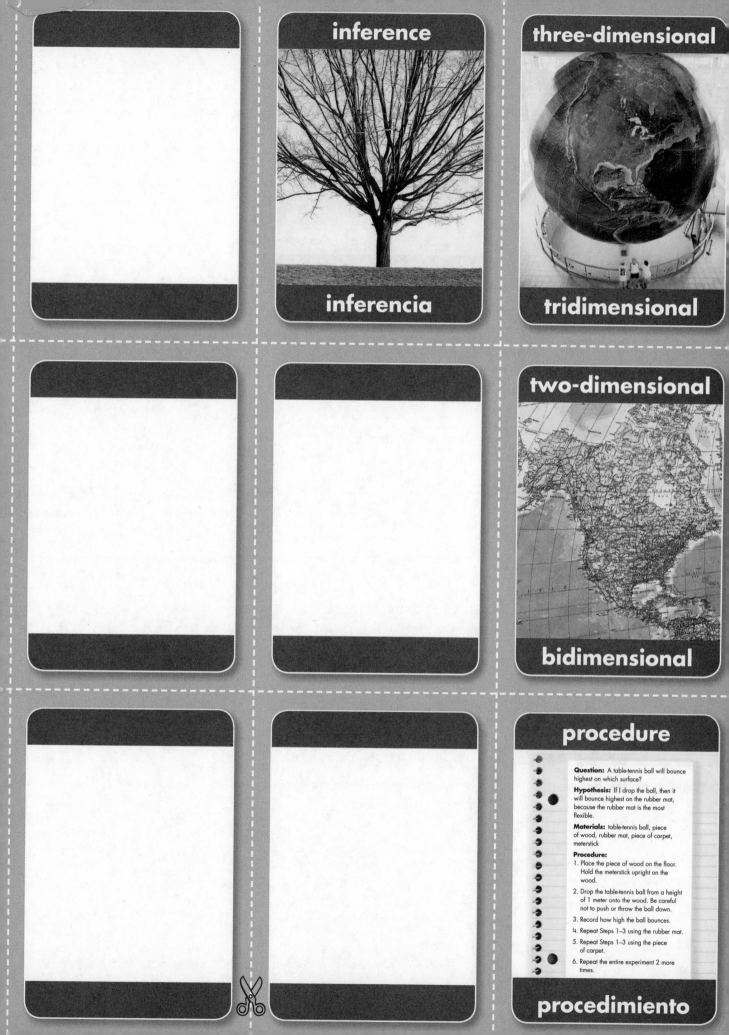

inference

inferencia

three-dimensional

tridimensional

two-dimensional

bidimensional

procedure

Question: A table-tennis ball will bounce highest on which surface?

Hypothesis: If I drop the ball, then it will bounce highest on the rubber mat, because the rubber mat is the most flexible.

Materials: table-tennis ball, piece of wood, rubber mat, piece of carpet, meterstick

Procedure:

1. Place the piece of wood on the floor. Hold the meterstick upright on the wood.

2. Drop the table-tennis ball from a height of 1 meter onto the wood. Be careful not to push or throw the ball down.

3. Record how high the ball bounces.

4. Repeat Steps 1–3 using the rubber mat.

5. Repeat Steps 1–3 using the piece of carpet.

6. Repeat the entire experiment 2 more times.

procedimiento

describes objects that have length, width, and height

Write three examples.

....
....
....
....

describe objetos que tienen largo, ancho y altura

a conclusion drawn from data and observations

Write a sentence using the verb form of this word.

....
....
....

conclusión que se saca de los datos y de las observaciones

....
....
....
....
....

describes something that has length and width, but not height

Draw an example.

describe algo que tiene largo y ancho, pero no tiene altura

....
....
....
....
....
....

....
....
....
....
....

a set of step-by-step instructions

Write three related words.

....
....
....
....

instrucciones paso por paso

....
....
....
....

....
....
....
....

Lesson 1

What questions do scientists ask?

- Scientists ask questions about the natural world.
- Scientists observe and do research while conducting investigations.
- Scientists develop hypotheses based on collected data.

Lesson 2

How do scientists use tools?

- A tool is an object or device used to perform a task.
- Scientists use many tools, including thermometers, microscopes, balances, and computers.

Lesson 3

How do scientists answer questions?

- Scientific methods are organized steps for doing an investigation.
- Evidence is used to develop reasonable answers to questions.
- Scientists compare their results with other scientists' results.

Lesson 4

How do scientists draw conclusions?

- Procedures are step-by-step instructions for how to perform tests.
- Scientists keep detailed and accurate records in order to share their findings with others.

SavvasRealize.com

Part 1 Review

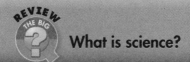
Lesson 1

What questions do scientists ask?

1. **Vocabulary** Inquiry is the process of
   A. doing work.
   B. asking questions.
   C. analyzing data.
   D. reporting results.

2. **Explain** How can scientists develop explanations about data?

   ....

   ....

   ....

   ....

3. **Ask Questions** A team of scientists is studying the formation of islands in the Pacific Ocean. Provide a question that the team might ask.

   ....

   ....

   ....

   ....

Lesson 2

How do scientists use tools?

Measurement Long Ago
   Long ago, people measured by using familiar objects. They used a forearm or a foot to measure length. For smaller measurements, they might have used the width of a man's thumb. They measured weight with stones or even with seeds from different plants.

4. **Text Features** What does the heading in the passage above tell you?

   ....

   ....

   ....

5. **Recognize** A graduated cylinder is used to measure
   A. temperature.
   B. mass.
   C. volume.
   D. weight.

6. **Explain** Why do scientists use tools to measure things and gather information?

   ....

   ....

   ....

Lesson 3

How do scientists answer questions?

7. Summarize What are some of the organized steps that scientists use to answer questions and solve problems?

....

....

....

....

....

....

8. Evaluate In an experiment, the thing you are trying to measure or observe is the

A. controlled variable.

B. dependent variable.

C. independent variable.

D. hypothesis.

Lesson 4

How do scientists draw conclusions?

9. Write about It Why do scientists keep detailed and accurate records?

....

....

....

....

....

....

10. APPLY THE BIG **?** **What is science?**

....

What does it mean to be a scientist?

....

....

....

....

....

....

Benchmark Practice

Read each question and choose the best answer.

1 Scientific knowledge is based on

  A opinions.
  B evidence.
  C guesses.
  D predictions.

2 What is a hypothesis?

  A an observation
  B a possible answer to a question
  C a problem to be solved
  D an accurate measurement

3 Which of these is <u>not</u> a measuring tool?

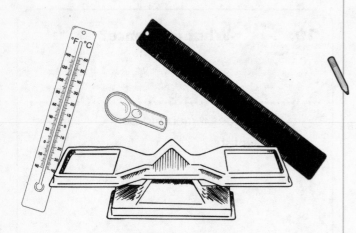

  A a thermometer
  B a pan balance
  C a meterstick
  D a hand lens

4 In a fair test, how many variables will change?

  A 1
  B 2
  C 3
  D 4

5 An inference is

  A a question to be answered.
  B a conclusion based on observations.
  C a measurement that is not exact.
  D the result of an experiment.

6 How might a three-dimensional model of a house be useful to the people constructing the house? Explain your answer.

....

....

....

....

....

....

Observing Plants

You can practice the skill of observation by carefully examining a plant. Go outside with an adult and a notebook. Bring a hand lens if you like. Find a plant that interests you. It can be in a garden, or it can be growing wild. Do not touch the plant. Observe the plant carefully. Draw the plant. Then write down observations about how it looks.

Illustrate Draw the plant.

Record observations about how it looks.

....

....

Use reference materials from your school media center to identify the plant. Write down the name of the plant and the title of the reference material you used.

....

....

What can you test in a wind tunnel?

Technology and Design

Scientists and engineers use wind tunnels to test how air moves around cars, planes, people, or other objects. The smoother the air flows around an object, the faster the object can travel and the less energy it will need to move.

Predict What can a downhill skier learn from wind tunnel tests? Explain your answer.

....

....

....

....

THE BIG ? How does technology affect our lives?

How can you design a hovercraft?

☐ **1. Design** a hovercraft. Use a spool for the nozzle. The nozzle will direct the airflow from the balloon to the body of the hovercraft.

☐ **2.** As part of the design, you will need to **choose materials.** Choose a balloon, a hovercraft body, and a way to attach the nozzle to the hovercraft body.

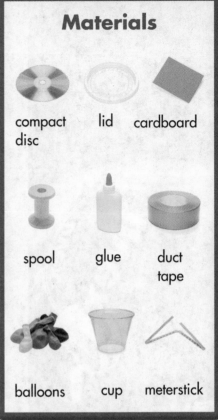

Materials

compact disc   lid   cardboard

spool   glue   duct tape

balloons   cup   meterstick

☐ **3.** Which materials will you use?

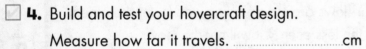

....

....

Inquiry Skill
You can **make and use a model** to test different designs you make.

☐ **4.** Build and test your hovercraft design.
Measure how far it travels. .... cm

☐ **5. Redesign** your hovercraft so it travels farther.
Communicate your changes to others.

Explain Your Results

6. As a class, which combination of materials worked best?

....

....

7. **UNLOCK THE BIG ?** **Interpret Data** How did your **redesign** affect the distance the hovercraft traveled?

....

....

Cause and Effect

- A **cause** is why something happens.
- An **effect** is what happens.
- When you read, sometimes clue words such as *because* and *since* indicate a relationship of cause and effect.

Rubber Tires

Before the 1800s, wheels were made of wood and metal. A thin metal tire was wrapped around a wood rim. Riding in a vehicle with these rigid tires was very bumpy. Because of this, some inventors decided to use rubber to make tires. The flexibility of rubber made the ride less bumpy. Today, rubber tires are used on bikes, cars, tractors, and trucks.

Practice It!

Use the graphic organizer below to list one cause and one effect found in the example paragraph.

Cause

Effect

What's Inside?

Can you see what's inside the building holding it up? Under the bricks, siding, and sheetrock, many buildings have frames made of wood or steel. Like your skeleton, the frame of a building provides support. The shapes used in the frame must be sturdy and stable.

To win first prize in the Tiny Towers contest downtown, **design and build** the tallest tower possible using no more than 30 straws.

Identify the Problem

☐ **1.** What is your task? _____

_____

Do Research

Examine the photos of building frames.

☐ **2.** What is the purpose of a building frame? _____

_____

☐ **3.** What shapes do you see in the frames? _____

_____

☐ **4.** Explain why there is often a reinforcing piece in corners of rectangle frames. _____

_____

Go to the materials station(s). Gather 10 paper clips and two straws. Cut one of the straws into four equal pieces. Hook two paper clips together as if you were going to make a chain. Insert one of the paperclips into the end of one of the straw pieces. Insert the second paperclip into a second straw piece. This will make one corner of a straw square, as shown. Finish making the square.

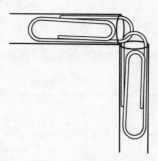

5. How can you use the other straw and paperclips to stabilize the square you made so

that it doesn't rock back and forth? _____

_____

Try out your idea.

6. What other stable shapes can you make with straws and paperclips? **List** them, and

then try to make them. _____

_____

_____

Go to the materials station(s). Pick up each material one at a time. Think about how it may
or may not be useful in your design. Leave the materials where they are.

7. What are your design constraints? _____

_____

Develop Possible Solutions

8. **List** five possible shapes you could use in your tower. _____

_____

9. What shapes could you use for the base of your tower? _____

_____

Choose One Solution

☑ **10.** What shapes will you use in your tower? _____

_____

☑ **11.** What shape will the base of your tower be? _____

☑ **12. Draw** a diagram of the three-dimensional, self-supporting tower you will build.

Design and Construct a Prototype

Gather your materials plus a ruler and compass. You may use a maximum of 30 straws.

13. To record the design details of your prototype, **draw** a picture of each two-dimensional shape you will use in your tower. **Label** the angles in each shape and the length in centimeters (cm) of each shape's sides.

Test the Prototype

Test your design. **Build** your three-dimensional, self-supporting tower. Keep building until your tower falls or you use the maximum number of straws.

14. How high were you able to build your tower? _____

Communicate Results

15. Compare your results with your classmates' results. Fill in a class table with the following information.

Designer	Height	Shapes Used	Shape of Base

Evaluate and Redesign

16. Explain how you would change your design to make your tower more stable or taller.

_____

_____

_____

_____

What is technology?

Tell what problem this communications satellite might help solve.

MY PLANET DIARY

Ray Harroun's 1911 racecar

Side-view mirror

Rear-view camera in automobile

Connections

Sometimes adding older technology to something new can help solve problems. The first Indianapolis 500 automobile race was held in 1911. Racecars at the time carried two people. A mechanic would ride with the driver. The mechanic would fix the car and warn the driver about cars behind them.

Driver Ray Harroun was also an automobile designer. He designed a racecar with room for only one person. To see behind the car, Harroun attached a mirror above the steering wheel. It became the first known rear-view mirror on an automobile. Driving without a mechanic was risky, but it paid off. Harroun became the first Indy 500 winner.

Cars today are still built with rear-view and side-view mirrors. However, there is new technology to help drivers know what is around them. Some cars use video cameras so drivers can see behind them. Some cars have sensors in the bumpers. Sounds or computerized voices may signal the driver if a car is too close to a curb.

What other technologies can improve a car's safety?

....

....

I will know how technology solves problems and makes work easier.

Word to Know

technology

Scientific Discoveries

Scientific discoveries change our lives. The discovery of bacteria helped us develop modern medicine. Discoveries about how electricity works brought us telephones, computers, refrigerators, light bulbs, and many more devices. Scientific discoveries often lead to new technologies. **Technology** is the knowledge, processes, and products that solve problems and make work easier.

Just as scientific methods are used to answer scientific questions, people often use a process to design technology. This process involves identifying a problem, researching and testing possible solutions, and then redesigning if necessary.

1. **Identify** Underline the definition of technology.

2. ◉ **Cause and Effect** Write one cause and effect related to technology.

Cause	Effect
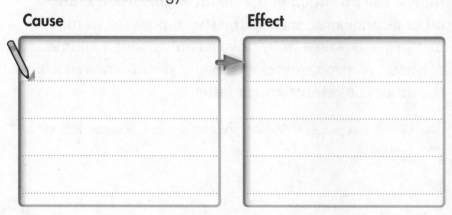	

This smartphone combines many technologies into one device. The icons show some of its functions. A high-tech device like this receives and decodes information. It changes voices to digital data and back again.

3. **Identify** What can a smartphone do besides make phone calls?

....

....

....

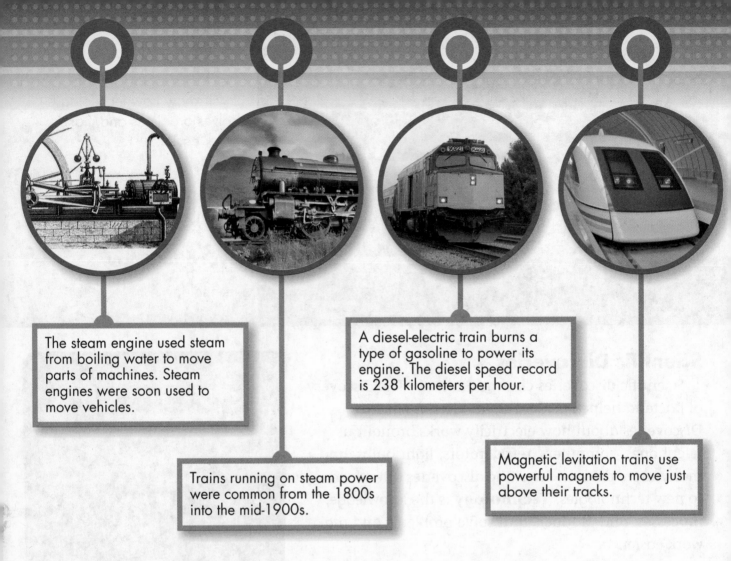

The steam engine used steam from boiling water to move parts of machines. Steam engines were soon used to move vehicles.

A diesel-electric train burns a type of gasoline to power its engine. The diesel speed record is 238 kilometers per hour.

Trains running on steam power were common from the 1800s into the mid-1900s.

Magnetic levitation trains use powerful magnets to move just above their tracks.

5. Predict Many large cities have problems with heavy traffic. What technology might be developed in the future to help solve this problem?

Technology and Transportation Systems

Transportation systems move people and goods from place to place. Technology has made transportation systems faster and safer. Long trips that once took days or weeks may now take only hours.

During the 1700s, steam engines were being developed. They first were used to operate machines in factories and mines. The invention of the steam engine led to many other technologies, such as the steam-powered train. The first steam-powered train traveled only about 6 kilometers per hour. As people developed better steam-powered trains, the trains could travel much faster.

4. Give Examples What are some other transportation systems?

Steam trains had some disadvantages. Water was heated inside a boiler, changing the water to steam. As the water changed to steam, pressure would build up inside the boiler. Sometimes the heat inside the boiler would melt a hole in the steel. The sudden release of steam out of the hole would cause the boiler to explode.

Electric, diesel, and magnetic levitation trains have replaced steam-powered trains. These trains are safer since they do not have a boiler that could explode. These trains are also faster. Magnetic levitation trains can reach speeds of more than 500 kilometers per hour.

GPS device

GPS technology keeps track of this city bus's location.

Today's transportation systems often use computer technology. Computers keep systems running properly and on time. Global Positioning System (GPS) technology sends location data from satellites orbiting Earth. A driver using a GPS device can get directions to a destination. Some city bus systems now have GPS in their buses. People waiting for a bus can use cell phones to find out if their bus is running on time.

6. **Apply** What is another problem a GPS device might solve?

Kitchen Technology

Carefully examine a can opener. Draw a diagram of the can opener and identify its parts. Write about how you think the can opener works.

Everyday Technologies

You may be surprised at the technology you can find in your home or at school. Can openers, microwave ovens, refrigerators, windows, pens, computers, clocks, and microphones are all technologies.

Technology at Home

In the past, people would have to eat fresh fruits and vegetables soon after they bought them. As fruits and vegetables ripen, they release a gas that causes them to spoil. When they are kept cool, the spoiling process slows down. The invention of the refrigerator helped solve the problem of fruits and vegetables quickly spoiling. Today, new technologies are still being developed to keep food fresh. There are certain minerals that absorb the gas that causes fruits and vegetables to spoil. Special green food-storage bags are made with these minerals. Fruits and vegetables stored in these bags stay fresh even longer.

There are other technologies for heating food. You can have an entire meal ready in minutes using a microwave oven. Some new stoves use electromagnets. They use less energy than gas or electric stoves.

A computer connects you to the Internet from your home or anywhere else. You can communicate instantly with people all over the world. Digital data can be sent over long distances without losing quality or content.

7. **Cause and Effect** How has the technology to keep food fresh affected how you eat?

....

....

Green food-storage bag technology solves the problem of food quickly spoiling.

computer

microwave oven

Technology at School

Many schools have public address systems so that announcements can be made to the entire school. These systems are a form of technology. The announcer speaks into a microphone where the sound is changed into electricity. The electricity travels through wires to speakers throughout the school. The speakers turn the electricity back into sound and you hear the announcement.

Many teachers have started using electronic white boards to teach. These white boards allow the students to learn lessons in a different way. Students can interact with the white board.

public address system

8. Infer How do you think an electronic white board could be used in your classroom?

....

....

electronic white board

Got it?

9. Explain How has train transportation changed over time?

....

....

....

10. UNLOCK THE BIG ? Identify one technology you use everyday. How does it affect your life?

....

....

⬛ **Stop!** I need help with ....

⏸ **Wait!** I have a question about ....

▶ **Go!** Now I know ....

Lesson 2

What is the design process?

Envision It!

Why do you think these aircraft have different designs?

Inquiry **Explore It!**

How can the design of a model help you learn about the real thing?

☐ **1.** Make 2 paper planes **(models)** with wings of different shapes but the same size (area). Plane A has wide, short wings. Plane B has long, narrow wings.

☐ **2.** Make a plan to test how far each plane flies. Test each plane 3 times. **Record** your **data.**

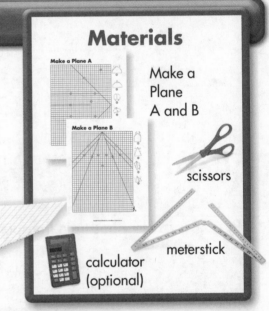

Materials

Make a Plane A and B

scissors

meterstick

calculator (optional)

Explain Your Results

3. Draw a Conclusion How might the shape of a plane's wings affect how far it flies?

4. Communicate Based on what you learned, discuss the shape of wings on passenger planes.

Effect of Wing Shape on Distance Traveled

Trial	Distance Traveled (meters)	
	Plane A (wide, short wings)	Plane B (long, narrow wings)
1		
2		
3		
Average		

Words to Know

design process
prototype

Design Process

People often have problems that can be solved with a new product or an improved process. For example, people have always looked for faster ways to travel from one place to another. Engineers develop or improve technologies to offer more benefits, to make products or processes safer, and to meet the demands of people.

Orville and Wilbur Wright had a dream to design the world's first piloted and powered flying machine. Other inventors had created gliders. A glider is a kind of aircraft that can sail from a high place to a lower one without a motor. Early gliders were difficult to control. After many experiments, Orville and Wilbur invented a way to control flight. On December 17, 1903, their motorized airplane, the *Flyer,* flew for 12 seconds.

The way the Wright brothers designed the airplane can show how the design process is used. The **design process** is a set of steps for developing products and processes that solve problems.

1. **Identify** **Underline** the definition of the design process.

2. **Predict** Why is it important to use the design process when developing a new product?

....

....

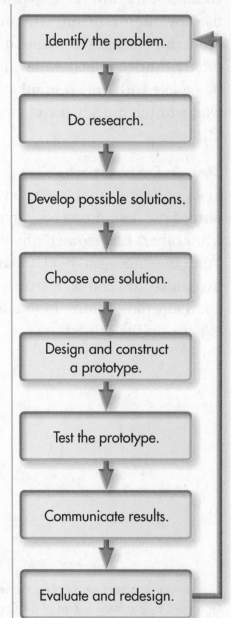

Identify the problem.

Do research.

Develop possible solutions.

Choose one solution.

Design and construct a prototype.

Test the prototype.

Communicate results.

Evaluate and redesign.

Steps of the Design Process

Many people, such as engineers and scientists, use the design process when forming a solution to a problem. They may use different steps or use them in a different order. However, the goal of finding a solution to a problem remains the same.

Step 1: Identify the problem.

The first step in the design process is to identify the problem. One of the problems the Wright brothers noticed was that aircraft could not turn easily.

When you identify the problem, it is also important to identify who will benefit from your solution. If they could control how the airplane turned, then it could be used by almost anyone who wanted to learn how to fly. Modern passenger airplanes are designed to be used by highly trained pilots, while other airplanes can be used by people with only a small amount of training. People who want to quickly travel long distances benefit from the airplane.

Step 2: Do research.

Researching what others have learned is an important part of the design process. Orville and Wilbur researched what others had learned about flight. They talked to other inventors and read about the experiments of other inventors. You can do research by using the Internet, encyclopedias, informational books, and by interviewing experts on the subject.

3. Identify Name a problem that can be solved by a new design. Who would use your design?

....

....

....

....

....

4. Infer Why do you think research is important?

....

....

....

....

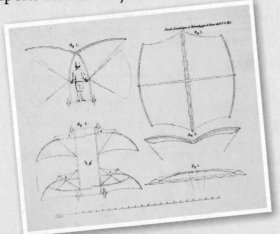

The Wright brothers researched the work of Sir George Cayley. Here is one of Sir Cayley's diagrams.

This picture shows one of Otto Lilienthal's gliding experiments. His work was also part of the Wrights' research.

Step 3: Develop possible solutions.

The next step is to think of one or more solutions to the problem. Wilbur decided to make airplane wings that could be twisted. The wings could then be moved to turn the plane. Orville and Wilbur called twisting the wings of the plane "wing-warping."

It is important to measure the size and weight and identify the shape of each part of your design. How much each part weighs can affect how your design works. Drawing or building a model of your solution helps you determine which solution is best.

Math and science will help you develop possible solutions to your design problem. The Wright brothers made careful measurements and calculations to perfect the design of the airplane. Knowledge of scientific principles related to motion helped them develop solutions.

Orville and Wilbur adjusted the wing shape of this kite to experiment with wing-warping.

5. **Compare** Look at the captions and images on this page. How has adjusting an aircraft's wing-shape changed?

_____

_____

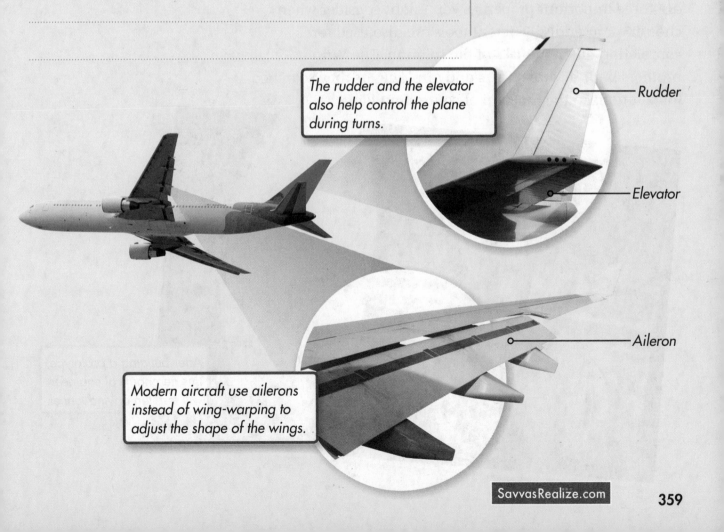

The rudder and the elevator also help control the plane during turns.

Rudder

Elevator

Aileron

Modern aircraft use ailerons instead of wing-warping to adjust the shape of the wings.

Step 4: Choose one solution.

In the design process, several factors can influence the solution that you choose. The solution must solve the problem you identified. The solution must also be affordable. If your solution costs too much, you may not be able to sell it. The amount of time you have can also affect which solution you choose. Safety is another factor to consider when choosing a solution.

When choosing a solution, engineers have to make trade-offs. If a plane design is fast, but not safe, a safer design should be chosen. You should save all the plans you have for other possible solutions because you may need them in the future.

Step 5: Design and construct a prototype.

Next, you need to carefully construct a prototype using the plans you have created for that solution. A **prototype** is the first fully working product that uses your design solution.

You should identify the materials and tools you need to construct your solution. Flexibility, strength, and hardness are three important properties you might consider when choosing materials. Different tools are also used for completing different tasks of the solution. The Wright brothers built several gliders and airplanes as they searched for solutions to the problem of controlling flight.

6. ◎ **Cause and Effect** <u>Underline</u> the factors that may affect which solution you choose to build.

7. **Explain** What materials do you think the Wright brothers used to construct the wings of their plane? Why?

....

....

....

....

....

After building a prototype, this aeronautical engineer will test it in a wind tunnel.

Step 6: Test the prototype.

The product needs to be carefully tested to see if it works safely and solves the problem it was designed for. Tests should use careful measurements. Recording the results of the tests you do will help you make adjustments to your design. After the tests, you should evaluate whether or not your product solved the problem.

Orville and Wilbur tested their gliders and planes. They observed how well each was controlled and made changes to their design to improve control during turns.

The Wright brothers used this glider to test their ideas.

8. **Infer** Why do you think it is important to record your measurements and observations?

....

....

Do the math!

Elapsed Time

The Wrights measured the elapsed time from take-off to landing for each flight. Elapsed time is the amount of time that passes from the start time to the end time. A flight departs at 7:00 A.M. and arrives at 11:20 A.M. How long is the flight?

Find the starting time.

Count the hours.   Count the minutes.

The flight lasted 4 hours, 20 minutes.

Find the elapsed time for each flight.

1 Departure Time: 9:00 A.M.
Arrival Time: 10:45 A.M.

....

2 Departure Time: 1:30 P.M.
Arrival Time: 3:55 P.M.

....

3 Departure Time: 11:00 A.M.
Arrival Time: 2:15 P.M.

....

Step 7: Communicate results.

Many times, a team of people work together to design a solution to a problem. It is important to document and communicate with your team members the solution and the data, or evidence, you collect. There are many ways to document and communicate this information. Tables and graphs can help you communicate data. Labeled diagrams, graphic organizers, and lists are also helpful in communicating your solution to others. The procedure for building the solution and for the tests performed on it should be written carefully.

Other team members should be able to use your procedures, observations, and diagrams to do their own investigations. After you have communicated your results to others, they may help you find solutions to problems with your product.

Solving one problem may create new problems. You should think of ways your solution will affect society. The invention of the airplane made travel much quicker. This benefits the lives of many people. Some inventions can have harmful effects. Noise pollution is a common problem related to airplane technology.

9. Identify (Circle) two things you need to communicate to others about your product.

10. Explain Tell why diagrams can be an effective way to communicate information.

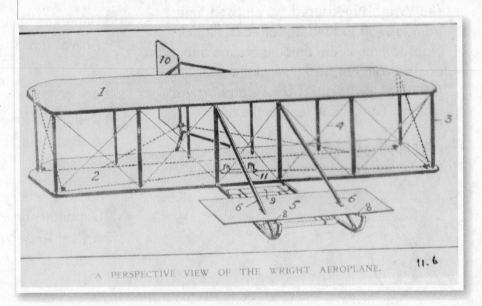

A PERSPECTIVE VIEW OF THE WRIGHT AEROPLANE.

This diagram was used to communicate information about the design of the Wright brothers' invention to the U.S. Patent Office.

Step 8: Evaluate and redesign.

After testing your prototype, you should evaluate how well it solves the problem. You may need to redesign your product. Orville and Wilbur redesigned their airplane many times. Since then, airplanes have been redesigned many times by many other people. Modern airplanes have many different designs because they have different purposes. Planes travel faster and farther today than the planes the Wright brothers made.

Redesigning your product will help solve some of the problems that you discovered as you tested it. The new solution should go through the design process again.

This modern jet solves the problem of turning in a different way.

11. Contrast Explain one way this modern airplane is different from the Wright brothers' first successful airplane.

....

....

Got it?

12. Identify What are the steps in the design process?

....

....

....

13. Judge Why do you think it is important to communicate your solution to others?

....

....

Stop! I need help with ....

Wait! I have a question about ....

Go! Now I know

Which boat design will hold more cargo?

Materials

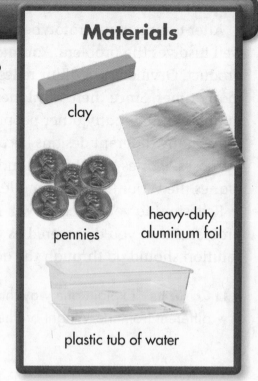

clay

heavy-duty
aluminum foil

pennies

plastic tub of water

Follow a Procedure

☐ **1. Make a Model**
Make a boat out of clay.
Make a boat of the same size and shape out of foil.
Pennies are the cargo your boat will hold.

☐ **2.** Place each boat in water.
Record your **observations.**

☐ **3. Predict** which boat will hold more pennies.
Record your prediction.

☐ **4.** Dry off the clay boat. Place it back in the water.
Place a penny in the boat.
Keep adding pennies until the boat sinks.
Record your **data.**

☐ **5.** Repeat Step 4 with the foil boat.

Inquiry Skill
Making a model can help
you make inferences about
objects and events that are
too large to test.

Be sure your boats are
the same size and shape.

Observations of Boats With and Without Cargo		
Boat	**Without Cargo**	**With Cargo**
Clay		
Foil		

Analyze and Conclude

6. Which boat floated better without cargo?

....

....

7. How many pennies did each boat hold?
Did your **observations** support your **predictions**?

....

....

8. Infer Compare your boat **design** with those of other groups.
What inferences can you make about boat design based on this activity?

....

....

9. UNLOCK THE BIG ? How can physical **models** help engineers design
boats and ships?

....

....

....

....

STEM

Submersibles

Scientists use submersibles similar to this one to explore the bottom of the ocean.

Scientists and engineers have worked together to develop and build new technologies to explore the oceans. A submersible, a type of small submarine, is an example of this kind of technology. As the ocean becomes deeper, its pressure increases. The increased pressure makes exploring the ocean difficult and unsafe. Scientists needed a vehicle that was strong enough to withstand the pressure. Engineers designed submersibles with strong glass and metals to protect humans from the high pressure of the deep ocean.

Using submersibles, scientists have discovered new, unusual animals. One unusual animal was the dumbo octopus. This species of octopus can live far below the surface of the ocean. Some can live more than 5,500 meters below sea level. Scientists can use a submersible to safely explore the habitat of the dumbo octopus. Submersibles are an example of science, engineering, and technology working together!

dumbo octopus

Determine Why is it important for scientists and engineers to work together to design new submersibles?

....

....

....

Vocabulary Smart Cards

technology
design process
prototype

Play a Game!

Cut out the Vocabulary Smart Cards.

Work with a partner. Choose a Vocabulary Smart Card. Do not let your partner see your card.

Draw a picture to show what the term means. Have your partner guess the term. Take turns drawing and guessing.

technology

tecnología

design process

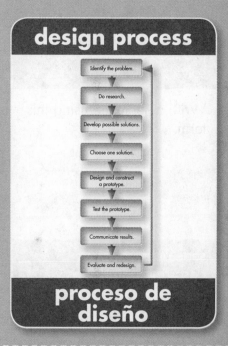

proceso de diseño

prototype

prototipo

the knowledge, processes, and products that solve problems and make work easier

Write two examples.

....

....

el conocimiento, los procesos y los productos con que se resuelven los problemas y se facilita el trabajo

a set of steps for developing products and processes that solve problems

Write a sentence using this term.

....

....

serie de pasos para desarrollar productos y procesos que resuelven problemas

first fully working product that uses a design solution

What is the prefix in this word and what does it mean?

....

....

el primer producto que demuestra una solución de diseño

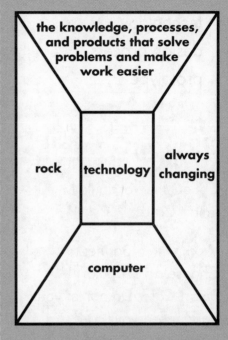

the knowledge, processes, and products that solve problems and make work easier

rock | technology | always changing

computer

Make a Word Square!

Choose a vocabulary term and write it in the center of the square. Fill in the other spaces with a definition, a characteristic, an example, and something that is not an example.

Lesson 1

What is technology?

- Technology can help solve problems and make work easier.
- Transportation technologies help move people and products quickly and safely from place to place.

Lesson 2

What is the design process?

- The design process is a set of steps for developing products and processes that solve problems.
- A prototype is the first fully working product that uses your solution.

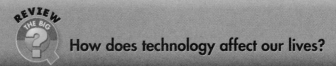
Lesson 1

What is technology?

1. Infer Why is technology important?

....

....

....

....

....

....

2. Write About It Explain how trains have changed over time.

....

....

....

....

....

3. **Do the math!** Suppose a car travels 70 kilometers per hour. How far will the car travel in 3 hours and 30 minutes?

....

....

....

4. Predict How do you think a magnetic levitation train would affect your community?

....

....

....

....

....

5. ◉ **Cause and Effect** Explain how technology affects your school.

....

....

....

....

....

Lesson 2

What is the design process?

6. Vocabulary Which of the following is NOT a step in the design process?
   A. Do research.
   B. Construct a prototype.
   C. Identify and control variables.
   D. Redesign.

7. Explain How might cost affect which prototype you choose to build?

....

....

....

....

....

....

8. Infer Why do you think engineers build prototypes of their designs?

....

....

....

....

....

9. Identify What are two steps in the design process that the Wright brothers used when building their plane?

....

....

....

....

....

....

....

....

10. **APPLY THE BIG ?** **How does technology affect our lives?**

··

Choose a transportation technology and explain how it affects your life.

....

....

....

....

....

....

....

....

Part 2
Benchmark Practice

Science,
Engineering,
and
Technology

Read each question and choose the best answer.

1 **What is a prototype?**

A a procedure for building a solution

B the first fully working product that uses a design solution

C a final solution

D a set of steps that solve problems

2 **Some cars have a Global Positioning System (GPS). A GPS uses data from _____ to provide information about a car's location.**

A engineers

B public address systems

C microwaves

D satellites

3 **The knowledge, processes, and products that solve problems and make work easier are called**

A discoveries.

B technology.

C science.

D computers.

4 **What is the last step in the design process?**

A Communicate results.

B Choose one solution.

C Evaluate and redesign.

D Test the prototype.

5 **Explain how an engineer might use the design process to build a bridge.**

....

....

....

....

....

....

....

....

....

....

....

....

Green Transportation

One of the biggest problems with transportation today is air pollution. Cars, trains, planes, and ships all release pollutants. Many transportation technologies release carbon dioxide. Carbon dioxide is a pollutant that contributes to global climate change.

You may wonder how you can reduce air pollution. There are many ways. You can choose to walk to a friend's house instead of getting a ride. If you need to go a longer distance, you can ride a bike, take a bus, or ride on a train. Some people travel in carpools. A carpool is when two or more people meet to travel together. Using a bus, train, or carpool helps to reduce the number of cars on the road. Fewer cars mean less pollution.

Some technologies help to reduce the amount of pollution cars produce. Hybrid cars can run on electricity and gasoline. This reduces the amount of pollution they produce. Cars today have catalytic converters. This technology changes some of the toxic gases given off by an engine to less harmful gases.

REVIEW THE BIG ?

What is a positive effect of transportation technology?

....

....

What is a negative effect of transportation technology?

....

What design will carry cargo best?

Cargo must be moved from one place to another and delivered on time. Different transportation systems may be used to move the cargo. Many times cargo of different weights and shapes must be moved on trains and trucks. The cargo must be arranged and secured in the vehicle so nothing shifts or falls off. The way the cargo is loaded onto the truck is a design.

You need to design a way to load a group of objects on a cart. Your cargo is a metric ruler, a wooden block, 15 cm of tape, 4 unsharpened pencils, 4 table-tennis balls, 4 large rubber bands, 100 cm of string, a half-full bottle of water, $\frac{1}{2}$ stick of clay, and an inflated balloon. After the cart is loaded you will test your loading design by pulling it through a course your teacher has provided.

Identify the problem.

☑ **1.** Identify the problems you need to address in your **design.**

....

....

....

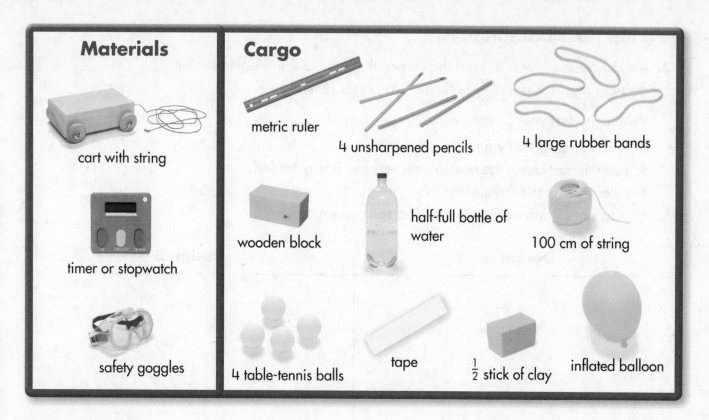

Materials

cart with string

timer or stopwatch

safety goggles

Cargo

metric ruler

4 unsharpened pencils

4 large rubber bands

wooden block

half-full bottle of water

100 cm of string

4 table-tennis balls

tape

$\frac{1}{2}$ stick of clay

inflated balloon

Do research.

☐ **2.** Consider the problems you have identified. Research **design** solutions others have used that address those problems. Brainstorm ideas with others. List three examples of solutions others have used or suggested.

Develop possible solutions.

3. As you design a way to load the cargo, think about the problems your **design** must solve and the solutions you researched.

When you test your prototype:

- load the cargo on your cart.
- pull the cart along the course your teacher has provided.
- time each of the three trials.
- stop after 3 trials or when the load spills when moving.

Design A	Design B

Choose one solution.

4. Choose one **design** to build and **test.** Tell which design you chose. Explain why you chose that design.

....

....

....

....

Design and construct a prototype.

☐ **5.** Draw the **design** you will use to make a prototype.
Explain why you chose that design.

☐ **6.** Tell how to load the cart.

....

....

....

....

....

....

....

....

....

Test the prototype.

☑ **7.** Test your **design** on the course. Use the timer to record the time it takes to complete one lap of the course.

Prototype Testing Results

Trial	Time (seconds)	Notes
1		
2		
3		

Communicate results.

☑ **8.** What elements of your **design** worked in your prototype? Use your **test** results and your **observations** to support your **conclusions.**

....

....

....

☑ **9.** What elements of your design could be improved?

....

....

....

....

Evaluate and redesign.

10. Evaluate what did and did not work in your prototype.
Use what you learned from testing to **redesign** your prototype.
Write or draw your design changes.

REVIEW
THE BIG
?

Performance-Based Assessment

Science,
Engineering,
and
Technology

Conduct a Survey

Choose a question to ask each of your classmates. You might ask them what their favorite fruit is or how many pets they have. Collect all the answers. Graph the results of your survey.

Write a Report

Choose one kind of transportation system. You may choose airplanes, cars, trucks, or boats. Research how that transportation system has changed society. Write a report about what you learn. Identify the books or other sources in which you found your information.

Design a Package

Suppose you want to send fresh flowers to a friend. Design a package that will keep the flowers fresh. The flowers and stems should not bend or break. Make sure the flowers can get the light and water that they need.

Science and Engineering Practices

1. Ask a question or define a problem.
2. Develop and use models.
3. Plan and carry out investigations.
4. Analyze and interpret data.
5. Use math and computational thinking.
6. Construct explanations or design solutions.
7. Engage in argument from evidence.
8. Obtain, evaluate, and communicate information.

Measurements

Metric and Customary Measurements

The metric system is the measurement system most commonly used in science. Metric units are sometimes called SI units. SI stands for International System. It is called that because these units are used around the world.

These prefixes are used in the metric system:

kilo- means *thousand*
1 kilometer = 1,000 meters

milli- means *one thousandth*
1,000 millimeters = 1 meter, or 1 millimeter = 0.001 meter

centi- means *one hundredth*
100 centimeters = 1 meter, or 1 centimeter = 0.01 meter

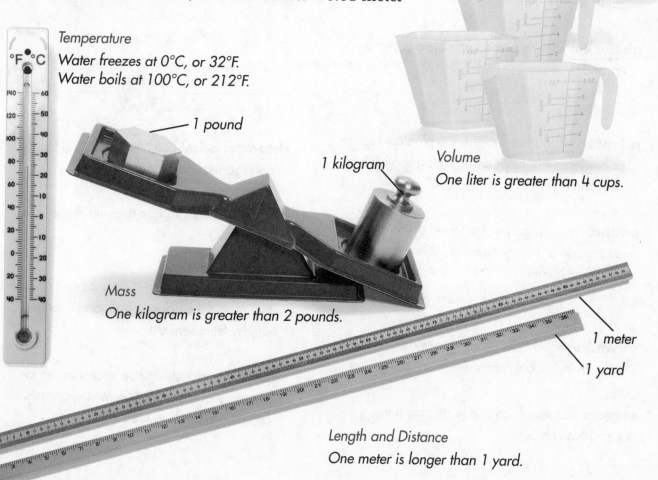

1 liter

1 cup

Temperature
Water freezes at 0°C, or 32°F.
Water boils at 100°C, or 212°F.

1 pound

1 kilogram

Volume
One liter is greater than 4 cups.

Mass
One kilogram is greater than 2 pounds.

1 meter
1 yard

Length and Distance
One meter is longer than 1 yard.

Glossary

The glossary uses letters and signs to show how words are pronounced. The mark ′ is placed after a syllable with a primary or heavy accent. The mark ′ is placed after a syllable with a secondary or lighter accent.

To hear these vocabulary words and definitions, you can log on to the digital path's Vocabulary Smart Cards.

Pronunciation Key

a in hat	ō in open	sh in she
ā in age	ȯ in all	th in thin
â in care	ô in order	ᵺH in then
ä in far	oi in oil	zh in measure
e in let	ou in out	ə = a in about
ē in equal	u in cup	ə = e in taken
ėr in term	u̇ in put	ə = i in pencil
i in it	ü in rule	ə = o in lemon
ī in ice	ch in child	ə = u in circus
o in hot	ng in long	

A

absorption (ab sôrp′ shən) occurs when an object takes in light waves

absorción ocurre cuando un objeto captura las ondas de luz

adaptation (ad′ ap tā′ shən) a physical feature or behavior that helps an organism survive in its environment

adaptación rasgo físico o forma de conducta que ayuda a un organismo a sobrevivir en su medio ambiente

advantage (ad van′ tij) a characteristic that can help an individual compete

ventaja característica que le permite a un individuo competir

amplitude (am′ plə tüd) the height of a wave measured from its midline

amplitud altura de una onda medida desde su punto medio

C

characteristics (kar′ ik tə ris′ tiks) the qualities an organism has

rasgos cualidades que tiene un organismo

chlorophyll (klôr′ ə fil) the substance in plants that makes their parts green and captures energy from sunlight

clorofila sustancia que se encuentra en las plantas y que da color verde a sus partes y capta energía de la luz solar

classify (klas′ ə fī) to arrange or sort objects or living things according to their properties or characteristics

clasificar ordenar o agrupar objetos o seres vivos según sus propiedades o características

cleavage (klē′ vij) property of minerals to break along smooth, flat surfaces

fractura propiedad que les permite a los minerales romperse por superficies lisas y planas

competition (kom′ pə tish′ ən) occurs when two or more living things need the same resources in order to survive

competencia situación en la que dos o más seres vivos necesitan los mismos recursos para sobrevivir

conduction (kən duk′ shən) the transfer of heat that occurs when one thing touches another

conducción transmisión de calor que ocurre cuando un objeto toca otro objeto

conductor (kən duk′ tər) a material through which an electric charge can move easily

conductor material a través del cual las cargas eléctricas se mueven fácilmente

convection (kən vek′ shən) the transfer of thermal energy as matter moves

convección transferencia de energía térmica mientras se mueve la material

design process (di zīn′ pros′ es) a set of steps for developing products and processes that solve problems

proceso de diseño serie de pasos para desarrollar productos y procesos que resuelven problemas

ecosystem (ē′ kō sis′ təm) all the living and nonliving things in an environment and the many ways they interact

ecosistema todos los seres vivos y las cosas sin vida que hay en un medio ambiente y las múltiples interacciones entre ellos

electric current (i lek′ trik kėr′ ənt) an electric charge in motion

corriente eléctrica carga eléctrica en movimiento

energy (en′ ər jē) the ability to cause motion or create change

energía capacidad de producir movimiento o causar cambio

erosion (i rō′ zhən) process of carrying away weathered bits of rock

erosión proceso por el cual se transportan pedacitos de roca desgastada

evidence (ev′ ə dəns) observations and facts gained from experiments

evidencia observaciones y datos obtenidos de experimentos

extinct (ek stingkt′) no longer existing as a species

extinto ya no existe más como especie

F

fault (fôlt) a break or crack in rocks where Earth's crust can move suddenly

falla fisura o grieta en las rocas donde la corteza terrestre puede desplazarse en forma repentina

fertilization (fėr′ tl ə zā′ shən) the process in which a sperm cell and an egg cell combine

fertilización proceso por el cual se unen un óvulo y un espermatozoide

filament (fil′ ə mənt) a thin, coiled wire that can get very hot without melting

filamento alambre fino y enrollado que puede calentarse mucho sin derretirse

force (fôrs) any push or pull

fuerza empujón o jalón

fossil (fos′ əl) remains or mark of an animal or plant that lived long ago

fósil restos o marca de un ser vivo que existió hace mucho tiempo

frequency (frē′ kwən sē) number of waves that pass a point in a certain amount of time

frecuencia número de ondas que pasan por un punto en un tiempo determinado

G

germinate (jėr′ mə nāt) to start to grow

germinar empezar a crecer

gravity (grav′ ə tē) the force that pulls all objects toward each other

gravedad fuerza que atrae a todos los objetos entre sí

groundwater (ground′ wȯ′ tər) any water that is underground

agua subterránea agua que está debajo del suelo

H

habitat (hab′ ə tat) area or place where an organism lives in an ecosystem

hábitat área o lugar de un ecosistema donde vive un organismo

hardness (härd′ nis) how easily the surface of a mineral can be scratched

dureza facilidad con la que se puede rasgar la superficie de un mineral

hypothesis (hī poth′ ə sis) a possible answer to a question

hipótesis respuesta posible a una pregunta

I

igneous (ig′ nē əs) rocks that form from molten rock

ígnea rocas que se forman a partir de roca derretida

inference (in′ fər əns) a conclusion drawn from data and observations

inferencia conclusión que se saca de los datos y de las observaciones

inherit (in her′ it) to receive characteristics from an organism's parents

heredar recibir rasgos de los padres de un organismo

inquiry (in kwī′ rē) the process of asking questions and searching for answers

indagación proceso que consiste en preguntar y buscar respuestas

instinct (in′ stingkt) a behavior that is inherited

instinto conducta que se hereda

insulator (in′ sə lā′ tər) a material through which an electric charge moves with difficulty

aislante material a través del cual una carga eléctrica se mueve con dificultad

invertebrates (in vėr′ tə brits) animals without backbones

invertebrados animales que no tienen columna vertebral

investigation (in ves′ tə gā′ shən) a careful way of looking for something

investigación manera cuidadosa de buscar algo

kinetic energy (ki net′ ik en′ ər jē) energy of motion

energía cinética energía de movimiento

landform (land′ fôrm′) a natural land feature on Earth's surface

accidente geográfico formación natural en la superficie terrestre

luster (lus′ tər) the way the surface of a mineral reflects light

brillo reflejo de la luz en la superficie de un mineral

M

metamorphic (met′ ə môr′ fik) rocks that have changed as a result of heat and pressure

metamórfica rocas que han cambiado a causa del calor y la presión

mineral (min′ ər əl) natural, nonliving solid crystals that make up rocks

mineral cristal natural, sólido y sin vida del que se componen las rocas

motion (mō′ shən) a change in the position of an object

movimiento cambio en la posición de un objeto

nonrenewable resource (non′ ri nü′ ə bəl rē′ sôrs) a type of energy resource that cannot be replaced at all or cannot be replaced as fast as people use it

recurso no renovable tipo de recurso energético que no se puede reemplazar o que no se puede reemplazar con la misma rapidez con que se lo usa

paleontologist (pā′ lē on tol′ ə jist) a scientist who studies fossils

paleontólogo científico que estudia los fósiles

parallel circuit (par′ ə lel sėr′ kit) a circuit that has two or more paths through which electric charges may flow

circuito en paralelo circuito que tiene dos o más vías por las que pueden fluir las cargas eléctricas

photosynthesis (fō′ tō sin′ thə sis) the process in which plants make sugar

fotosíntesis proceso en el cual las plantas producen azúcar

pistil (pis′ tl) a female structure in plants that produces egg cells

pistilo estructura femenina de las plantas donde se producen los óvulos

pitch (pich) how high or low a sound is

tono cuán agudo o grave es un sonido

pollination (pol′ ə nā′ shən) the movement of pollen from stamen to pistil

polinización proceso por el cual el polen se mueve del estambre al pistilo

population (pop′ yə lā′ shən) all the members of one species that live within an area of an ecosystem

población todos los miembros de una especie que viven en un área de un ecosistema

potential energy (pə ten′ shəl en′ ər jē) energy that is stored in an object

energía potencial energía que está almacenada en un objeto

precipitation (pri sip′ ə tā′ shən) any form of water that falls to Earth

precipitación cualquier forma de agua que cae a la Tierra

procedure (prə sē′ jər) a set of step-by-step instructions

procedimiento instrucciones paso por paso

prototype (pro′ tə tīp) first fully working product that uses a design solution

prototipo el primer producto que demuestra una solución de diseño

R

radiation (rā′ dē ā′ shən) energy that is sent out in waves

radiación energía transmitida a través de ondas

reference point (ref′ ər əns point) a place or object used to determine if an object is in motion

punto de referencia lugar u objeto usado para determinar si algo está en movimiento

reflection (ri flek′ shən) occurs when light rays bounce off a surface

reflexión ocurre cuando los rayos de luz rebotan en una superficie

refraction (ri frak′ shən) the bending of light when it passes into a new medium

refracción desviación que sufre la luz cuando pasa de un medio a otro

renewable resource (ri nü′ ə bəl rē′ sôrs) a type of energy resource that can be replaced

recurso renovable tipo de recurso energético que puede reemplazarse

S

scientific methods (sī′ ən tif′ ik meth′ ədz) organized ways to answer questions and solve problems

métodos científicos maneras organizadas de responder a preguntas y resolver problemas

sedimentary (sed′ ə men′ tər ē) rocks that form when layers of sediments settle on top of one another and harden

sedimentaria rocas que se forman cuando varias capas de sedimento se acumulan, una sobre otra, y se endurecen

sepal (sē′ pəl) one of the leaflike parts that cover and protect the flower bud

sépalo una de las partes en forma de hoja que cubren y protegen el botón de las flores

series circuit (sir′ ēz sėr′ kit) a circuit in which electric charge can flow in only one circular path

circuito en serie circuito en el cual las cargas eléctricas sólo pueden fluir en una trayectoria circular

sound (sound) energy in the form of vibrations passing through matter

sonido energía en forma de vibraciones que pasa a través de la materia

speed (spēd) the rate at which an object changes position

rapidez ritmo al cual cambia la posición de un objeto

stamen (stā′ mən) male structure in plants that makes pollen

estambre estructura masculina de las plantas que produce el polen

stimulus (stim′ yə ləs) something that causes a reaction in a living thing

estímulo algo que provoca una reacción en un ser vivo

streak (strēk) color of the powder that a mineral leaves when it is scratched across a special plate

surco color del polvo que sale de un mineral cuando se le rasga en una placa especial

T

technology (tek nol′ ə jē) the knowledge, processes, and products that solve problems and make work easier

tecnología el conocimiento, los procesos y los productos con que se resuelven los problemas y se facilita el trabajo

three-dimensional (thrē′ də men′ shə nəl) describes objects that have length, width, and height

tridimensional describe objetos que tienen largo, ancho y altura

tool (tül) an object or device used to perform a task

instrumento objeto o herramienta que se usa para hacer un trabajo

....

two-dimensional (tü′ də men′ shə nəl) describes something that has length and width, but not height

bidimensional describe algo que tiene largo y ancho, pero no tiene altura

velocity (və los′ ə tē) the speed and the direction an object is moving

velocidad rapidez y dirección en que se mueve un objeto

....

vertebrates (vėr′ tə brits) animals that have backbones

vertebrados animales que tienen columna vertebral

volume (vol′ yəm) a measure of how strong a sound seems to us

volumen medida de cuán fuerte nos parece un sonido

water cycle (wȯ′ tər sī′ kəl) the movement of water from Earth's surface to the atmosphere and back again

ciclo del agua recorrido de ida y vuelta que realiza el agua entre la atmósfera y la superficie de la Tierra

....

wavelength (wāv′ lengkth) distance between a point on one wave and a similar point on the next wave

longitud de onda distancia entre un punto de una onda y un punto similar de la onda que sigue

....

weathering (weŦH′ ər ing) process of rocks in Earth's crust slowly being broken into smaller pieces

meteorización proceso de las rocas de la corteza terrestre que se van rompiendo en trozos más pequeños

Index

Credits

Staff Credits

The people who made up the *Interactive Science* team—representing core design digital and multimedia production services, digital product development, editorial, manufacturing, and production—are listed below.

Geri Amani, Alisa Anderson, Jose Arrendondo, Amy Austin, Lindsay Bellino, Jennifer Berry, Charlie Bink, Bridget Binstock, Holly Blessen, Robin Bobo, Craig Bottomley, Jim Brady, Laura Brancky, Chris Budzisz, Mary Chingwa, Sitha Chhor, Caroline Chung, Margaret Clampitt, Karen Corliss, Brandon Cole, Mitch Coulter, AnnMarie Coyne, Fran Curran, Dana Damiano, Nancy Duffner, Susan Falcon, Amanda Ferguson, David Gall, Mark Geyer, Amy Goodwin, Gerardine Griffin, Chris Haggerty, Laura Hancko, Jericho Hernandez, Autumn Hickenlooper, Guy Huff, George Jacobson, Marian Jones, Abigail Jungreis, Kathi Kalina, Chris Kammer, Sheila Kanitsch, Alyse Kondrat, Mary Kramer, Thea Limpus, Dominique Mariano, Lori McGuire, Melinda Medina, Angelina Mendez, Claudi Mimo, John Moore, Phoebe Novak, Anthony Nuccio, Jeffrey Osier, Rachel Pancare, Dorothy Preston, Julianne Regnier, Charlene Rimsa, Rebecca Roberts, Camille Salerno, Manuel Sanchez, Carol Schmitz, Amanda Seldera, Sheetal Shah, Jeannine Shelton El, Geri Shulman, Greg Sorenson, Samantha Sparkman, Mindy Spelius, Karen Stockwell, Dee Sunday, Dennis Tarwood, Jennie Teece, Lois Teesdale, Michaela Tudela, Oscar Vera, Dave Wade, Melissa Walker, Tom Wickland, James Yagelski, Tim Yetzina, Diane Zimmermann

Illustrations

vi, vii, viii, 1, 41, 43, 44, 47, 73, 75, 76, 79, 101, 103, 104, 111 ©Aleksi Markku/Shutterstock; **ix, x, xiv, 113, 169, 171, 172, 175, 219, 221, 222, 229** ©Jens Stolt/Shutterstock; **xi, 231, 285, 287, 288, 295** Leonello Calvetti/Getty Images; **xii, xiii, 297, 337, 339, 340, 343, 369, 371, 372, 380** ©James Thew/Shutterstock; **vi, 12–13, 138, 165, 270, 280, 283** Precision Graphics; **xvii** (TR) Jeff Grunewald, (CL) Alan Bernard; **139, 165, 184** Robert Ulrich; **202–203, 210** Alan Male; **263, 283** Adam Benton; **58, 71** Peter Bollinger; **207** Jon Hughes/Bedrock Studios/DK Images; **208** DK Images; **252–253** Andy Crawford/Donks Models – modelmaker/DK Images
All other illustrations Chandler Digital Art

Photographs

Photo locators denoted as follows: Top (T), Center (C), Bottom (B), Left (L), Right (R), Background (Bkgd)

COVER: Ondrej Prosicky/Shutterstock

Front Matter
i (C) Ondrej Prosicky/Shutterstock; **ii** (BR) Ondrej Prosicky/Shutterstock; **iv–v** Thinkstock; **vii** (TR) ©Peter Cade/Getty Images; **viii** (TR) szpeti/Shutterstock; **ix** (TR) Alan & Linda Detrick/Photo Researchers, Inc.; **x** (TR) ©Larisa Lofitskaya/Shutterstock; **xi** (TR) ©Savanah Stewart/Danita Delimont/Alamy; **xii** (TR) ©Alexis Rosenfeld/Photo Researchers, Inc.; **xiii** (TR) ©Neo Edmund/Shutterstock; **xiv** (C) clabert/Fotolia; **xv** (CL) Getty Royalty Free, (TRT) Fotolia, (TRCL) ©Adisa/Shutterstock, (TRCR) ©Mytho/Shutterstock, (TRBR) ©aleks.k/Shutterstock, (TRBC) ©Daniel Aguilar/Reuters/Corbis; **xvi** (LTC) ©Foto011/Shutterstock, (LTR) ©Petr Jilek/Shutterstock, (L Bkgd) ©Pakhnyushcha/Shutterstock, (LC) Time & Life Pictures/Getty Images, (RTL) ©Wheatley/Shutterstock, (RTC) ©Caryn Becker/Alamy Royalty Free, (RBC) ©EcoPrint/Shutterstock; **xvii** (BR) Masterfile Royalty Free; **xviii** (TC) ©Elena Yakusheva/Shutterstock, (CR) ©Jan Hopgood/Shutterstock; **xix** (TR) ©Ilja Masik/Shutterstock; **xxiii** Mikiradic/Fotolia

Chapter 1 Energy and Heat
xxiv–1 ©Raul Touzon/Getty Images; **3** (Bkgd) Laurentiu Iordache/Alamy; **8–9** (T) ©Pete Ryan/Getty Royalty Free; **9** (CR) ©Cade Martin/Getty Images; **10** (TR) ©TebNad/Shutterstock, (CR) Thinkstock, (BR) ©U.P.images_photo/Shutterstock; **11** (TL) ©Lawrence Roberg/Shutterstock, (CL) Zeljko Radojko/Shutterstock, (BL) Callum Parsons/Alamy; **14** (TL) ©Philip J. Brittan/Getty Images; **15** (TL) TMPhoto/Alamy; **16** (C) DK Images; **16–17** (T) ©Gary Conner/Getty Images; **17** (CR) ©RubberBall/SuperStock Royalty Free; **18** (TR) Getty Images/Getty Royalty Free; **19** (BL) Clive Streeter/Courtesy of Marconi Instruments Ltd./DK Images; **20** (TL) Getty Royalty Free; **22–23** (T) ©Dan Suzio/Photo Researchers, Inc.; **23** (CR) ©Anita Patterson Peppers/Shutterstock; **24–25** (Bkgd) Alan Sirulnikoff/Photo Researchers, Inc.; **25** (TR) ©David Parker/Photo Researchers, Inc.; **26** (TL) ©Southern Illinois University/Photo Researchers, Inc., (B) Gail Johnson/Shutterstock; **27** (TR) ©Callahan/Shutterstock; **28–29** (T) Kinsman Physics Productions/Photo Researchers, Inc. **29** (B) Peter Van Nostrand/Fotolia; **30** (B) ©Foodcollection/Alamy Royalty Free; **31** (B) ©apply pictures/Alamy; **32** (B) ©GIPhotoStock/Photo Researchers, Inc.; **33** (TR) ©isifa Image Service s.r.o./Alamy; **36** (Bkgd) ©piotrwzk/Shutterstock, (BL) Tony Freeman/PhotoEdit, Inc.; **37** (TC) ©RubberBall/SuperStock Royalty Free, (TR) ©Cade Martin/Getty Images, (CC) Clive Streeter/Courtesy of Marconi Instruments Ltd./DK Images, (CR) ©Lawrence Roberg/Shutterstock, (BC) Clive Streeter/Courtesy of Marconi Instruments Ltd./DK Images, (BR) Callum Parsons/Alamy; **39** (TL) Peter Van Nostrand/Fotolia, (TC) ©Southern Illinois University/Photo Researchers, Inc., (TR) Getty Royalty Free, (CL) ©apply pictures/Alamy Royalty Free, (CC) ©Southern Illinois University/Photo Researchers, Inc., (CR) ©Gary Conner/Getty Images, (BL) ©apply pictures/Alamy Royalty Free, (BC) ©Callahan/Shutterstock; **41** (TLT) ©Pete Ryan/Getty Royalty Free, (TLB) ©Gary Conner/Getty Images, (CLT) ©Dan Suzio/Photo Researchers, Inc., (CLB) Kinsman Physics Productions, (B) ©Raul Touzon/Getty Images; **42** (BR) Getty Images/Getty Royalty Free; **45** (Bkgd) ©Craig Aurness/Corbis, (CR) Gabriele Simbriger-Williams/Solar Cookers International

Chapter 2 Motion
46–47 (Bkgd) ©Mark Scott/Getty Images; **54** (Bkgd) ©Losevsky Pavel/Shutterstock; **54–55** (T) ©Ted Kinsman/Photo Researchers, Inc.; **55** (CR) Getty Royalty Free; **56** (C) ©Peter Cade/Getty Images; **57** (B) ©Cindy Charles/Photo

©DK Images, (TR) Shutterstock; **199** (TR) ©Ryan Mcvay/Getty Images, (TR) ©Saul Gravy/Getty Images; **200** (TR) ©Gabrielle Hovey/Shutterstock, (CR) AFP/Getty Images, (BR) ITAR-TASS Photo Agency/Alamy; **201** (TL) John Foxx/Imagestate, (B) Colin Keates/DK Images; **202** (TL) ©EIGHTFISH/Alamy Royalty Free; **203** (TL) ©Pylypenko/Shutterstock, (TR) Sora/Fotolia, (CR) ©psamtik/Shutterstock; **204** (T) DK Images, (CL) ©Steve Hamblin/Alamy; **205** (CL) ©Falk Kienas/Shutterstock, (CC) ©Anton Foltin/Shutterstock; **206** (R) Catmando/Fotolia, **206–207** (T) ©Geoff Hardy/Shutterstock, **207** (BR) ©AFP/Getty Images; **208** (BL) ©John Cancalosi/Alamy, (BR) ©Emilio Ereza/Alamy; **209** (B) American Museum of Natural History, (CR) ©Jamie York/iStock International, Inc.; **214** (TC) George Rinhart/Corbis, (R) Simpson/Photri Images/Alamy; **215** (TC) ©Brad Mitchell/Alamy, (TR) cherie/Fotolia, (CC) ©loriklaszio/Shutterstock, (CR) Masterfile Royalty Free, (BC) Shutterstock, (BR) Masterfile Royalty Free; **217** (TR) ©Gabrielle Hovey/Shutterstock, (CR) Colin Keates/DK Images, (BR) ©AFP/Getty Images; **219** (TLT) Juliec/123RF, (TLB) David Gowans/Alamy, (CLT) Shutterstock, (CLB) ©Gabrielle Hovey/Shutterstock, (BL) ©Geoff Hardy/Shutterstock, (B) Jetta/Fotolia; **220** (CL) ©Rich Lindie/Shutterstock; **221** (TL) Sora/Fotolia, (BL) ©Edgewater Media/Shutterstock; **223** (TL) B. G. Thomson/Photo Researchers, Inc., (CL) Mark Newman/Photo Researchers, Inc., (Bkgd) Andy Rouse/Photo Researchers, Inc; **228** (CL) ©Melinda Fawver/Shutterstock; **229** (TR) Getty Royalty Free, (B) ©Chris Selby/Alamy

Chapter 6 Earth's Resources
230–231 (Bkgd) Masterfile Royalty Free; **233** (T) Getty Royalty Free; **238** (TR) Gary Ombler/DK Images; **239** (TL) ©Steffen Foerster Photography/Shutterstock, (CR) Harry Taylor/DK Images, (BR) Papa1266/Shutterstock; **240** (BR) ©M. Claye/Jacana Scientific Control/Photo Researchers, Inc., (TR, TCR) Colin Keates/Courtesy of the Natural History Museum, London/©DK Images, (TCL) Colin Keates/The Natural History Museum, London/©DK Images, (TL, TCR, TC, CR, BL) DK Images; **241** (TR, CR) Colin Keates/Courtesy of the Natural History Museum, London/©DK Images, (TL, TCL, TC, CL, BC) DK Images; **242** (TR) Harry Taylor/DK Images, (CR) Harry Taylor/DK Images, (BL) ©Charles D. Winters/Photo Researchers, Inc.; **243** (TR) Tim Ridley/DK Images; **244–245** (T) ©George Burba/Shutterstock; **245** (Bkgd) ©Presniakov Oleksandor/Shutterstock; **246** (BL) Natural History Museum, London/DK Images, (BC) Colin Keates/Courtesy of the Natural History Museum, London/DK Images, (BR) Dave King/Courtesy of The Science Museum, London/DK Images; **246–247** (C) ©beboy/Shutterstock; **247** (BL) DK Images, (BC) Harry Taylor/DK Images, (BR) DK Images; **248** (TRT) Gary Ombler/DK Images, (TRB) Linda Burgess/DK Images, (CR) Harry Taylor/Courtesy of the Royal Museum of Scotland, Edinburgh/DK Images; **248–249** (Bkgd) Nozyer/Fotolia; **250–251** (Bkgd) ©Thomas R. Fletcher/Alamy; **251** (TL) Colin Keates/Courtesy of the Natural History Museum, London/DK Images, (CLT) DK Images, (CLB) DK Images, (BL) Harry Taylor/DK Images; **254–255** (T) geogphotos/Alamy; **256–257** (Bkgd) Savanah Stewart/Danita Delimont/Alamy; **258** (B) ©kavram/Shutterstock; **259** (TR) ©Martin Maun/Shutterstock, (CR) ©canadabrian/Alamy Royalty Free; **260** (BR) AP Images; **260–261** (T) ©Rick Strange/Alamy; **261** (B) ©Bart Nedobre/Alamy Royalty Free; **262** (CL) ©Douglas Peebles Photography/Alamy Royalty Free,

(B) Krafft/Photo Researchers, Inc.; **264** (TL) ©Daniel and Flossie White/Alamy; **266–267** (T) ©imagebroker/Alamy Royalty Free; **267** (R) ©Darren Baker/Shutterstock; **268–269** (TC) ©kwest/Shutterstock, (CT) ©Serg64/Shutterstock, (CB) ©Ishbukar Yalilfatar/Shutterstock, (BC) ©Ivonne Wierink/Shutterstock; **271** (TR) ©Marmaduke St. John/Alamy Royalty Free; **272–273** (T) ©Karin Claus/Shutterstock; **273** (R) ©Beata Becia/Shutterstock; **274–275** (Bkgd) ©Yuriy Kulyk/Shutterstock; **276** (BL) szpeti/Shutterstock, (BC) ©Tony Campbell/Shutterstock, (BR) ©ollirg/Shutterstock; **277** (TR) ©Corbis/SuperStock Royalty; **280** (Bkgd) ©Michael Zysman/Shutterstock; **281** (TC) DK Images, (TR) Harry Taylor/DK Images, (CC) Harry Taylor/DK Images, (CR) DK Images, (BC) ©beboy/Shutterstock, (BR) Colin Keates/Courtesy of the Natural History Museum, London/©DK Images; **283** (TC) Savanah Stewart/Danita Delimont/Alamy, (TR) Nozyer/Fotolia, (CL) ©Beata Becia/Shutterstock, (CC) ©kavram/Shutterstock, (CR) ©Thomas R. Fletcher/Alamy, (BL) ©Yuriy Kulyk/Shutterstock, (BR) geogphotos/Alamy; **285** (TLT) ©Steffen Foerster Photography/Shutterstock, (TLB) ©George Burba/Shutterstock, (CLT) geogphotos/Alamy, (CLB) ©Rick Strange/Alamy, (BLT) ©imagebroker/Alamy Royalty Free, (BLB) ©Karin Claus/Shutterstock, (B) Masterfile Royalty Free; **289** (TL) ©Sam Toren/Alamy, (Bkgd) ©Johner Images/Alamy Royalty Free; **294** (TL) ©beboy/Shutterstock; **295** (TR) ©Daniel and Flossie White/Alamy, (B) ©Serg64/Shutterstock

Science, Engineering, and Technology Skills Handbook
Part 1 The Nature of Science
296–297 (Bkgd) Morgan Lane Photography/Shutterstock; **299** (C, Bkgd) ©Linda Sikes/Alamy, (C, TL) ©Robbie Shone/Alamy; **304** (Bkgd) Demetrio Carrasco/DK Images; **304–305** (T) ©Inga Spence/Alamy; **305** (CR) ©Harald Sund/Getty Images; **306** (TL) ©Robbie Shone/Alamy; **306–307** (Bkgd) ©Linda Sikes/Alamy; **307** (TR) Colin Keates/Courtesy of the Natural History Museum, London/DK Images; **310** (C) Getty Royalty Free; **312** (C) ©Photoroller/Shutterstock, (BR) Steve Shott/DK Images; **313** (TC) Mike Dunning/DK Images; **314–315** (T) ©Grant Faint/Getty Images; **315** (BR) ©Maria Stenzel/National Geographic Stock; **320** (TL) Robert F. Bukaty/AP Images, (BL) ©Tim Ridley/DK Images; **322–323** (T) ©Alexis Rosenfeld/Photo Researchers, Inc.; **323** (R) ©Photoroller/Shutterstock; **326** (TL) ©Leslie Banks/iStock International, Inc., (BL) Tim Ridley/DK Images, (BC) Jupiter Royalty Free; **327** (BL) ©Alyda De Villers/iStock International, Inc., (BC) DK Images; **328** (TR) ©image100/Alamy Royalty Free; **332** (Bkgd) ©Cultura Limited/SuperStock Royalty Free, (TL) ©fStop/Alamy Royalty Free; **333** (TC) ©Maria Stenzel/National Geographic Stock, (TR) ©Harald Sund/Getty Images, (CR) ©Robbie Shone/Alamy; **335** (TC)©Leslie Banks/iStock International, Inc.; (TR) Robert F. Bukaty/AP Images, (CR) ©Tim Ridley/DK Images, (BR) ©Photoroller/Shutterstock; **337** (TL) ©Inga Spence/Alamy, (CLT) ©Grant Faint/Getty Images, (CLB) ©Alexis Rosenfeld/Photo Researchers, Inc., (B) Morgan Lane Photography/Shutterstock; **341** (Bkgd) ©Alexey Stiop/Shutterstock, (CL) Image Source Royalty Free

Part 2 Technology and Design
342–343 (Bkgd) Nathan Denette/CP/AP Images; **345** (TR) ©Gary Crabbe/Alamy, (C) ©Andrew Holt/Getty Royalty Free;